Classics in Consciousness / Russell Targ Editions

Some of the twentieth century's best texts on the scientific study of consciousness are out of print, hard to find, and unknown to most readers; yet they are still of great importance. Their insights into human consciousness and its dynamics are still valuable and vital. Hampton Roads Publishing Company—in partnership with physicist and consciousness research pioneer Russell Targ—is proud to bring some of these texts back into print, introducing classics in the fields of science and consciousness studies to a new generation of readers. Upcoming titles in the *Classics in Consciousness* series will cover such perennially exciting topics as telepathy, astral projection, the after-death survival of consciousness, psychic abilities, long-distance hypnosis, and more.

OTHER BOOKS IN THE SERIES

Spring 2001
_____

An Experiment with Time

Fall 2001
_____

Human Personality and Its Survival of Bodily Death
Mind to Mind
Experiments in Mental Suggestion

CLASSICS IN (C@ CONSCIOUSNESS
Russell Targ Editions

Mental Radio

Upton Sinclair

HAMPTON ROADS
PUBLISHING COMPANY, INC.

MENTAL RADIO

Upton Sinclair

Publisher's Note copyright © 2001
by Russell Targ
Cover copyright © 2001
by Mayapriya Long

Originally copyrighted 1930 by Upton Sinclair.

Cover photographic images by Digital Stock

For information write:

Hampton Roads Publishing Company, Inc.
1125 Stoney Ridge Road
Charlottesville, VA 22902

Or call: 804-296-2772
Fax: 804-296-5096
e-mail: hrpc@hrpub.com
Web site: www.hrpub.com

If you are unable to order this book from your local
bookseller, you may order directly from the publisher.
Call 1-800-766-8009, toll-free.

Library of Congress Catalog Card Number: 00-111233

ISBN 1-57174-235-2

10 9 8 7 6 5 4 3 2 1

Printed on acid-free paper in Canada

CONTENTS

PUBLISHER'S NOTE

Hampton Roads is proud to inaugurate the publication of *Classics in Consciousness*—a new series of books featuring the pioneers in psychical research, from its beginnings to the present day. In this series, we will reprint the original classic investigations with their remarkable insights into the paranormal and its relationship to consciousness itself.

The series is published in collaboration with physicist and ESP researcher Russell Targ. Scientific research into extrasensory perception (ESP) has made enormous progress since the founding of the Society for Psychical Research in 1882 by a distinguished group of Cambridge University scholars. The Society's purpose was to examine allegedly paranormal phenomena in a scientific and unbiased way—the first organization of its kind in the world. Now, in the twenty-first century, the evidence has become overwhelming that our thoughts and bodies can be directly influenced by the thoughts of another person, or by events and activities at a distant location blocked from ordinary perception. Although we do not presently understand the mechanisms underlying psychical abilities, thousands of experiments have been successfully carried out, in hundreds of laboratories around the world, establishing the existence of some form of ESP.

In spite of our lack of understanding of the physics of ESP, we have learned a great deal about its psychology, and how to make this elusive phenomena appear with ever-increasing reliability in laboratory experiments. For example, today's remote viewing experiments—in which we can often describe and experience places thousands of miles away—have shown more than ten times the statistical power or "psychic strength" than those of J. B. Rhine's original ESP card-guessing experiments seventy years ago at Duke University. These new results have been published in the world's most prestigious scientific journals, such as *Nature*, the *Proceedings of the Institute of Electrical and Electronics Engineers*, and the *Proceedings of the American Academy of Science*.

The books in this series will deal with the physics and psychology of ESP, which today is often called psi research. We will let the courageous researchers describe, in their own words, what they found as they looked at and experienced phenomena such as hypnosis at a distance, survival of bodily death, precognition of future events, out of body experiences, and mind-to-mind connections over thousands of miles.

This first volume, *Mental Radio*, describes the imaginative and highly successful research in mind-to-mind communication carried out by the distinguished and visionary novelist Upton Sinclair (1878–1968) and his psychic and very discerning wife, Mary Craig. In the introduction, psychologist William McDougall presents a penetrating analysis of these thoughtful and ground-breaking experiments in telepathic picture-drawing carried out in the 1920s. We chose this highly acclaimed book to launch our series because of the care and awareness of the experimenters, and the self-evident strength shown in hundreds of psychic matches between Sinclair's target pictures and his wife's drawn responses.

> FRANK DEMARCO, publisher
> RUSSELL TARG, series editor

INTRODUCTION

MR. UPTON Sinclair needs no introduction to the public as a fearless, honest, and critical student of public affairs. But in the present book he has with characteristic courage entered a new field, one in which reputations are more easily lost than made, the field of Psychic Research. When he does me the honor to ask me to write a few words of introduction to this book, a refusal would imply on my part a lack either of courage or of due sense of scientific responsibility. I have long been keenly interested in this field; and it is not necessary to hold that the researches of the past fifty years have brought any solidly established conclusions in order to feel sure that further research is very much worth while. Even if the results of such research should in the end prove wholly negative that would be a result of no small importance; for from many points of view it is urgently to be wished that we may know where we stand in this question of the reality of alleged supernormal phenomena. In discussing this question recently with a small group of scientific men, one of them (who is perhaps the most prominent and influential of American psychologists) seems to feel that the whole problem was settled in the negative when he asserted that at the present time no American psychologist of standing took any interest in this field. I do not know whether he meant to deny my Americanism or my standing, neither of which I can establish. But his remark if it were true, would not in any degree support his conclusion; it would rather be a grave reproach to American psychologists. Happily it is possible to name several younger American psychologists who are keenly interested in the problem of telepathy.

And it is with experiments in telepathy that Mr. Sinclair's book is chiefly concerned. In this part, as in other parts of the field of Psychic Research, progress must largely depend upon such work by intelligent educated laymen or amateurs as is here reported. For facility in obtaining seemingly supernormal phenomena seems to be of rare and sporadic occurrence; and it is the duty of men of science to give whatever encouragement and sympathetic support may be possible to all amateurs who find themselves in a position to observe and carefully and honestly to study such phenomena.

Mrs. Sinclair would seem to be one of the rare persons who have telepathic power in a marked degree and perhaps other supernormal powers. The experiments in telepathy, as reported in the pages of this book, were so remarkably successful as to rank among the very best hitherto reported. The degree of success and the conditions of experiment were such that we can reject them as conclusive evidence of some mode of communication not at present explicable in accepted scientific terms only by assuming that Mr. and Mrs. Sinclair either are grossly stupid, incompetent, and careless persons or have deliberately entered upon a conspiracy to deceive the public in a most heartless and reprehensible fashion. I have unfortunately no intimate personal knowledge of Mr. and Mrs. Sinclair; but I am acquainted with some of Mr. Sinclair's earlier publications; and that acquaintance suffices to convince me, as it should convince any impartial reader, that he is an able and sincere man with a strong sense of right and wrong and of individual responsibility. His record and his writings should secure a wide and respectful hearing for what he has to tell us in the following pages.

Mrs. Sinclair's account of her condition during successful experiments seems to me particularly interesting; for it falls into line with what has been observed by several other workers; namely, they report that a peculiar passive mental state or attitude seems to be a highly favorable, if not essential, condition of telepathic communication. It would seem that if the faint and unusual telepathic processes are to manifest themselves, the track of the mind must be kept clear of other traffic.

Other experiments reported in the book seem to imply some supernormal power of perception of physical things such as is commonly called clairvoyance. It is natural and logical that alleged instances of clairvoyance should have from most of us a reception even more skeptical than that we accord to telepathic claims. After all, a mind at work is an active agent of whose nature and activity our knowledge is very imperfect; and science furnishes us no good reasons for denying that its activity may affect another mind in some fashion utterly obscure to us. But when an experimenter seems to have large success in reading printed words shut in a thick-walled box, words whose identity is unknown to any human being, we seem to be more nearly in a position to assert positively— That cannot occur! For we do seem to know with very fair completeness the possibilities of influence extending from the printed word to the experimenter; and under the conditions all such possibilities seem surely excluded. Yet here also we must keep the open mind, gather the facts, however unintelligible they may seem at present, repeating observations under varied conditions.

And Mrs. Sinclair's clairvoyant successes do not stand alone. They are in line with the many successful "book-tests" recorded of recent years by competent workers of the English Society for Psychical Research, as well as with many other less carefully observed and recorded incidents.

Mr. Sinclair's book will amply justify itself if it shall lead a few (let us say two per cent) of his readers to undertake carefully and critically experiments similar to those which he has so vividly described.

WILLIAM McDOUGALL
Duke University, N. C.
September 1929

PREFACE

ICH HABE DAS BUCH von Upton Sinclair mit grossem Interesse gelesen und bin überzeugt, dass dasselbe die ernsteste Beachtung, nicht nur der Laien, sondern auch der Psychologen von Fach verdient. Die Ergebnisse der in diesem Buch sorgfältig und deutlich beschriebenen telepathischen Experimente stehen sicher weit ausserhalb desjenigen, was ein Naturforscher für denkbar hält. Andererseit aber ist es bei einem so gewissenhaften Beobachter und Schriftsteller wie Upton Sinclair ausgeschlossen, dass er eine bewusste Täuschung der Leserwelt anstrebt; seine bona fides und Zuverlässigkeit darf nicht bezweifelt werden. Wenn also etwa die mit grosser Klarheit dargestellten Tatsachen nicht auf Telepathie, sondern etwa auf unbewussten hypothischen Einflüssen von Person zu Person beruhen sollten, so wäre auch dies von hohem psychologischen Interesse. Keinesfalls also sollten die psychologisch interessierten Kreise an diesem Buch achtlos vorübergehn.

gez A. EINSTEIN den 23. Mai 1930

I HAVE READ THE BOOK of Upton Sinclair with great interest and am convinced that the same deserves the most earnest consideration, not only of the laity, but also of the psychologists by profession. The results of the telepathic experiments carefully and plainly set forth in this book stand surely far beyond those which a nature investigator holds to be thinkable. On the other hand, it is out of the question in the case of so conscientious an observer and writer as Upton Sinclair that he is carrying on a conscious deception of the reading world; his good faith and dependability are not to be doubted. So if somehow the facts here set forth rest not upon telepathy, but upon some unconscious hypnotic influence from person to person, this also would be of high psychological interest. In no case should the psychologically interested circles pass over this book heedlessly.

[signed] A. EINSTEIN
May 23, 1930

FOREWORD

I CONTEMPLATED A STATEMENT introducing this book to the reader, but on further thought I realized that the book introduces itself and speaks for itself all the way through. I will only say that Mary Craig Kimbrough was my wife for almost half a century. She guarded me, managed me, and worried about me during that period—for the task was an unending one. I was often engaged in politically and socially dangerous tasks, and Craig was the one who realized the dangers and undertook the task of saving me. This went on all through our marriage, and in the end her heart weakened, and for almost ten years I dropped all my other tasks and devoted myself to keeping her alive. She died in April 1961.

I wrote the text of *Mental Radio, 1929,* under her direction; she revised every word and had it exactly the way she wanted it. She was the most conscientious and morally exacting person I have ever known. Loyalty to the truth was her religion; and every sentence in this book was studied so that it would be exactly true and so clear that nobody could misunderstand it. She knew just how we did our experiments; she had told me exactly what to do, and I had done it; if I set it down wrong in the manuscript, she made it right.

She has told of her early psychic experiences, and they were enough to fill her with determination to make sure they were real, and if possible to find out what they meant. It was she who laid down all the procedures in our tests. It was she who studied the results and got the record exact to the last comma. In reading this book bear in mind, there are no errors. If the book says that the experiment was done in a certain precise way, that is the way it was done; and always it was done without prejudice, without a preconception or anything that could affect the result. When the record was put on paper every word had to be studied, and every little mistake that I made had to be corrected by her tenacious memory.

So trust this book. Understand that what is told here happened exactly as it has been told. Don't think that maybe there was a slight slip, or that there is a careless word. I remember in the course of the years some learned psychologist suggesting that maybe Craig had unconsciously got some idea of what the drawings were by seeing the movement of my pen or pencil. This meant just one thing—the learned gentleman didn't want to believe, and hadn't taken the trouble to go back and study the book. You who are going to read now will note again and again that I went into another room to make the drawing, and I shut the door. Make note now and bear it in mind all through the book, I never made a drawing in the same room with Craig; and always the door was shut. To have done otherwise would have been to waste her time as well as mine, and she saw to it that I did not waste either. She wanted to *know*; she was *determined* to *know*; she laid down the law, and I obeyed it. The only way you can reject the evidence in this book is to decide that we were a pair of unconscionable rascals. I'll give you one opinion about that. Albert Einstein, possessor of one of the greatest modern brains, and also of a high character, was one of our close friends. He came to our home, and we came to his, and he witnessed some of our experiments. When this book was ready for publication in 1929 I sent him a set of the proofs and asked him if he would care to write a preface for the German edition. He consented and wrote the letter in German to the German publisher. Unfortunately, the publisher went out of business.

What you are going to read is the exact text of Craig's book as it was written in the year 1929 and published in the next year. The only changes I have made have to do with the lapse of thirty years since the text was written. Near the end are one or two references to friends who have since died, but you probably never knew those persons, so it doesn't matter.

At the end of the book I have published a few comments on it, and an account, written by myself, of later experiments. Also I give an extensive summary of the results of a study of the drawings published by Dr. Walter Franklin Prince, a Boston clergyman who resigned from his pulpit in order to become Research Officer of the Boston Society for Psychic Research. Dr. Prince asked if we would be willing to entrust the documents to his examination, and I immediately bundled them up and sent them to him by registered mail. The long commentary which he wrote appeared in the *Bulletin* of the society for April 1932.

Perhaps the most important single item concerning *Mental Radio* is the following:

Prof. William McDougall, who had been head of the Department of Psychology at Oxford University and later head of the Department of Psychology at Harvard—and who had won the title of "Dean of American Psychology"— came to see us in Pasadena soon after the publication of this book. He told Craig that he had just accepted the job of head of the Department of Psychology at Duke University, Durham, North Carolina, and would have at his disposal a considerable fund for research. He had read *Mental Radio* and had written the preface which is in this book, and he said that he would like to be able to say that he himself had witnessed a test of the genuineness of Craig's telepathic power.

Craig had always shrunk from anything of that sort because her power depended entirely upon solitude and concentration; but her respect for McDougall was great, and she told him she would do her best. He said that he had some pictures in his inside coat pocket, and he would like to see if she could describe them. She sat quietly with her eyes closed and presently said that she saw a building with stone walls and narrow windows, and it seemed to be covered with green leaves. McDougall took from his inside coat pocket a postcard of one of the buildings at Oxford covered with ivy.

Other tests with him will appear later. Here I add one more story, how we took the good man for a test with Arthur Ford, who was then head of a spiritualistic church in Los Angeles. I had picked out four letters or postcards from well-known persons, one of them Jack London and another Georg Brandes, the Danish critic, highly respected. I wrapped each of these documents in a sheet of green paper to remove any possibility of holding them up to the light or otherwise getting a glimpse. I showed this to McDougall, and he agreed that the concealment was effective. We then sealed them in four numbered envelopes, and in a little ante-room of the church Arthur Ford lay back in his chair, covered his eyes with a handkerchief, and put the envelopes one by one on his forehead.

I subsequently wrote an article about the experiment which was published in the *Psychic Observer,* but I do not have the text at hand. Ford told us significant things about the contents of all those envelopes, and I remember that afterwards McDougall, Craig, and I strolled down the street and stopped at a little kiosk where we ordered lemonade or orange juice. I said, "Well, what do you think of it?" and McDougall's answer was, "I should say that it is undoubtedly supernormal."

He then told Craig that what she had done had already decided him—he was going to Duke University in a week or two and his first action would be to set up a Department of Parapsychology. That was a little over thirty years ago, and I think it is correct to say that what McDougall did, with the help of J. B. Rhine, his assistant and later his successor, has made the subject of Parapsychology scientifically respectable throughout the United States and Europe.

And now, to the text, as published, 1930.

UPTON SINCLAIR

1

IF YOU WERE BORN as long as fifty years ago, you can remember a time when the test of a sound, commonsense mind was refusing to fool with "new-fangled notions." Without exactly putting it into a formula, people took it for granted that truth was known and familiar, and anything that was not known and familiar was nonsense. In my boyhood, the funniest joke in the world was a "flying machine man"; and when my mother took up a notion about "germs" getting into you and making you sick, my father made it a theme for no end of domestic wit. Even as late as twenty years ago, when I wanted to write a play based on the idea that men might some day be able to make a human voice audible to groups of people all over America, my friends assured me that I could not interest the public in such a fantastic notion.

Among the objects of scorn, in my boyhood, was what we called "superstition"; and we made the term include, not merely the notion that the number thirteen brought you bad luck, not merely a belief in witches, ghosts, and goblins, but also a belief in any strange phenomena of the mind which we did not understand.

We knew about hypnotism, because we had seen stage performances, and were in the midst of reading a naughty book called *Trilby;* but such things as trance mediumship, automatic writing, table-tapping, telekinesis, telepathy and clairvoyance—we didn't know these long names, but if such ideas were explained to us, we knew right away that it was "all nonsense."

In my youth I had the experience of meeting a scholarly Unitarian clergyman, the Rev. Minot J. Savage of New York, who assured me quite seriously that he had seen and talked with ghosts. He didn't convince me, but he sowed the seed of curiosity in my mind, and I began reading books on psychic research. From first to last, I have read hundreds of volumes; always interested, and always uncertain—an uncomfortable mental state. The evidence in support of telepathy came to seem to me conclusive, yet it never quite became real to me. The consequences of belief would be so tremendous, the changes it would make in my view of the universe so revolutionary, that I didn't believe, even when I said I did.

But for thirty years the subject has been among the things I hoped to know about; and, as it happened, fate was planning to favor me. It sent me a wife who became interested, and who not merely investigated telepathy, but learned to practice it. For three years I watched and assisted in this work, day by day and night by night, in our home. So I could say that I was no longer guessing. Now I really know. I am going to tell you about it, and hope to convince you; but regardless of what anybody can say, there will never again be a doubt about it in my mind. I KNOW!

2

TELEPATHY, OR MIND-READING: that is to say, can one human mind communicate with another human mind, except by the sense channels ordinarily known and used—seeing, hearing, feeling, tasting and touching? Can a thought or image in one mind be sent directly to another mind and there reproduced and recognized? If this can be done, how is it done? Is it some kind of vibration, going out from the brain, like radio broadcasting? Or is it some contact with a deeper level of mind, as bubbles on a stream have contact with the water of the stream? And if this power exists, can it be developed and used? Is it something that manifests itself now and then, like a lightning flash, over which we have no control? Or can we make the energy and store it, and use it regularly, as we have learned to do with the lightning which Franklin brought from the clouds?

These are the questions; and the answers, as well as I can summarize them, are as follows: Telepathy is real; it does happen. Whatever may be the nature of the force, it has nothing to do with distance, for it works exactly as well over forty miles as over a few feet. And while it may be spontaneous and may depend upon a special endowment, it can be cultivated and used deliberately, as any other object of study, in physics and chemistry. The essential in this training is an art of mental concentration and autosuggestion, which can be learned. I am going to tell you not merely what you can do, but how you can do it, so that if you have patience and real interest, you can make your own contribution to knowledge.

Starting the subject, I am like the wandering book agent or peddler who taps on your door and gets you to open it, and has to speak quickly and persuasively, putting his best goods foremost. Your prejudice is against this idea; and if you are one of my old-time readers, you are a little shocked to find me taking up a new and unexpected line of activity. You have come, after thirty years, to the position where you allow me to be one kind of "crank," but you won't stand for two kinds. So let me come straight to the point— open up my pack, pull out my choicest wares, and catch your attention with them if I can.

Here is a drawing of a table fork. It was done with a lead-pencil on a sheet of ruled paper, which has been photographed, and then reproduced in the ordinary way. You note that it bears a signature and a date (Fig. 1):

Fig. 1

This drawing was produced by my brother-in-law, Robert L. Irwin, a young businessman, and no kind of "crank," under the following circumstances. He was sitting in a room in his home in Pasadena at a specified hour, eleven-thirty in the morning of July 13, 1928, having agreed to make a drawing of any object he might select, at random, and then to sit gazing at it, concentrating his entire attention upon it for a period of from fifteen to twenty minutes.

At the same agreed hour, eleven-thirty in the morning of July 13, 1928, my wife was lying on the couch in her study, in our home in Long Beach, forty miles away by the road. She was in semi-darkness, with her eyes closed; employing a system of mental concentration which she has been practicing off and on for several years, and mentally suggesting to her subconscious mind to bring her whatever was in the mind of her brother-in-law. Having become satisfied that the image which came to her mind was the correct one—because it persisted, and came back again and again—she sat up and took pencil and paper and wrote the date, and six words, as follows (Fig. 1a):

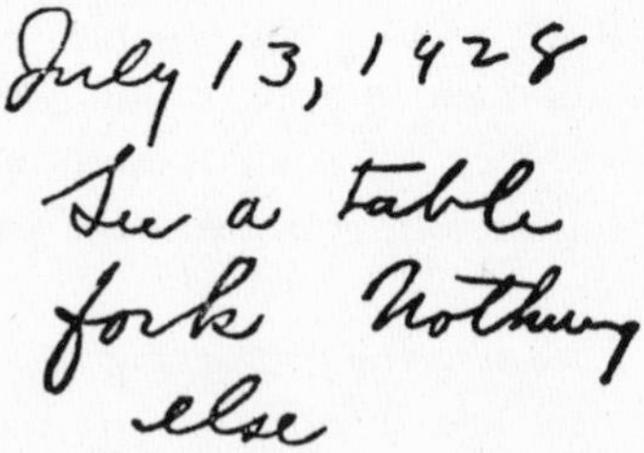

July 13, 1928
See a table
fork Nothing
else

Fig. 1a

A day or two later we drove to Pasadena, and then in the presence of Bob and his wife, the drawing and writing were produced and compared. I have in my possession affidavits from Bob, his wife, and my wife, to the effect that the drawing and writing were produced in this way. Later in this book I shall present four other pairs of drawings, made in the same way, three of them equally successful.

Second case. Here is a drawing (Fig. 2), and below it a set of five drawings (Fig. 2a).

Fig. 2

Fig. 2a

The drawings were produced under the following circumstances. The single drawing (Fig. 2) was made by me in my study at my home. I was alone, and the door was closed before the drawing was made, and was not opened until the test was concluded. Having made the drawing, I held it before me and concentrated upon it for a period of five or ten minutes.

The five drawings (Fig. 2a) were produced by my wife, who was lying on the couch in her study, some thirty feet away from me, with the door closed between us. The only words spoken were as follows: When I was ready to make my drawing, I called, "All right," and when she had completed her drawings, she called "All right"—whereupon I opened the door and took my drawing to her and we compared them. I found that in addition to the five little pictures, she had written some explanation of how she came to draw them. This I shall quote and discuss later on. I shall also tell about six other pairs of drawings, produced at this same time.

Third case: Another drawing (Fig. 3a), produced under the following circumstances. My wife went upstairs, and shut the door which is at the top of the stairway. I went on tip-toe to a cupboard in a downstairs room and took from a shelf a red electric-light bulb—it having been agreed that I should select any small article, of which there were certainly many hundreds in our home. I wrapped this bulb in several thicknesses of newspaper, and put it, so wrapped, in a shoebox, and wrapped the shoe-box in a whole newspaper, and tied it tightly with a string. I then called my wife and she came downstairs, and lay on her couch and put the box on her body, over the solar plexus. I sat watching, and never took my eyes from her, nor did I speak a word during the test. Finally she sat up, and made her drawing, with the written comment, and handed it to me. Every word of the comment, as well as the drawing, was produced before I said a word, and the drawing and writing as here reproduced have not been touched or altered in any way (Fig. 3a):

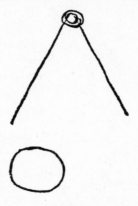

Fig. 3a

The text of my wife's written comment is as follows:

"First see round glass. Guess nose glasses? No. Then comes V shape again with a 'button' in top. Button stands out from object. This round top is of different color from lower part. It is light color, the other part is dark."

To avoid any possible misunderstanding, perhaps I should state that the question and answer in the above were my wife's description of her own mental process, and do not represent a question asked of me. She did not "guess" aloud, nor did either of us speak a single word during this test, except the single word, "Ready," to call my wife downstairs.

The next drawings were produced in the following manner. The one at the top (Fig. 4) was drawn by me alone in my study, and was one of nine, all made at the same time, and with no restriction upon what I should draw—anything that came into my head. Having made the nine drawings, I wrapped each one in a separate sheet of green paper, to make it absolutely invisible, and put each one in a plain envelope and sealed it, and then took the nine sealed envelopes and laid them on the table by my wife's couch. My wife then took one of them and placed it over her solar plexus, and lay in her state of concentration, while I sat watching her, at her insistence, in order to make the evidence more convincing. Having received what she considered a convincing telepathic "message," or image of the contents of the envelope, she sat up and made her sketch (Fig. 4a) on a pad of paper.

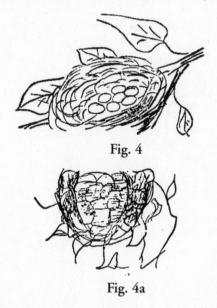

Fig. 4

Fig. 4a

The essence of our procedure is this: that never did she see my drawing until hers was completed and her descriptive words written; that I spoke no word and made no comment until after this was done; and that the drawings presented here are in every case exactly what I drew, and the corresponding drawing is exactly what my wife drew, with no change or addition whatsoever. In the case of this particular pair, my wife wrote, "Inside of rock well with vines climbing on outside."

Such was her guess as to the drawing, which I had meant for a bird's nest surrounded by leaves; but you see that the two drawings are for practical purposes identical.

Many tests have been made, by each of the different methods above outlined, and the results will be given and explained in these pages. The method of attempting to reproduce little drawings was used more than any other, simply because it proved the most convenient; it could be done at a moment's notice, and so fitted into our busy lives. The procedure was varied in a few details to save time and trouble, as I shall later explain, but the essential feature remains unchanged: I make a set of drawings, and my wife takes them one by one and attempts to reproduce them without having seen them. Here are a few samples, chosen at random because of their picturesque character. If my wife wrote anything on the drawing, I add it as "comment"; and you are to understand here, and for the rest of this book, that "comment" means the exact words which she wrote *before* she saw my drawing. Often there will be parts of this "comment" visible in the photograph. I give it all in print. Note that drawings 1, 2, 3, etc. are mine, while 1a, 2a, 3a, etc., are my wife's.

In the case of my drawing numbered Fig. 5, my wife's comment was: "Knight's helmet."

On Fig. 6, the comment was: "Desert scene, camel, ostrich, then below"—and the drawing in Fig. 6a:

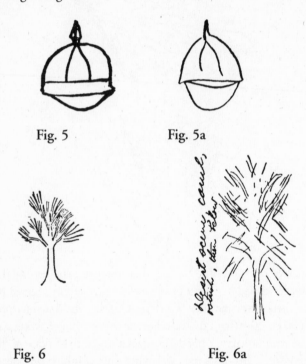

Fig. 5   Fig. 5a

Fig. 6   Fig. 6a

On the reverse side of the page is further comment: "This came in fragments, as if I saw it being drawn by invisible pencil."

And here is a pair with no comment, and none needed (Figs. 7, 7a):

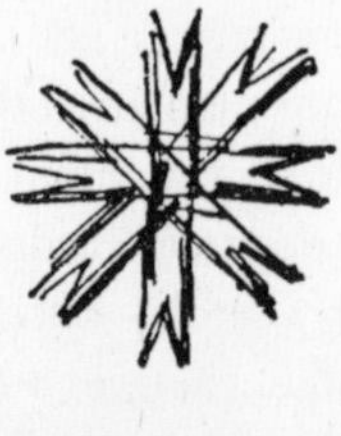

Fig. 7    Fig. 7a

On the following, also, no comment is written (Figs. 8, 8a):

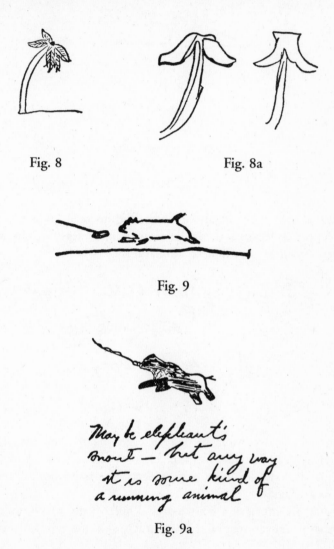

Fig. 8   Fig. 8a

Fig. 9

Fig. 9a

I drew Fig. 9, and my wife drew 9a, a striking success, and wrote the comment: "May be elephant's snout—but anyway it is some kind of a running animal. Long thing like rope flung out in front of him."

Next, a series of three pairs, which, as it happened, were done one after the other, numbers three, four, and five in the twenty-third series of my drawings. They are selected in part because they are amusing. First, I tried to draw a bat, from vague memories of boyhood days when they used to fly into the ballrooms at Virginia springs hotels, and have to be massacred with brooms, because it was believed that they sought to tangle themselves in the hair of the ladies (Figs. 10, 10a):

Fig. 10

Fig. 10a

My wife's comment on the above reads: "Big insect. I know this is right because it moves his legs as if flying. Beetle working its legs. Legs in motion!" And next, my effort at a Chinese mandarin (Figs. 11, 11a):

Fig. 11 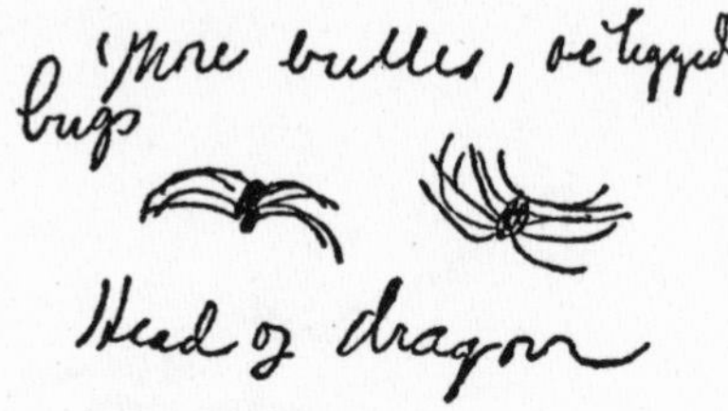   **Fig. 11a**

The comment reads: "More beetles, or legged bugs"—and she draws the mustaches of the mandarin and his hair. "Head of dragon with big mouth. See also a part of his body—in front, or shoulders." The association of mandarins with dragons is obvious.

And finally, my efforts at a boy's foot and roller-skate, which undergoes a strange telepathic transformation. I have put it upside down for easier comparison (Figs. 12, 12a):

Fig. 12   **Fig. 12a**

The comment, complete, reads: "Profile of head and neck of animal—lion or dog—a muzzle. Maybe pig snout."

The above are samples of our successes. Altogether, of such drawings, 38 were prepared by my secretary, while I made 252, a total of 290. I have classified the drawings to the best of my ability into three groups: successes, partial successes, and failures. The partial successes are those drawings which contain some easily recognized element of the original drawing: such as, for example, the last one above. The profile of a pig's head is not a roller skate, but when you compare the drawings, you see that in my wife's first sketch the eyes resemble the wheels of the roller-skates, and in her second sketch the snout resembles my shoe-tip; also there is a general similarity of outline, which is what she most commonly gets.

In the 290 drawings, the total of successes is 65, which is roughly 23 per cent. The total of partial successes is 155, which is 53 per cent. The total of failures is 70, which is 24 per cent. I asked some mathematician friends to work out the probabilities on the above results, but I found that the problem was too complicated. Who could estimate how many possible objects there were, which might come into my head to be drawn? Any time the supply ran short, I would pick up a magazine, and in the advertising pages find a score of new drawings to imitate. Again, very few of the drawings were simple. We began with such things as a circle, a square, a cross, a number or a letter; but soon we were doing Chinese mandarins with long mustaches, and puppies chasing a string. Each of these drawings has many different features; and what mathematician could count the number of these features, and the chances of reproducing them?

It is a matter to be judged by common sense. It seems to me any one must agree that the chances of the twelve drawings so far shown have been reproduced by accident is too great to be worth considering. A million years would not be enough for such a set of coincidences.

3

MUCH OF THE EVIDENCE which I am using rests upon the good faith of Mary Craig Sinclair; so, before we go further, I ask your permission to introduce her. She is a daughter of the far South; her father a retired planter, bank president and judge, of Mississippi. The fates endowed his oldest child with the blessings of beauty, health, wealth, and wisdom—and then spoiled it, by adding a curse in the shape of a too tender heart. The griefs of other people overwhelm Craig like a suffocation. Strangers take one glance at her, and instantly decide that here is one who will "understand." I have seen her go into a store to buy a piece of ribbon, and come out with tears in her eyes, because of a tragic story which some clerk was moved to pour out to her, all in a moment, without provocation. She has always said that she "gets" the feelings of people, not by their words, but by intuition. But she never paid any attention to this gift; never associated it with "psychic" matters. She was always too busy, first with eight younger brothers and sisters, and then with the practical affairs of an unpractical author-husband.

Early in childhood, things like this would happen: her mother would say to a little negro servant, "Go and find Miss Mary Craig"; but before the boy could start, Craig would know that her mother wanted her, and would be on the way. This might, of course, have been coincidence; if it stood alone, it would have no value.

But the same thing happened with dreams. Craig dreamed there was a needle in her bed, and woke up and looked for it in vain; in the morning she told her mother, who slept in another room. The mother said: "How strange! I dreamed the same thing, and I woke up and really found one!"

Of her young ladyhood, Craig told this story, one of many: Driving with a girlfriend, miles from home, she suddenly remarked: "Let's go home; Mr. B is there." Now this was a place to which Mr. B had never come; it was three hundred miles from his town. But Craig said: "I have just had an impression of him, sitting on our front porch." Going home, they found him there.

Another instance, of more recent date. Shortly after our coming to California, my wife all at once became greatly worried about Jack London; she insisted that he was in terrible mental distress. As it happened, George Sterling had told us much about Jack's troubles, but these were of old standing, and there was nothing to account for the sudden notion which my wife took up on a certain day. We had a lot of conversation about it; I offered to take her to the London ranch, but she said she would not attempt to meddle in the affairs of a married man, unless at his wife's request. I made the laughing suggestion that she go alone, in the guise of a gypsy fortune-teller—a role which in her young ladyhood she had played with social éclat. Two days later we read that Jack London was dead, and very soon came letters from George Sterling, telling us that he had taken his own life. This, again, might be coincidence; if it stood alone I would attach no importance to it. But taken with this mass of evidence, it has a share of weight.

When we were married, seventeen years ago, we spent some time in England, and there we met a woman physician, interested in "mental healing," and full of ideas about "psychic" things. Both Craig and I were in need of healing, having been through a siege of trouble. Craig was suffering with intense headaches, something hitherto unknown in her life; while I had an ancient problem of indigestion, caused by excess of brain work and lack of body work. We began to experiment with healing by the "laying on of hands"—without knowing anything about it, just groping in the dark. I found that I could cure Craig's headaches—and get them myself; while she found that she could take my indigestion, a trouble she had never known hitherto. Each of us was willing to take the other's pains, but neither was willing to give them, so our experiments came to a halt.

We forgot the whole subject for more than ten years. I was busy trying to reform America, while Craig was of the most intensely materialistic convictions. Her early experiences of evangelical religion had repelled her so violently that everything suggestive of "spirituality" was repugnant to her. Never was a woman more "practical," more centered upon the here and now, the things which can be seen and touched. I do not go into details about this, but I want to make it as emphatic as possible, for the light it throws upon her attitude and disposition.

But shortly after the age of forty, her custom of carrying the troubles of all who were near her resulted in a breakdown of health. A story of suffering needless to go into: suffice it that she had many ills to experiment upon, and mental control became suddenly a matter of life and death. In the course of the last five or six years Craig has acquired a fair-sized library of books on the mind, both orthodox scientific, and "crank." She has sat up half the night studying, marking passages and making notes, seeking to reconcile various doctrines, to know what the mind really is, and how it works, and what can be done with it. Always it was a practical problem: things had to *work*. If now she believes anything, rest assured that it is because she has tried it out in the crucibles of pain, and proved it in her daily regimen.

She was not content to see psychic phenomena produced by other persons. Even though authorities warned her that trances might be dangerous, and that *rapport* with others might lead to dissociations of personality—even so, she had to find out for herself. A hundred times in the course of experiments of which I am going to tell, she has turned to me, saying: "Can you think of any way this can be chance? What can I do to make it more sure?" When I said, the other night: "This settles it for me. I am going to write the story," her reply was, "Wait a while!" She wants to do more experimenting; but I think that enough is enough.

| 4

TWO YEARS AGO Craig and I heard of a "psychic," a young foreigner who was astounding physicians of Southern California, performing feats so completely beyond their understanding that they were content to watch without trying to understand. We went to see this young man, and befriended him; he came to our home every day, and his strange demonstrations became familiar to us. He had the ability to produce anaesthesia in many parts of his body, and stick hatpins through his tongue and cheeks without pain; he could go into a deep trance in which his body became rigid and cold; and I put his head on one chair and his heels on another, and stood in the middle, as if he were a two-inch plank. We have a motion picture film, showing a 150-pound rock being broken with a sledge-hammer on his abdomen while he lay in this trance. The vital faculties were so far suspended in this trance that he could be shut up in an airtight coffin and buried underground for several hours; nor was there any hocus-pocus about this—I know physicians who got the coffins and arranged for the tests and watched every detail; in Ventura, California, it was done in a ball park, and a game was played over the grave.

In our home he gave what appeared to be a demonstration of levitation without contact. I do not say that it really was levitation; I merely say that our friends who witnessed it—physicians, scientists, writers and their wives, fourteen persons in all—were unable even to suggest a normal method by which the event could have happened. There was no one present who could have been a confederate, and the psychic had been searched for apparatus; it was in our home, where he had no opportunity whatever for preparation. His wrists and ankles were firmly held by persons whom I know well; and there was sufficient light in the room so that I could see the outline of his figure, slumped in a chair. Under these circumstances a 34-pound table rose four feet into the air and moved slowly a distance of eight feet over my head.

We saw this; our friends saw it; yet, in my mind, and likewise in theirs, the worm of doubt would always creep in. There are so many ways to fool people; so many conjuring tricks—think of Houdini, for example! I was unwilling to publish what I had seen; yet, also, I was unwilling not to publish it—for think of the possible importance of faculties such as this, locked up in our minds! Here was my wife, ill, suffering pain; and these facilities might perhaps be used for healing. If by concentration and auto-suggestion it was possible for the mind to control the body, and put a veto upon even a few of its disorders, certainly it was worthwhile for us to prove the fact. I could not escape the moral obligation to probe these matters.

This "psychic" claimed also to possess and demonstrate the power of telepathy, or mind-reading. He would go out of the room while one of us selected mentally some object in the room, not revealing the choice to anyone else. The "psychic" would then come back, and tell us to stand behind him and concentrate our thoughts upon that object, and follow close behind him, thinking of it. He would wander about the room for awhile, and in the end pick up the object, and do with it whatever we mentally "willed" him to do.

We saw him make this test not less than a hundred times, in California, New York, and Boston; he succeeded with it more than half the time. There was no contact, no word spoken, nothing that we could imagine as giving him a clue. Did we unconsciously make in our throats some faint pronunciation of words, and did the young man have a super-acuity of hearing? Again, you see, the worm of doubt, and we never could quite decide what we really believed about this performance. After puzzling over it for a year or more, my wife said: "There is only one way to be certain. I am going to learn to do these things *myself!*"

This young man, whom I will call Jan, was a peculiar person. Sometimes he would be open and frank, and again he would be mysterious and secretive. At one time he would agree to teach us all he knew, and again he would hold on to his arts, which he had had to go all the way to India to get. Was it that he considered these forces too dangerous for amateurs to play with? Or was it merely that he was considering his means of livelihood?

Jan was a hypnotist; and my wife had come to realize that all illness is more or less amenable to suggestion. She had had the idea of being hypnotized and given curative suggestions; but she did not know enough about this stranger, and was unwilling to trust him. After she got to know him better, her purposes changed. Here was a fund of knowledge which she craved, and she put her woman's wits to work to get it. She told him to go ahead and hypnotize her—and explained to me her purpose of trying to turn the tables on him. Jan fixed his eyes upon hers in the hypnotic stare, and made his magnetic passes; at the same time his patient stared back, and I sat and watched the strange duel of personalities.

An essential part of Jan's technique, as he had explained it, was in outstaring the patient and never blinking his eyes. Now suddenly he blinked; then he closed his eyes and kept them closed. "Do your eyes hurt?" asked his patient, in pretended innocence. "No," he replied. "Are you tired?" she asked. "No, thank you," said he. "What was I thinking?" she asked. "To hypnotize me," he replied, sleepily. But Craig wanted further proof, so she closed her eyes and willed that Jan should get up and go to the telephone. "Shall I go on treating you?" he asked. "Yes," said she. He hesitated a moment, then said, "Excuse me, I have to telephone to a friend!"

I am telling about these matters in the order of time, as they came to us. I am sorry that these stories of Jan come first, because they are the strangest, and the least capable of proof. In the hope of taking part of the onus from our shoulders, let me quote from a book by Charles Richet, a member of the Institute of Medicine in France, and a leading scientist; he is citing Pierre Janet, whose name is known wherever in the world the human mind is studied. The statement reads:

"P. Janet, a most eminent French psychiatrist, and one of the founders of the famous Salpetriere school of psychology in Paris, and a careful and skeptical observer, has verified that a patient of his, Leonie B., being put into hypnotic sleep by himself, or his brother (from whom Leonie in her hypnotic sleep was unable to distinguish him), could recognize *exactly* the substance that he placed in his mouth—sugar, salt, pepper. One day his brother, J. Janet, in an adjoining room, scorched his right arm above the wrist. Leonie, who could have known nothing about it normally, gave signs of real pain, and showed to P. Janet (who knew nothing of the occurrence), the exact place of the burn."

Or let me cite the late Professor Quackenbos, of Columbia University, who wrote many books on hypnotism as a therapeutic agency, and tells of numerous cases of the same kind. He himself would sometimes go involuntarily into hypnotic sleep with his patient, and so, sometimes, would the nurse. Frequently between the hypnotist and the subject comes what is called *rapport*, whereby each knows what is in the other's mind, and suggestions are taken without their being spoken. You may believe this, or refuse to believe it—that [is] your privilege. All I want to do is to make clear that my wife is claiming no special achievement, but merely repeating the standard experiences of the textbooks on this subject.

This *rapport* between Craig and her protege was developed to such an extent that she could tell him what was in his mind, and what he had been doing; she told him many stories about himself, where he had been and what he had done at a certain hour. This was embarrassing to a young man who perhaps did not care to have his life so closely overseen; also, possibly, he was wounded in his *amour propre*, that a mere amateur—and a woman at that—should be coming into possession of his secret arts.

The trick depends upon a process of intense concentration, which will later be described in detail. After this concentration, Craig would give to her subconscious mind the suggestion, or command, that it should bring to her consciousness a vision of what Jan was doing. This giving an order to the subconscious mind is much the same sort of thing that you do when you seek to remember a name; whether you realize it or not, you order your subconscious mind to get that bit of information and bring it to you. Whatever came to Craig, she would write it out, and when next she met Jan, she would use her woman's wits to verify it without Jan's knowing what was happening. At times it would be very amusing—when he would find himself accused of some youthful misdemeanor which his preceptress was not supposed to know about. In his efforts to defend himself, he would fail entirely to realize the telepathic aspects of the matter.

| 5

PLEASE LET ME REPEAT, I am not telling here a set of fairy tales and fantasies; I am presenting a record of experiments, conducted in strict scientific fashion. All the results were set down day by day in writing. For an hour or two every day for the past three years my wife has been scribbling notes of her experiments, and there are eight boxes full in her study, enough to fill a big trunk. No statement in all the following rests upon our memories; everything is taken from memoranda now in my hands. Admitting that new facts can be learned about the mind, I do not see how anyone can use more careful methods than we have done.

My wife "saw" Jan carrying a bouquet of flowers, wrapped in white paper, on the street, and she wrote this down. She later ascertained that at this hour Jan had carried flowers to a friend in a hospital in Los Angeles, and she telephoned this friend and verified the facts. On another occasion when Jan was in Santa Barbara, a hundred miles from our home, she "saw" him escorting a blonde girl in a blue dress from an auto to a hotel over a rainy pavement; she wrote this down, and later ascertained that it had actually been happening. The details were verified, not merely by Jan, but by another member of the party. I ought to add that in no case did my wife tell the other persons what she had "seen" until after these persons had told her what had happened. No chance was taken of their making up events to conform to her records. Always Craig kept her cold-blooded determination to know what was real in this field where so much is invented and imagined.

Again, she "saw" Jan preparing to commit suicide, dressed in a pair of yellow silk pajamas; then she "saw" him lying dead on the floor. She was much disturbed—until Jan reminded her that he had been seven times publicly "buried" in Southern California before she met him. Several weeks later she learned that in one of these "burials" he had worn yellow silk pajamas. Jan had forgotten this, but Dr. Frank Sweet, of Long Beach, who had overseen the procedure, remembered the pajamas, and how they had been ruined by mud.

Craig saw a vision of a bride, at a time when Jan, in his room in a far part of the city, was awakened from sleep with a dream about a friend's wedding. On two occasions, while "concentrating," she got the impression that Jan and a friend of his had returned unexpectedly from Santa Barbara to Hollywood. In both cases she made careful record, and it turned out to be correct; I have a written statement of the two young men, confirming the second instance, and saying that it could not have been normally known to my wife.

I have also a detailed record—some twenty pages long—of a "clairvoyant" vision of Jan's movements about the city of Long Beach, including his parking of a car, carrying something over his arm, visiting a barbershop and a flower-shop, and stopping and hesitating and then going on. The record includes a detailed description of the streets and their layout, a one-story white building, etc. Jan had been doing all this at approximately the time specified. He had carried his trousers to a tailorshop, with a barber-shop directly opposite; he had stopped in front of a flower-shop and debated whether to buy some flowers; he had taken a letter to be copied by a typist, and had stopped on the street, hesitating as to whether to wait for this copying to be done. All these details he narrated to my wife *before* he knew what was in her written record.

Another curious experience: I took Jan to the home of Dr. John R. Haynes of Los Angeles, to give a demonstration of his mind-reading. Jan said he felt ill, and would not be successful. Only one [or] two [of] the tests succeeded. But meanwhile my wife was at home concentrating, and ordering her subconscious mind to show her what Jan and I were doing. When I returned I found that she had written a detailed description of Dr. Haynes' home, including a correct ground plan of the entrance hall, stairs and drawing-room, and a description of the color and style of decorations, furniture, lamps, vases, etc., in good part correct. Craig has never been in this house.

Jan goes into one of his deep states—a cataleptic trance, he calls it—in which his body is rigid and cold. He has the power to fix in advance the time when he will come out of the trance, and his subconscious mind apparently possesses the power to keep track of time, days, hours, minutes, even seconds. I have seen him amaze a group of scientists by coming out on the second, while they held stop-watches on him.

But now my wife thinks she will vary this procedure. Jan goes into the trance in our home and Craig sits and silently wills, "Your right leg will come out; you will lift it; you will put it down again. You will sit erect"—and so on. Without speaking a word, she can make him do whatever she pleases.

Another incident, quite a long one. I ask you to have patience with the details, promising that in the end you will see what it is all about. I am in the next room, and I hear Jan and my wife having one of their regular evening arguments, because he will not tell her how he does this or that; at one moment he insists that he has told her, and the next moment he insists that he does not know. My wife finally asks him to concentrate upon an object in the room, and she will see if she can "get" it. He selects the gas stove, in which a fire is burning, and Craig says, "I see a lot of little flames." Jan insists that is "no good," she didn't get the stove, which annoys her very much—she thinks he does not want to allow any success to a woman. He is a "continental male," something she makes fierce feminist war upon.

Craig is suffering from neuralgia in her neck and shoulder, and Jan offers to treat her. He will use what he calls "magnetism"; he believes there is an emanation from his finger-tips, and so, with his two forefingers he lightly traces the course of the nerves of her neck and shoulder and arm. For ten or fifteen minutes his two fingers are tracing patterns in front of her.

Then it is time for him to go home, and he is unhappy, and she succeeds in drawing the explanation from him—he has to walk, and his shoes are tight and hurt him. He has to have them stretched, he tells her. She offers him a pair of my big tennis shoes to wear home, and then she scolds him because he has the fashionable notion that white canvas tennis shoes are not proper footwear for eleven o'clock in the evening. Finally he puts them on and departs, and my wife lies down and makes her mind a blank, and orders it to tell her what Jan is doing.

She has a pencil and paper, and presently she is writing words. They are foreign words, and she thinks they must be in Jan's native language; they come drifting through her mind for several minutes. Next day comes Jan for the daily lesson, and she shows him this record. He tells her that the words are not in his language, but German—which he knows, but never uses. My wife knows no German; except possibly sauerkraut and kindergarten. But here she has written a string of German and near-German words. I have the original sheet before me, and I give it as well as I can make out the scrawl: "ei einfinen ein-fe-en swefenz fingen sweizzen czie ofen weizen ofen fingen swienfen swei fingern efein boden fienzen meifen bogen feingen Bladen Meichen frefen eifein."

Some of this is nonsense; but there are a few German words in it, and others which are guesses at German words, such as might be made by a person hearing a strange language, and trying to set down what he hears. Part of the effort seems to be concentrated on getting one expression, "zwe Fingern"—two fingers! You remember the two fingers moving up and down over Craig's neck and shoulder! And "Ofen"—the argument about the stove! And "bladen"—to stretch shoes over a block of wood. Where these ideas came from seems plain enough. But where did the German come from—unless from the subconscious mind of Jan?

A further detail, especially curious. Jan gave my wife the meaning for the word "bladen": "to stretch shoes over a block of wood"; I have the memo which he wrote at the time. But looking up the word in the dictionaries, I do not find it, nor can I find any German who knows it. Apparently there is no such word; and this would clearly seem to indicate that my wife got her German from Jan. If so, it was by telepathy, for he spoke no word of it that evening.

It is the fashion among young ladies of the South to tease the men, and Craig found in this episode a basis for tormenting her psychic instructor. He had assured his patient that during the treatment he was sending her "curative thoughts." But what kind of telepathic healer was it who sent gas-stoves and shoe-blocks into a neuralgic shoulder? Jan, missing the humor, and trying to save his reputation, declared that he hated the German language so greatly, he did not even allow himself to think in it! Germany was associated in his mind with the most painful memories, and all that previous day he had been fighting depression caused by these memories. You see, in this blundering defense, a significant bit of evidence. Jan had really had the German language in his thoughts at the time Craig got them!

I have before me a letter from Jan to my wife, postmarked Santa Barbara, October 19, 1927. He says: "May these lovely Cosmos bring you such peace and contentment as they have brought me." He has cut a double slit in the paper, and inserted cosmos blossoms and violets. Prior to the receipt of this letter, my wife was making the record of a dream, and here is what she wrote down: "I dreamed Jan had a little basket of flowers, pink roses and violets, shaped like this." (A drawing.) "He lifted them up and said they were for me, but a girl near him took them and said, 'But I want them.'" When Jan came to see us again, my wife asked about the circumstance, and learned the following: a woman friend, who had given Jan the flowers, had accused him of meaning to send them to a girl; but he had answered that they were for "a middle-aged and distinguished lady."

I present here the basket of "pink roses and violets" which my wife drew, and then the spray of pink double cosmos and violets which met her eyes when she opened the young "psychic's" letter a day or two later. I explain that my wife's drawing (Fig. 13) is partly written over by the words of her notes; while in Jan's letter the violets had to be at once traced in pencil, as they would not last. My wife drew pencil marks around them and wrote the word "violet" in three places, to indicate what the marks meant. The cosmos flowers, pressed

Fig. 13

Fig. 13a

and dried, are still exactly as Jan stuck them into position and as they remained until I took them to be photographed (Fig. 13a).

6

AS I HAVE SAID, I hesitate to tell about incidents such as these. They are hard to believe, and the skeptic may say that my wife was hypnotized by Jan, and made to believe them. But it happens that Craig has been able to establish exactly the same *rapport* with her husband, who has never had anything to do with hypnosis, except to watch it a few times. A Socialist "muckraker," much wrapped up in his job, the husband sits and reads, or revises manuscript, while the wife works her white magic upon his mind. Suddenly his train of thought is broken by an exclamation; the wife has "willed" him to do such and so—and he has done it! Or maybe she has been asleep, and come out with the tail end of a dream, and has written down what appears to be a lot of rubbish—but turns out to be a reproduction of something the husband has been reading or writing at that very moment! Here are one or two instances of such events, all written down at the time.

Colonel Lindbergh has flown to France, but Craig does not know much about it, because she is not reading the papers, she is asking, "What is life?" A year passes, and in the mail I receive a monthly magazine, the Lantern, published by Sacco-Vanzetti sympathizers in Boston. I open it, and find an article by a young radical, assailing Lindbergh because he does not follow in his father's footsteps; his father was a radical congressman, but now the son allows himself to be used by the army and navy people, and by the capitalist press, to distract the minds of the masses from social justice. So runs the charge; and before I am through reading it, my wife comes downstairs from a nap. "What are you reading?" she asks, and I answer: "Something about Lindbergh." Says my wife: "Here are my notes about a dream I just had." She hands me a sheet of paper, I have it before me now as I write, and I give it with misspelling and abbreviations exactly as she wrote it in a hurry, not anticipating that it would ever become public:

"'I do not believe that Lindberg flew across the ocean in order to take a ransome from a foreign gov as well as from his own. Nor in order to induce the nations of the earth to a war in the air.' Words which were in my mind as I awoke from nap on aft May 25."

I should add that my wife had had no opportunity to look at the Boston magazine, whether consciously or unconsciously. She tells me that Lindbergh had not been in her conscious mind for a long time, and she had no remotest idea that the radicals were attacking him.

Another instance: I am reading the latest "book of the month," which has just come in the mail, and to which my wife has paid no attention. She interrupts me with a question: "Are there any flowers in what you are reading?" I answer, "Yes," and she says: "I have been trying to concentrate, and I keep seeing flowers. I have drawn them." She hands me two drawings (Figs. 14a, 14b).

The book was Mumford's *Herman Melville,* and I was at page 346, a chapter entitled, "The Flowering Aloe." On this page are six lines from a poem called

Fig. 14a   Fig. 14b

"The American Aloe on Exhibition." On the preceding page is a discussion of the habits of this plant. While my wife was making the left-hand drawing (Fig. 14a), I had been reading page 344: "the red clover had blushed through the fields about their house"; and "he would return home with a handful of clover blossoms."

Of experiences like this there have been many. Important as the subject is, I find it a bother, because I am called upon to listen to long narratives of dreams and telepathy, while my mind is on Sacco and Vanzetti, or the Socialist presidential campaign, or whatever it is. Sometimes the messages from the subconscious are complicated and take patience to disentangle. Consider, for example, a little drawing (Fig. 15)—one of nearly three hundred which this long-suffering husband has

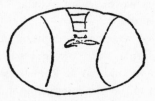 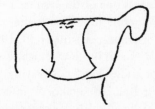

Fig. 15   Fig. 15a

made for his witch-wife to reproduce by telepathy: a football, you see, neatly laced up. In her drawing (Fig.15a) Craig gets the general effect perfectly, but she puts it on a calf. Her written comment was: "Belly-band on calf."

While Craig was making this particular experiment, her husband was reading a book; and now, wishing to solve the mystery, she asks, "What are you reading?" The husband replies, wearily: "DeKruif's *Hunger Fighters,* page 283." "What does it deal with?" "It is a treatise on the feeding of cows." "Really?" says Craig. "Will you please write that down for me and sign it?"

But why did the cow become a calf? That, too, is something to be explained. Says Craig: "Do you remember what I used to tell you about old Mr. Bebb and his calves?" Yes, the husband knows the story of the half-crazy old Welshman, who thirty or forty years ago was the caretaker of the Kimbrough summer home on the Mississippi Sound. Old Mr. Bebb made his hobby the raising of calves by hand, and turning them into parlor pets. He would teach them to use his three fingers as a nursing bottle, and would make fancy embroidered belly-bands for them, and tie them up in these. So to the subconscious mind which was once little Mary Craig Kimbrough of Mississippi, the idea of a calf sewed up like a football is one of the most natural in the world.

Since my wife and I have no secrets from each other, it does not trouble me that she is able to see what I am doing. While I am away from home, she will "concentrate" upon me, and immediately afterwards write out what she "sees." On one occasion she described to me a little red book which I had got in the mail at the office. By way of establishing just what kind of book she had "seen," she had gone to my bookcase and picked out a French dictionary—and it happened that I had just received the Italian dictionary of that same series, uniform in binding. On another occasion, while making a study of dream-material, she wrote out a dream about being lost in long and involved concrete corridors—while I was trying to find my way through the lockerrooms of a Y. M. C. A. basement, running into one blind passage after another, and being much annoyed by doors that wouldn't open.

Dreams, you understand, are products of subconscious activity, and to watch them is one method of proving telepathy. By practice Craig has learned to lie passive, immediately after awakening, and trace back a long train of dreams. Here is one of the results, a story worth telling in detail—save that I fear you will refuse to believe it after it is told.

On the afternoon of January 30, 1928, I was playing tennis on the courts of the Virginia Hotel, in Long Beach, California, and my wife was taking a nap. She did not know that I was playing tennis, and has no knowledge about the places where I play. She takes no interest in the game, regarding it as a foolish business which will some day cause her husband to drop dead of heart failure—and she declines to be present on the occasion. When I entered the house, she said: "I woke up with a long involved dream, and it seemed so absurd I didn't want to write it out, but I did so." Here are the opening sentences verbatim:

"Dreamed I was on a pier, watching a new kind of small, one or two seated sport-boat, a little water car into which a woman got and was shot by machinery from the pier out to the water, where she skidded around a minute or two and was drawn back to the pier. With us on the pier were my sister and child, and two young men in white with white caps. These appeared to be in charge of this new sport-boat. This boat is not really a boat. It is a sort of miniature car. I've never seen anything like it. Short, so that only one or two people could sit in it. An amusement thing, belonging to the pier. The two young men were intensely interested, and stood close together watching it out on the water," etc., etc.

Understand that this dream was not supposed to have anything to do with me. It was before Craig had come to realize the state of rapport with me; she had not been thinking about me, and when she told me about this dream, she had no thought that any part of it had come from my mind. But here is what I told her about my afternoon:

The Virginia Hotel courts are close to what is called "The Pike," and there is an amusement pier just across the way, and on it a so-called "Ferris wheel," with little cars exactly like the description, which go up into the air with people in them. That afternoon it happened that the tennis courts were crowded, so my partner and I waited out a set or two. We sat on a bench, in white tennis suits and hats, and watched this wheel, and the cars which went up in the air, and at a certain point took a slide on long rods, which made them "skid around," and caused the women in them to scream with excitement. Underneath the pier was the ocean, plainly visible along with the little cars.

(Footnote, 1962: The hotel and the Pike no longer exist, so do not waste your time trying to verify all this.)

I should also mention the case of our friend, Mrs. Kate Crane-Gartz, with whom there is a *rapport* which my wife does not tell her about. My wife will say to me, "Mrs. Gartz is going to phone," and in a minute or two the phone will ring. She will say, "Mrs. Gartz is coming. She wants me to go to Los Angeles with her." Of course, a good deal of guessing might be possible, in the case of two intimate friends. But consider such guessing as this: My wife had a dream of an earthquake and wrote it down. Soon thereafter occurred this conversation with Mrs. Gartz. I heard it, and my wife recorded it immediately afterwards, and I quote her written record:

"Mrs. Gartz dreamed of earthquake. 'Wasn't it queer that I dreamed of swaying slowly from side to side.'"

"'I dreamed the same,' I said. 'But I was in a high building.'"

"'So was I,' she replied."

Craig calls attention to the word "slowly," as both she and Mrs. Gartz commented on this. They didn't believe that an earthquake would behave that way; but I pointed out that it would happen just so with a steelframe building.

7

I come now to a less fantastic and more convincing series of experiments; those made with the husband of my wife's younger sister, Robert L. Irwin. Eight years ago the doctors gave Bob only a few months to live, on account of tuberculosis. Needless to say, he has much time on his hands, waiting for the doctors' clairvoyance to be verified. He proved to be a good "subject"—the best of all in the tests with Jan. One day in our home, a series of five tests were made, with Bob holding an object in mind, while sitting several feet away from Jan. The latter found the object, and made the correct disposition of it, as willed by Bob, in four out of the five trials. This included such unlikely things as picking up a striped blanket and wrapping it about my shoulders.

Bob and Craig made the arrangement that at a certain hour each day, Bob, in his home in Pasadena, was to take pencil and paper and make a drawing of an object, and sit and concentrate his mind upon that drawing. At the same hour Craig, in our home in Long Beach, forty miles away, was to go into her state of "concentration," and give orders to her subconscious mind to find out what was in Bob's mind. The drawings were to be dated, and filed, and when the two of them met, they would compare the results, in the presence of myself and Bob's wife. If there should turn out to be a correspondence between the drawings, greater than could be attributed to chance, it would be evidence of telepathy, as good as any that could be imagined or desired.

The results were such as to make me glad that it was another person than myself, so as to afford a disinterested witness to these matters, so difficult of belief. I repeat that Bob is a young American businessman, priding himself on having no "crank" ideas; he has had a Socialist brother-in-law for ten years or more without being in the slightest degree affected in manners, morals, or convictions. Here is his first drawing, done on a half sheet of green paper. The word "CHAIR" underneath, and the date, were written by Bob, while the words "drawn by Bob Irwin" were added for purposes of record by Craig (Fig. 16):

Bob Irwin

CHAIR drawn by
July 8-1928

are a straight chair.
1st   2nd

Fig. 16   Fig. 16a

And now for Craig's results. I give her report verbatim, with the two drawings which are part of her text:

"At 10 o'clock or a little before, while sewing (without effort) I saw Bob take something from black sideboard—think it was the glass candlestick. At 11:15 (I concentrate now) I saw Bob sitting at dining room table—a dish or some small object in front of him (on N. E. corner table). I try to see the object on table—see white something at last. I can't decide what it is so I concentrate on seeing his drawing on a green paper as it is about 11:20 now and I think he has made his drawing. I try hard to see what he has drawn—try to see a paper with a drawing on it, and see a straight chair. Am not sure of second drawing. It does not seem to be on his paper. It may be his bed-foot. I distinctly see a chair like 1st on his paper." (Fig. 16a).

When Bob and my wife discussed the above test, she learned that he had sat at the northeast corner of the table, trying to decide what to draw, and facing the sideboard on which were silver candlesticks. Later he went to his bedroom and lay down, gazing through the foot of his bed at the chair which he had taken as his model for the drawing. The bed has white bars running vertically, as in my wife's second drawing. The chair, like Bob's drawing, has the strips of wood supporting the back running crossways, and this feature is reproduced in Craig's first drawing. Her report goes on to add that she sees a star and some straight lines, which she draws; they are horizontal parallel lines, as in the back of the chair. The back of the chair Bob had looked at had a carved star upon it.

The second attempt was the next day, and Bob drew his watch (Fig. 17). Craig first drew a chair, and then wrote, "But do not feel it is correct." Then she drew the following (Fig. 17a):

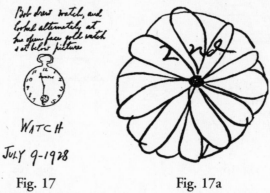

WATCH

JULY 9-1928

Fig. 17   Fig. 17a

The comment was: "I see this picture. Later I think it is not flower but wire (metal, shining). The 'petals' are not petals but wire, and should be uniform. This is hasty drawing so not exact as seen. What I mean is, I try to see Bob's drawing and not what he drew from. So I see no flower but shape of one on paper. Then decide it is of wire, but this may be merely because I see drawing, which would have no flower color. However, I see it shining as if it is metal. Later a glass circle." Drawings then show an ellipse, and then a drinking glass and a glass pitcher. It is interesting to note that Bob had in front of him a glass bowl with goldfish.

The next day Bob drew a pair of scissors (Fig. 18):

SCISSORS

JULY 10-1928

Fig. 18

The drawings of Craig follow without comment (Figs. 18a, 18b):

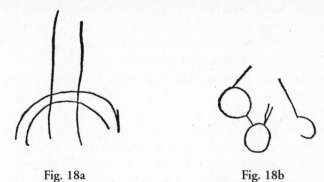

Fig. 18a   Fig. 18b

Three days later Bob drew the table fork, which has already been reproduced (Fig. 1), and Craig made the report which has been given in facsimile (Fig. 1a): "See a table fork. Nothing else."

One more test between Bob and Craig, the most sensational of all. It is quite a story, and I have to ask your pardon for the medical details involved. So much vital knowledge hangs upon these tests that I have asked my brother-in-law to forget his personal feelings. The reader will please consider himself a medical student or hospital nurse for the moment.

The test occurred July 1, 1928. My wife made her drawing, and then told me about the matter at once. Also she wrote out all the details and the record is now before me. She saw a feather, then a flower spray, and then she heard a scream. Her first thought in case of illness or danger is her aged parents, and she took it for her mother's voice, and this so excited her that she lost interest in the experiment. But soon she concentrated again, and drew a series of concentric circles, with a heavy black spot in the center. Then she saw another and much larger spot, and this began to spread and cover the sheet of paper. At the same time came a feeling of intense depression, and Craig decided that the black spot was blood, and that Bob had had a hemorrhage. Here is her drawing (Fig. 19a):

Fig. 19a

Two or three days later Bob's wife drove him to our home, and in the presence of all four of us he produced the drawing he had made. He had taken a compass and drawn a large circle; making, of course, a hole in the center of the paper. "Is that all you thought of during the time?" asked my wife. "No," said Bob, "but I'd hate to have you get the rest of it." "What was it?" "Well, I discovered that I had a hemorrhoid, and couldn't put my mind on anything else but the thought, 'My God, my lungs—my kidneys—and now this!'"

A hemorrhoid is, of course, apt to be accompanied by a hemorrhage; and it seems clear that my wife got the mood of depression of her brother-in-law, his thoughts of blood and bodily breakdown, as well as the circle and the hole in the paper. There is another detail which does not appear in the written record, but is fixed in my memory. My wife said: "I wanted to draw a little hill." Upon hearing that, I called up a physician friend who is interested in these tests, and asked him what a drawing of a hemorrhoid would look like, and he agreed that "a little hill" was about as near as one could come. I hope you will note that this particular drawing test is supported by the testimony of four different persons, my wife, her sister, the sister's husband, and myself. I do not see how there could possibly be more conclusive evidence of telepathic influence—unless you suspect all four of us of a series of stupid and senseless falsehoods. Let me repeat that Bob and his wife have read this manuscript and certified to its correctness so far as concerns them. The comment written by my wife reads: "All this dark like a stain—feel it is blood; that Bob is ill—more than usual."

(Note: Bob Irwin died not long afterwards.)

8

THE EXPERIMENTS JUST DESCRIBED were all that were done with Bob, because he found them a strain. Craig asked me to make some drawings for her, and I did so, sitting in the next room, some thirty feet away, but always behind a closed door. Thus you may verify my assertion that the telepathic energy, whatever it may be, knows no difference between thirty feet and forty miles. The results with Bob and with myself were about the same.

The first drawings made with me are those which have already been given (Figs. 2, 2a), but I give them again for the sake of convenience. I explain that in these particular drawings the lines have been traced over in heavier pencil; the reason being that Craig wanted a carbon copy, and went over the lines in order to make it. This had the effect of making them heavier than they originally were, and it made the whirly lines in Craig's first drawing more numerous than they should be. She did this in the case of two or three of the early drawings, wishing to send a report to a friend. I pointed out to her how this would weaken their value as evidence, so she never did it again.

After my wife and I had compared the above drawings, she wrote a note to the effect that just before starting to concentrate, she had been looking at her drawing of many concentric circles, which she had made in a test with Bob the previous day (Fig. 19a). So her first vision was of a whirl of circles. This turned sideways, and then took the shape of an arrowhead, and then of a letter A, and finally evolved into a complete star. As the agent in this test, I wish to repeat that I made my drawing in my study with the door closed, that I kept the drawing before my eyes the entire time, and that the door stayed closed until Craig called that she was through.

I do not find it easy to concentrate on a drawing, because my active mind wanders off to side issues. If I draw a lighted cigarette, I immediately think of the odious advertising now appearing in the papers; or I think: "Will Craig get this right, and what does it mean, and will the world accept evidence on this subject from me?"—and so on. Several times my wife has "got" such thoughts, and so we took to noting them on the record.

On July 29, I drew a cigarette, with two little curls for smoke, each running off like a string of the letter "eeeee," written by hand. Underneath I wrote as follows: "My thought: 'cigarette with curls of smoke.' I said to myself these words: 'she got the curls but not the cigarette.'" This would appear to be telepathy coming from Craig to me, for her drawing was found to contain a lot of different curves—a curly capital S, several other half circles twisted together, and three ??? one inside the other. She added the following words: "I can't draw it, but curls of some sort."

Again, here is a work of art from my facile pen, dated July 21, and having underneath my notation: "Concentrated on bald head" (Fig 20).

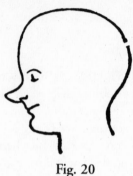

Fig. 20

My wife's note was: "Saw Upton's face." Then she drew a line through the words, and wrote the following explanation: "Saw two half circles. Then they came together making full circle. But I felt uncertain as to whether they belonged together or not. Then suddenly saw Upton's profile float across vision."

July 20 I drew a three-pronged fork, and made the note that I was not sure if it was a hay-fork or an oysterfork, and decided it was the latter, whereupon my mind went off to "society" people and their many kinds of forks. Craig wrote: "I thought it was an animal's head with horns and the head was on a long stick—a trophy mounted like this"—and she drew a two-pronged fork.

July 17 1 drew a large round stone with a smaller stone on top: at least so I thought, and then decided they were two eggs. Craig drew two almost tangent circles, and wrote: "I see two round things, not one inside the other, as in Bob's drawing of circles. Then the above vanished and I saw as below"—and she drew four little oblongs, tangent, which might be a cluster of fish-eggs or fly-eggs.

July 20 I drew two heavy straight lines making a capital letter T, and Craig drew a complete cross or square X, which is, of course, the T with vertical arm prolonged. July 14 I drew a sort of jack-o'-lantern. It is on this page (Fig. 21).

Fig. 21

I looked at this drawing and thought of the eyes of M.C.S., and said mentally, "I should have drawn the curves over eyes." Afterwards I told Craig about this, and she noted it down on the drawing. On the reverse side of the sheet she added the following: "I told U. it was shaped like a half moon with something in center—I supposed it must be a star, though I did not see it as star but as indistinct marks." Her drawing follows, turned upside down for greater convenience (Fig. 21a):

Fig 21a

9

A NEW METHOD OF EXPERIMENT invented itself by accident; and makes perhaps the strangest story yet. There came a letter from a clergyman in South Africa, saying that he was sending me a copy of his wife's novel dealing with South African life. I get many letters from strangers, and answer politely, and as a rule forget them quickly. Some time afterwards came two volumes, entitled, *Patricia*, by Marcus Romondt, and I did not associate them with the clergyman's letter. I glanced at the preface, and saw that the work had something to do with the religious cults of the South African natives. I didn't read more than twenty lines—just enough to classify the book as belonging in Craig's department. Everything having to do with philosophy, psychology, religion, and medicine is first read by her, and then fed back to me in her eager discourses. I took the volumes home and laid them on her table, saying, "This may interest you." The remark attracted no special attention, for the reason that I bring her a book, or a magazine, or some clippings at least once a day. She did not touch these volumes, nor even glance at the title while I was in the room.

I went into the kitchen to get some lunch, and when I was ready I called, "Are you going to eat?" "Let me alone," she said, "I am writing a story." That also is a common experience. I ate my lunch in silence, and then came into the living room again, and there was Craig, absorbed in writing. Some time later she came to me, exclaiming, "Oh, I have had the most marvelous idea for a story! Something just flashed over me, something absolutely novel—I never heard anything like it. I have a whole synopsis. Do you want to hear it?" "No," I said, "you had better go and eat"—for it was my job to try to keep her body on earth. "I can't eat now," she said, "I am too excited. I'll read a while and get quiet." So she went to her couch, and there was a minute or two of silence, and then an exclamation: "Come here!"

Craig had picked up one of the two volumes from South Africa, and was staring at it. "Look at this!" she said. "Look what I opened to!" I looked at a page in the middle of the book—she has the devilish habit of reading a book that way—and in the center of the page, in capital letters, I read the words: "THE BLACK MAGICIAN." "What about it?" I said. "Did you ever hear of that idea?" asked Craig. I answered that I had, and she said, "Well, I never did. I thought it was my own. It is the theme of the 'story' I have just been writing. I have made a synopsis of a whole chapter in this book, and without ever having touched it!"

So Craig had a new set of experiments to try all by herself, without bothering her busy husband. She would go to one of my bookcases, with which she had hitherto had nothing to do, since her own books are kept in her own place. With her back to the bookcase, she would draw a book, and take it to her couch and lie down, placing the book upon her solar plexus, and taking every precaution to make sure that it never came into her line of vision. Most of the books, being new, were in their paper jackets, so there was no lettering that could be felt with her fingers. This, you note, is not a test of telepathy, for no human mind knew what particular book Craig's hand had fallen upon. If she could tell anything about the contents of that book, it would appear to be clairvoyance, or what is known as "psychometry."

My books are oddly varied in character. There are new novels, and works of history, biography, travel, and economics. In addition, there are what I call "crank books"; the queerly assorted volumes which are destined by donors all over the world to convert me to vegetarianism, antivivisection, anarchism, Mormonism, Mohammedanism, infanticide, the abolition of money, or the doctrine that alopecia is caused by onanism. Believe me, the person who sets out to guess the contents of the books that come to me in the course of a month has his or her hands full!

But Craig was able to do it. She did it on so many occasions that she would sit and stare at me and exclaim, "Now what do you *make of that?*" She would insist that I sit and watch the process, so as to be able to state that she never had the book in her line of vision. In my presence she picked out a volume, and keeping it hidden from both of us, she said, "I see a blue cover, with a rising sun and a bare landscape." It happened to be a volume circulated by the followers of "Pastor Russell," and as the preface tells me that 1,405,000 have been sold, it may be that you too have it in your library. The title is *Deliverance*, by J. F. Rutherford, and it has a blue cloth cover, with a gold design of a sun rising behind a mass of clouds and a globe.

On another occasion Craig wrote: "One big eye, with nothing else distinct— then lines or spikes came around it, or maybe these project from the head like stiff long hairs, or eyelashes. Can't tell what kind of head—but feel it must be a tropical something, tho the eye looks human," etc. The book was *Mr. Blettsworthy on Rampole Island,* by H. G. Wells, and in this book is a chapter headed, "The Friendly Eye," with the following sentences: "I became aware that an Eye observed me continually . . . It was a reddish brown eye. It looked out from a system of bandages that also projected a huge shock of brown hair upward and a great chestnut beard . . . the eye watched me with the illuminating but expressionless detachment of a head-lamp . . . Polyhemus, for that was my private name for the man."

A long string of such surprises! Craig picked up a book and wrote: "Black wings—a vampire flying by night." The title of the book was *The Devil's Jest*. She picked up one and wrote: "A Negro's head with a light around it." It is a German volume, called *Africa Singt*, and has a big startling design exactly as described. She picked up a book by Leon Trotsky, and wrote the word "Checkro"—which may not sound like Russian to Trotsky, but does to Craig! And a book with Mussolini on the cover, wearing a black coat and feeding a lion: she got the shape of the Duce's figure, only she labeled him "Black Bird." And here is a part of the jacket design of "wings" on the "Literary Guide" books—and below is what Craig made of it. She added the comment: "Motion—the thing is traveling, point first" (Fig. 22, 22a).

Another volume was described as follows: "A pale blue book. Lonely prairie country, stretch of flat land against sky, and outlined against it a procession of people. Had feeling of moving—wheeled vehicle which seemed to be baby-carriage. This was strange, because country was covered with snow." Upon examination, the book proved

Fig. 22

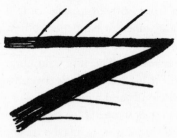

Fig. 22a

to be bound in mottled pale blue boards, title, *I'm Scairt*, with subtitle, "Childhood Days on the Prairies." On the first page of the preface occurs the following: "It was in those days that a company of Swedes left their beloved homeland in the far North and came to make a home for themselves and their children on the Kansas prairie."

Finally, I have obtained the publisher's consent to reproduce the jacket design of a recent book, so that I may put Craig's telepathy alongside it, and give you a laugh or two. Observe the jolly little tourists, and what they have turned into! And then the efforts of Craig's subconscious mind at French. They taught it to her in a "finishing school" on Fifth Avenue, and you can see that it was finished before it began (Figs. 23, 23a).

Yet another form of experiment invented itself under the pressure of necessity. Impossible to have such a witch-wife without trying to put her to use!

of frenchmen

by. lewis galantière

payson & clarke ltd

Fig. 23

Fig. 23a

I have the habit of working out a chapter of a new book in my head, and writing down a few notes on a scrap of paper, and sticking it away in any place that is handy; then, next day, or whenever I am ready for work, it is gone, and there is the devil to pay. I wander about the house for an hour or two, trying to imagine where I can have put that scrap of paper, and reluctant to do the work all over again. On one occasion I searched every pocket, my desk, the trash-baskets, and then, deciding that I had dropped it outdoors, where I work with my typewriter, I figured the direction of the wind, and picked up all the scraps of paper I saw decorating the landscape of our beach home. Then I decided it must be in a manuscript which I had given to a friend in Los Angeles, and I was about to phone to that friend, when Craig asked what the trouble was, and said, "Come, let's make an experiment. Lie down here, and describe the paper to me."

I told her, a sheet off a little pad, written on both sides, and folded once. She took my hand, and went into her state of concentration, and said, "It is in the pocket of a gray coat." I answered, "Impossible; I have searched every coat in the house half a dozen times." She said, "It is in a pocket, and I will get it." She got up off the couch, and went to a gray coat of mine, and in a pocket I had somehow overlooked, there was the paper! Let me add that Craig had had nothing to do with my clothing in the interim, and had never seen the paper, nor heard of it until I began roaming about the house, grumbling and fussing. Neither of us knows of any "normal" way by which her subconscious mind could have got this information.

My secretary lost two screw-caps of the office typewriter, and I said to my wife, "I will bring him over, and you see if you can tell him where to look." But my wife was ill, and did not want to meet anyone, so she said, "I will see if I can get it through you." Be it understood, Craig has not been in the office in a year, and has met my secretary only casually. She said, "I see him standing up at his typewriting." That is an unusual thing for a typist to do, but it happened to be true. Said Craig: "He has put the screw-caps on something high. They are in the south room, above the level of any table or desk." I went to the phone to ask my secretary, and learned that he had just found the screws, which he had put on top of a window-sash in the south room.

The third incident requires the statement that, a few months back, while my wife was away, our home had been loaned to friends, and I had camped at the little house which I was using as an office. Some medical apparatus had been left there; at least I had a vague impression that I had had it there, and I said, "I'll go and look." Said Craig: "Let's try an experiment." She took my hand, and told me to make my mind a blank, and presently she said, "I see it under the kitchen sink." I went over to the office, and found the object, not under the sink, but under the north end of the bathtub. I took it back to the house, and before I spoke a word, my wife said: "I tried to get you on the phone. I concentrated again, and saw the thing and wrote it out." She gave me a slip of paper, from which I copy: "Down under something, wrapped in paper—on N. side of room—under laundry tub on floor or under bathtub on floor in N. corner."

You may say, of course, if you are an incurable skeptic: "The man's wife had been over to the office and seen the object; she had been searching his pockets, and had seen the paper." Craig is positive that she did nothing of the sort; but of course it is conceivable that she may have done it and then forgotten it. Therefore, I pass on to a different and more acceptable kind of evidence—a set of drawing tests, in which I watched and checked every step of the proceedings at my wife's insistence. Here again I am a co-equal witness with her, and the skeptic has no alternative but to say that the two of us have [contrived] this elaborate hoax, making nearly three hundred drawings with fake reproductions, in order to get notoriety, or to sell a few books. I really hope nobody will say that is possible. Very certainly I could sell more books with less trouble by writing what the public wants; and if I were a dishonest man, I should not have waited until the age of fifty-one to begin such a career.

10

CONCERNING THESE DRAWINGS, there are preliminary explanations to be made. They were done hastily, by two busy people. Neither is a trained artist, and our ability to convey what we wish is limited. When I start on a giraffe, I manage to produce a pretty good neck, but when I get to the body, I am disturbed to note it turning into a sheep or a donkey. When I draw a monkey climbing a tree, and Craig says, "Buffalo or lion, tiger—wild animal"—I have to admit that may be so; likewise when my limb of a tree is called a "trumpet," or when Craig's "wild animal" resembles a chorus girl's legs. I will let you see those particular drawings. Figure 24 is mine, while 24a and 24b are my wife's.

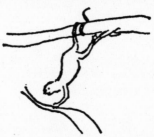

Fig. 24

Fig. 24a   Fig. 24b

Again, I draw a volcano in eruption, and my wife calls it a black beetle, which hardly sounds like a triumphant success; but study the drawings, and you see that my black smoke happens to be the shape of a beetle, while the two sides of the volcano serve very well for the long feelers of an insect (Figs. 25, 25a):

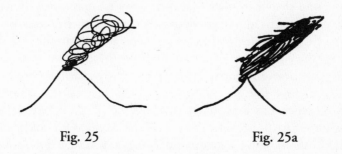

Fig. 25   Fig. 25a

The tests began with four series of drawings, thirty-eight in all, made by my secretary. Following these were thirty-one series drawn by myself, comprising 252 separate drawings. Each drawing would be wrapped in an extra sheet of paper, and sealed in a separate envelope, and the envelopes handed to my wife when she was ready for the tests. She would put them on the table by her couch, and lie down, putting the first envelope, unopened, over her solar plexus, covered by her hand. Her head would be lying back on a pillow, eyes closed, and head at such an angle that nothing but the ceiling could be seen if the eyes were open. A dim light to avoid sense stimulation; enough light to see everything plainly. When she had what she judged was the right image, she would take a pad and pencil and make the drawing or write the description of what she "saw." Then she would open the envelope and compare the two drawings, and number both for identification.

This recording was, of course, an interruption of her passive state, and made the task difficult. In a few cases she repeated a number or forgot the number, and this leaves a chance for confusion. I have done my best to clear up all such uncertainties, but there is a margin of error of one or two per cent to be noted. This is too small to affect the results, but is mentioned in the interest of exactness.

Since I found the sealing of envelopes tiresome, and Craig found the opening of them more so, we decided half way through the tests to abandon the sealing, and later we abandoned the envelopes altogether. We reasoned that acceptance of the evidence rests upon our good faith anyhow, and all that any sensible reader can ask is that Craig make sure of never letting a drawing get within her range of vision. She was doing this laborious work to get knowledge for herself, and she certainly made sure that she was not wasting her own time.

At present the practice is this: I make her a set of six or eight drawings on little sheets of pad paper, and lay them face down on her table, with a clean sheet of paper over them. She lies down, and with her head lying back on the pillow and her eyes closed, she reaches for one of the drawings, and slides it over and onto her body, covered by her hand. It is always out of her range of vision, even if the drawing were turned toward her eyes, which it never is.

For the comfort of the suspicious, let me add that the relaxing of the conditions caused no change in the averages. In the first four series, drawn by my secretary, and sealed by him in envelopes, there were only five complete failures in thirty-eight tests, which is thirteen per cent; whereas in the 252 drawings made by me there have been 65 outright failures, which is nearly twice as large a percentage. Series number six, which was carefully sealed up, produced four complete successes, five partial successes, and no failures; whereas series twenty-one, which was not put in envelopes at all, produced no complete successes, three partial successes, and six failures. Perhaps I should explain that by a "series" I mean simply a group of drawings which were done at one time. It is my custom to make from six to a dozen and when Craig has finished with them, they are put into an envelope and filed away.

I will add that Craig again and again begged me to sit and watch her work, so that I might be able to add my testimony to hers; I did so, watching tests both with envelopes and without, and assure you she left no loophole for self-deception. There was plenty of light to see by, and some of the most startling successes were produced under my eyes. I will add that no one could take this matter with more seriousness than my wife. She is the most honorable person I know, and she has worked on these experiments with rigid conscientiousness.

11

I SHALL give a number of the successful drawings, and some of the partial successes, but none of the failures, for these obviously are merely waste. When I draw a cow, and my wife draws a star or a fish or a horseshoe, all you want is the word "Failure," and then you want to know the percentage of failures, so that you can figure the probabilities. Failures prove nothing that you do not already believe; if your ideas are to be changed, it is successes that will change them.

I begin with series three, because of the interesting circumstances under which it was made. Late in the afternoon I phoned my secretary to make a dozen drawings; and then, after dark, Craig and I decided to drive to Pasadena, and on the way I stopped at the office and got the twelve sealed envelopes which had been laid on my desk. I picked them up in a hurry and slipped them into a pocket, and a minute or two later I put them on the seat beside me in the car.

After we had started, I said, "Why don't you try some of the drawings on the way?" We were passing through the Signal Hill oil-field, amid thunder of machinery and hiss of steam and flashing of headlights of cars and trucks. "It will be interesting to see if I can concentrate in such circumstances," said Craig, and took one envelope and held it against her body in the darkness, while I went on with my job of driving. After a few minutes Craig said, "I see something long and oblong, like a stand." She got a pad and pencil from a pocket of the car, and switched on the ceiling light, and made a drawing, and then opened the envelope. Here are the pictures; I call it a partial success (Figs. 26, 26a):

Fig. 26   Fig. 26a

Here is the next pair, done on the same drive to Pasadena (Figs. 27, 27a):

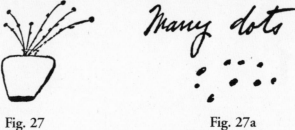

Fig. 27   Fig. 27a

Then came a drawing of an automobile. Considering the attendant circumstances, it was surely not surprising that Craig should report it as "a big light in the end of a tube or horn." There were many such lights in her eyes.

Then a fourth envelope: she said, "I see a little animal or bug with legs, and the legs are sticking out in bug effect." When she looked into the envelope, she was so excited that she tried to get to me look—at forty miles an hour on a highway at night! Here is the drawing, meant to be a skull and cross-bones, but so done that a "bug with legs" is really a fair description of it (Fig. 28):

Fig. 28

After we arrived at our destination, my wife did some more of the drawings, and got partial successes. On this telephone the comment was: "Goblet with another one floating near or above it inverted" (Figs. 29, 29a):

Fig. 29   Fig. 29a

And then this arrow (Figs. 30, 30a):

Fig. 30   **Fig. 30a**

Concerning the above my wife wrote: "See something that suggests a garden tool—a lawn rake, or spade." And for the next one (Fig. 31) she wrote: "A pullybone"—which is Mississippi "darky" talk for a wishbone of a chicken. I don't know whether it means a bone that you pull, or whether it is Creole for "poulet." Here is what my secretary had drawn (Fig. 31):

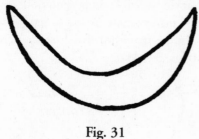

Fig. 31

I had asked my secretary at the outset to make simple geometrical designs, letters and figures, thinking that these would be easier to recognize and reproduce. But they brought only partial successes; Craig would get elements of the drawing but would not know how to put them together. There were seven in the first series, and there is some element right in every one. An oblong was drawn exactly, and then two fragments of oblongs added to it. A capital M in script had the first stroke done exactly, with the curl. A capital E in script was done with the curls left out.

And the same with the second series. Here is a square—but you see that the two halves of it are wandering about (Figs. 32, 32a):

Fig. 32   **Fig. 32a**

And here is a letter Y, but by telepathy it has been turned from script into print (Figs. 33, 33a):

Fig. 33   Fig. 33a

A quite different story began when my secretary allowed his imagination a little play. He knows that my wife lives in part on milk, and he knows that she is particular about the quality, because he has to handle the bills. So he has a little fun with her, and you see that immediately she gets, not the form, but the color and feeling of it (Figs. 34, 34a):

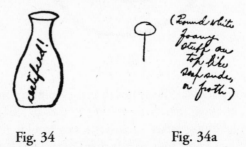

Fig. 34   Fig. 34a

The comment reads: "Round white foamy stuff on top like soap suds or froth." As she drinks her milk sour and whipped, you see that its foaminess is a prominent feature.

Then comes an oil derrick. We live in the midst of these unsightly objects, and are liable to be turned out of house and home by drilling nearby; moreover, I have written a book called *Oil!* and the exclamation mark at the end has been justified by the effect of it on our lives. My wife made a figure five with long lines going out, and wrote: "I don't know why the five should have such a thing as an appendage, but the appendage was most vivid, so there it is" (Figs. 35, 35a):

Fig. 35   Fig. 35a

After she had opened the envelope and seen the original drawing, the problem became, not why a figure five should have an appendage, but why an oil derrick should have a figure five. Craig puzzled over this, and then lay down and told her subconscious mind to bring her the answer. What came was this: the German version of my book, called *Petroleum*, has three oil derricks on the front, and a huge dollar sign on the back of the cover, and this was what Craig had really "seen." She had looked at this book when it arrived, a year or more back, and it had been filed away in her memory. Of course, this may not be the correct explanation, but it is the one which her mind brought to her.

12

THESE DRAWING TESTS afford a basis for psychoanalysis and it is interesting to note some of the facts thus brought up from the childhood of my wife. For example, fires! She was raised in the "black belt," where there are nine Negroes to one white, and the former are still close to Africa. When Craig was a girl, a nurse in the family, having been discharged, set fire to the home while the adults were away, and the children asleep. Another servant, jealous of an unfaithful husband, put her two babies into a barrel full of feathers and burned them alive. Other fires occurred; so now, in her home, Craig keeps an uneasy eye out for greasy rags, or overheated stoves, or whatever else her fears suggest. When in these drawing tests there has been anything indicating fire or smoke, she has "got" it, with only one or two failures out of more than a dozen cases. Sometimes she "got" the fire or smoke without the object; sometimes she supplied fire or smoke to an object which might properly have it, a pipe, for example. The results are so curious that I assemble them together—a series of fire-alarms, as it were.

You recall the fact that in one of the early drawing tests—those in which, instead of giving the drawings to my wife, I sat in my study and concentrated upon them—I drew a lighted cigarette, and thought of the curls of smoke. Craig filled up her drawing with curves, and wrote: "I can't draw it, but curls of some sort."

At this time the convention that curls stood for smoke had not been established. But now, in the series drawn by my secretary, appeared a little house with smoking chimney, and you will see that my wife got the smoke better than the house (Figs. 36, 36a):

Fig. 36

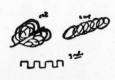

Fig. 36a

This apparently established in her mind the association of curls with smoke. So when, in series six, I drew a pipe with smoke-curls, my wife first drew an ellipse, and then wrote: "Now it begins to spin, round and round, and is attached to a stick." She then drew (Figs. 37, 37a):

Fig. 37   Fig. 37a

In series eight I drew a sky-rocket going up. My first impulse had been to draw a bursting rocket, with a shower of stars, but I realized that would be difficult, so I drew this instead (Fig. 38):

Fig. 38

My wife apparently took my first thought, rather than my drawing. Anyhow, she made half a dozen sketches of whirligigs and light (Figs. 38a, 38b, 38c):

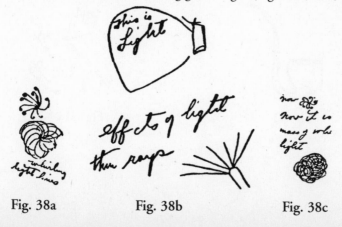

Fig. 38a   Fig. 38b   Fig. 38c

And here in series twenty-two is a burning lamp (Figs. 39, 39a):

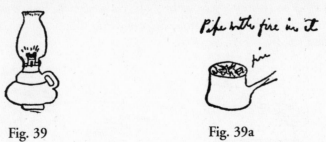

Fig. 39   Fig. 39a

And in series thirty-four another, with comment: "flame and sparks" (Figs. 40, 40a):

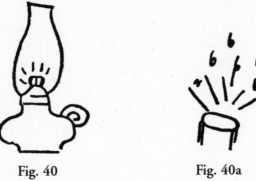

Fig. 40   Fig. 40a

I drew another pipe in series twenty-two, with the usual curls of smoke; and Craig wrote: "Smoke stack." I drew another in series thirty-three with the result that, five drawings in advance of the correct one, Craig drew a pipe with smoke. Of course, this may have been a coincidence; but wait till you see how often such coincidences happen! (Figs. 41, 41a):

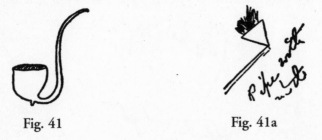

Fig. 41   Fig. 41a

In series twenty-one I drew a chimney, and Craig drew a chimney, and added smoke. In thirty-four I drew an old-fashioned trench-mortar; and here again she supplied the smoke (Figs. 42, 42a):

Fig. 42   Fig. 42a

Cannons are especially horrible things to her, as you may note again and again in her published war-sonnets:

The sharpened steel whips round, the black guns blaze,

Waste are the harvests, mute the songs of birds.

So when, in series eleven, I drew the muzzle half of an old-style cannon, Craig's imagination got to work one drawing ahead of time. She wrote: "Fire and smoke—smoke—flame," and then drew as follows (Fig. 43a):

Fig. 43a

The next drawing was the cannon, and I gave it, along with the drawing Craig made to go with it. The comment she wrote was: "Half circle—double lines—light inside—light is fire busy whirling or flaming" (Figs. 44, 44a):

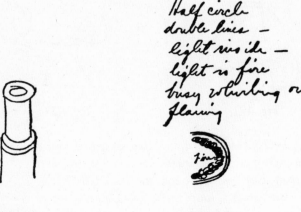

Fig. 44   Fig. 44a

So much for fires, and things associated with fire. Now consider another detail about life in the Yazoo delta, brought out in the course of our psycho-analysis. In the days of Craig's childhood, poisonous snakes were an ever-present menace, and fear of them had to be taught to children, and could hardly be taught too early.

There is a family story of a little tot crawling under the house and coming back to report, "I see nuffin wiv a tail to it!" In the swamps back of Craig's summer home on the Mississippi Sound I have counted a dozen copperheads and moccasins in the course of a half hour's walk. Also, her father has some childhood complex buried in his mind, which causes him to have a spell of nausea at the sight of a snake. All this, of course, strongly affected the child's early days, and now it is in her mental depths. So when I drew a hissing snake, just see the uproar I caused! She made no drawing but wrote a little essay. I give my drawing, and her essay following (Fig. 45):

Fig. 45

"See something like kitten with tail and saucer of milk. Now it leaps into action and runs away to outdoors. Turns to fleeing animal outdoors. Great activity among outdoor creatures. Know it's some outdoor thing, not indoor object—see trees, and a frightened bird on the wing (turned sidewise). It's outdoor thing, but none of above seems to be it."

In other words, little Mary Craig Kimbrough is back on the plantation, seeing terror among birds and poultry, and not knowing what causes it! Study the drawing, and you see that I got the action of the snake, but didn't get the coils very well, so they might be a "saucer of milk"—and a sure-enough kitten's tail sticking out from it. Another childhood horror here! Craig was a fat little thing, and she slipped and plumped down on her favorite pet kitten, and exploded it.

13

THE PERSON whom we are subjecting to this process of psychoanalysis has a strong color sense, and wanted to be a painter. So we note that she "gets" colors and names them correctly. Here is my drawing of what I meant to be a bouquet of pink roses (Figs. 46, 46a):

Fig. 46

Fig. 46a

Or take this case of a lobster. Craig's comment was: "Gorgeous colors, red and greenish tinges." Apparently I had failed to decide whether I was drawing a live lobster or a boiled one! My wife wrote further: "Now it turns into a lizard, camelian, reds and greens." When she sees this about to be made public, she is embarrassed by her bad spelling; but she says: "Please do not overlook the fact that a chameleon is a reptile—and so is a lobster." I dutifully quote her, even though her zoology is even worse than her spelling! (Figs. 47, 47a):

Fig. 47

Fig. 47a

While we are on the "reptiles," I include this menacing crab, which may have got hold of little Mary Craig's toe on the beach of the Mississippi Sound (Fig. 48):

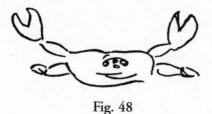

Fig. 48

For the crab, Craig made two drawings, on opposite sides of the paper (Figs. 48a, 48b):

Fig. 48a   Fig. 48b

The comments on the above read: "Wings, or fingers—wing effect, but no feathers, things like fingers instead of feathers. Then many little dots which all disappear, and leave two of them, O O, as eyes of something." And then, "Streamers flying from something."

Another color instance: I drew the head of a horse, and Craig drew a lot of apparently promiscuous lines, and at various places wrote "yellow," "white," "blue," "(dark)," and then a general description, "Oriental."

Afterwards she said to me: "That looks like a complete failure; yet it was so vivid, I can't be mistaken. Where did you get that horse?" Said I: "I copied it from a Sunday supplement." We got the paper from the trashbasket, and the page opposite the horse contained what Craig described. We shall note several other cases of this sort of intrusion of things I did not draw, but which I had before me while drawing.

Also anything with metal or shine seems to stand a good chance of being "got." For example, these nose-glasses (Figs. 49, 49a):

Fig. 49   Fig. 49a

The comment reads: "Opalescent shine or gleam. Also peafowl."

Or again, a belt-buckle; my wife writes the word "shines" (Figs. 50, 50a):

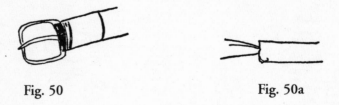

Fig. 50   Fig. 50a

Or this very busy alarm clock—she writes the same word "shines" (Figs. 51, 51a):

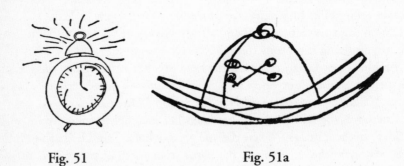

Fig. 51   Fig. 51a

She has got at least part of a watch whenever one has been presented. You remember the one Bob drew (Fig. 17). There was another in series thirty-three; Craig made a crude drawing and added: "Shines, glass or metal" (Figs. 52, 52a):

Fig. 52   Fig. 52a

Also, on the automobile ride to Pasadena, series three, there was a watch-face among the drawings, and Craig drew the angle of the hands, and added the words, "a complication of small configurations." Having arrived in Pasadena, she took the twelve drawings and tried them over again. This time, of course, she had a one in twelve chance of guessing the watch. She wrote: "A white translucent glimmering, or shimmering which I knew was not light but rather glass. It was like heat waves radiating in little round pools from a center . . . Then in the center I saw a vivid black mark . . . So it was bound to be the watch, and it was."

And here is a fountain. You see that it appears to be in a tub, and is so drawn by Craig. But you note that the "shine" has been got. "These shine!" (Figs. 53, 53a):

Fig. 53   Fig. 53a

Another instance, even more vivid. I made a poor attempt to draw a bass tuba, as one sees them on the stage—a lot of jazz musicians dressed up in white duck, and a row of big brass and nickel horns, polished to blind your eyes. See what Craig drew, and also what she wrote (Figs. 54, 54a):

Fig. 54   Fig. 54a

The comments, continued on the other side of the sheet, are: "Dull gold ring shimmers and stands out with shadow behind it and in center of it. Gleams and moves. Metal. There is a glow of gold light, and the ring or circle is out in the air, suspended, and moves in blur of gold."

You see, she gets the feeling, the emotional content. I draw a child's express-wagon, and she writes: "Children again playing but can't get exactly how they look. Just feel there are children." Or take this one, which she describes as "Egyptian." I don't know if my pillar is real Egyptian, but it seems so to me, and evidently to my wife, for you note all the artistry it inspired (Figs. 55, 55a):

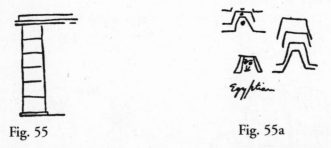

Fig. 55   Fig. 55a

Sometimes Craig will embody the feeling in some new form of her own invention; as for example, when I draw an old-fashioned cannon on wheels, and she writes: "Black Napoleon hat and red military coat." I draw a running fox—well drawn, because I copy it from a picture; she rises to the occasion with two crossed guns, and a hunting horn with a lot of musical notes coming out of it (Figs. 56, 56a):

Fig. 56   Fig. 56a

I draw an auto, and she replies with the hub and spokes of a wheel. Not satisfied with this, she sets it aside, and tries again a little later—without looking at the original drawing—and this time she produces a horn, with indication of a noise. I give both her drawings, which are on two sides of the same slip of paper (Figs. 57a, 57b):

Fig. 57a 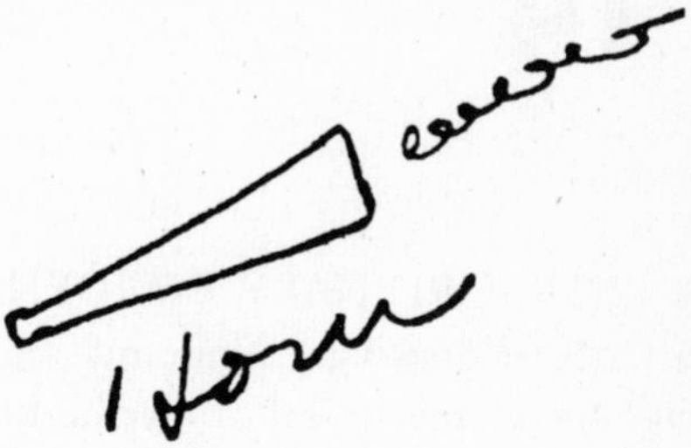   Fig. 57b

14

AN EXTRAORDINARY INCIDENT occurred in connection with the fourth series of drawings. While my secretary, E. M. Hart, was making the drawings, there came into the office his brother-in-law, R. H. Craig, Jr., a teller of the Security First National Bank of Long Beach, a person entirely unknown to my wife. He heard what was going on, and said, "I'll give her some that'll stump her." He took a pen and drew two pictures, which were duly wrapped in sheets of green paper and sealed in envelopes, and put with the rest of the series. I was not in the office, and nothing was said to me about Mr. Craig having taken part in the matter.

My wife did this series under my eyes; and when she came to the first of Mr. Craig's two drawings, she wrote, "Some sort of grinning monster," and added an elaborate description. Then she opened the envelope, and found a roller skate with a foot and leg attached. This, naturally, was called a failure; but seven drawings later in the same series came Mr. Craig's other drawing, which was as follows (Fig. 58):

Fig. 58

Now read the amazing description which my wife had written, seven drawings back, when the first of Mr. Craig's drawings had come under her hand:

"Some sort of grinning monster—see only the face and a vague idea of deformed neck and shoulders. It is a man, but it looks like a cat's face, cat eyes and whiskers. Don't know just how I know it is a man—it is a deformity. Not a cat. See color of skin which is deep, flat pink, as of a colored picture. The face of the creature is broad and weird. The flesh of neck, or somewhere, gives effect of rolls or creases."

I asked my secretary what this drawing was meant to be, and he said "a Happy Hooligan." My cultural backwardness is such that I wasn't sure just what a "Happy Hooligan" might be, but my secretary told me it is a comic supplement figure, and I then looked it up in the paper, and found that the face of the figure as printed is a very pale pink, and the little cap on top is a bright red. I called Mr. Craig on the phone and asked him this question: "If you were to think of a color in connection with a 'Happy Hooligan,' what color would it be?" He answered, "Red."

Now I ask you, what chance do you think there is of a person's writing a description such as the above by guess work? To be sure, my wife had eight guesses; but do you think that eight million guesses would suffice? And if we call it telepathy, do we say that my wife's mind has the power to dip into the mind of a young man whom she has never seen, nor even heard of? Or shall we say that his mind affected his brother-in-law's, the brother-in-law's affected mine, and mine affected my wife's? Or, if we decide to call it clairvoyance, or psychometry, then are we going to say there is some kind of vibration or emanation from Mr. Craig's drawing, so powerful that when one of his drawings is handed to my wife, she gets what is in another drawing which has been done at the same time? Whatever may be the explanation, here is the fact: Again and again we find Craig getting, not the drawing she is holding under her hand, but the next one, which she had not yet touched. When she picks up the first drawing, she will say, or write: "There is a little man in this series"; or: "There is a snow scene with sled"; or: "An elephant, also a rooster." I am going to show you these particular cases; but first a word as to how I have counted such "anticipations."

Manifestly, if I grant the right to more than one guess, I am increasing the chances of guesswork, and correspondingly reducing the significance of the totals. What I have done is this: where such cases have occurred, I have called them total failures, except in a few cases, where the description was so detailed and exact as to be overwhelming—as in the case of this "Happy Hooligan." Even so, I have not called it a complete success, only a partial success. In order to be classified as a complete success, my wife's drawing must have been made for the particular drawing of mine which she had in her hand at that time; and throughout this account, the reader is to understand that every drawing presented was made in connection with the particular drawing printed alongside it—except in cases where I expressly state otherwise.

Now for a few of the "anticipations." In the course of series six, drawn by me on Feb. 8, 1929, drawing number two was a daisy, and Craig got the elements of it, as you see (Figs. 59, 59a):

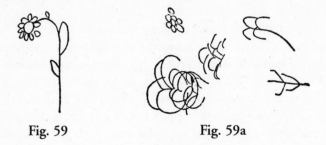

Fig. 59   **Fig. 59a**

Her mind then went ahead, and she wrote, "May be snow scene on hill and sled." The next drawing was an axe, which I give later (Fig. 145); she got the elements of this very well, and then added, on the back: "I get a feeling again of a snow scene to come in this series—a sled in the snow." That was number three; and when number five came Craig made this annotation: "Opened it by mistake, without concentrating. It's my expected sled and snow scene." Here is the drawing (Fig. 60):

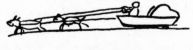

Fig. 60

Series number eight, on Feb. 10, brought even stranger results. This is the series in which the laced-up football was turned into a calf wearing a belly-band (Figs. 15, 15a). But even while I was engaged in making the drawings, sitting in my study apart, and with the door closed, Craig's busy magic, whatever it is, was bringing her messages. She called out: "I see a rooster!" I had actually drawn a rooster; but of course I made no reply to her words. She at once drew a rooster and several other things, and after I had brought my drawings into the room, but before she had started to work with them, she wrote as follows:

"While Upton was making these drawings I sat before the fire thinking how to dry felt slippers which I had washed. I had my mind on them. Hung them on grating to see if they would hang there without burning. Suddenly saw rooster crowing. Then thought, 'Can U be drawing rooster?' Decided to make note of this. Did so. Then saw"—and she draws a circle with eight radiating lines, like spokes of a wheel.

In due course came drawing number eight, and before looking at it, Craig wrote: "Rooster." Then she added, "But no—it looks like a picture of coffee-pot—see spout and handle." This is hard on me as an artist, but I give the drawing and let you judge for yourself (Fig. 61):

Fig. 61

What about the circle and the radiating spokes? That was, apparently, a fore-glimpse of drawing number five. I give you that, together with what Craig drew for that particular test when it came. Her effort suggests the kind of humor with which the newspaper artists used to delight my childhood; a series of drawings in which one thing turns into some other and quite unexpected thing by gradual changes. You will see here how the hub of a wagon-wheel may turn into the muzzle of a deer! (Figs. 62, 62a):

Fig. 62   Fig. 62a

15

WHAT ARE THE PRINCIPLES upon which I have classified the drawings, as between success, partial successes, and failures? I will use this series, number eight, to illustrate. There are eight drawings, and I have set them down as one success, six partial successes, one failure. The success is the rooster (Fig. 61), called "a rooster," even though it "looks like a coffee pot." The partial successes are, first, an electric light bulb, very crudely imitated as to shape in three drawings. Perhaps this was hardly good enough to be counted; it was a border-line case, and probably the poorest that I admitted to the classification of "partial successes" (Fig.63a):

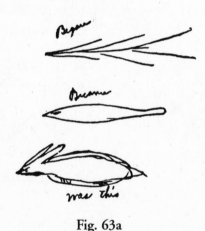

Fig. 63a

Second, the ascending sky-rocket, already printed as Fig. 38, giving rise to six different drawings of whirligigs and light. Third, the following drawing, for which Craig wrote: "See spider, or some sort of legged pest. If this is not a spider, there is a spider in the lot somewhere! This I know!" (Fig. 64):

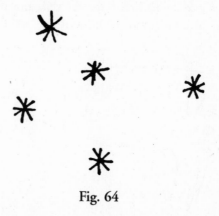

Fig. 64

The fourth partial success was a drawn bow, with arrow fitted, ready to be launched. Craig wrote as follows: "Picked this up and saw inside as it dropped on floor—so did not try it. Suddenly recall I have already 'seen' it earlier." Before starting the tests, along with her written mention of a "rooster," she had drawn a bow and crude arrow, and the resemblance is so exact that it seems to me entitled to be called a partial success (Figs. 65, 65a):

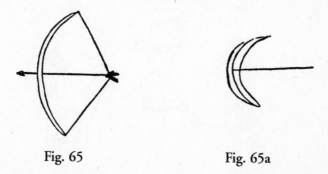

Fig. 65   Fig. 65a

Fifth, the wagon hub (Fig. 60), which became the deer's muzzle. And finally the laced-up football (Fig. 15), which became a belly-band on a calf (Fig. 15a).

As for the failure in this series, it is a cake of soap, which was called "whirls." There are a couple of other drawings in the series, marked: "Too tired to see it," and "Tired now and excited and keep seeing old things" —meaning, of course, the preceding drawings.

I tried to avoid drawing the same object more than once, but now and then I slipped up. In series eleven I drew another rooster, and there followed, not one "anticipation," but several. Drawing number one was a tooth; Craig wrote: "First see rooster. Then elephant." Drawing number two was an elephant; and Craig wrote: "Elephant came again. I try to suppress it, and see lines, and a spike sticking some way into something." She drew it, and it seems clear that the "spike" is the elephant's tusk, and the head of the "spike" is the elephant's eye (Figs. 66, 66a):

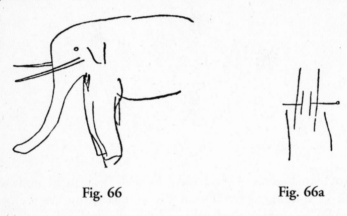

Fig. 66   Fig. 66a

Next, number three, was the rooster. But Craig had set "rooster" down in her mind as a blunder, so now she wrote: "I don't know what, see a bunch, or tuft clearly. Also a crooked arm on a body. But don't feel that I'm right." Here are the drawings, and you can see that she was somewhat right (Figs. 67, 67a):

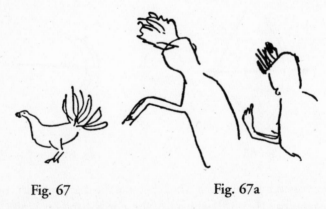

Fig. 67   Fig. 67a

This series eleven, containing fourteen drawings, is marked: "Did this lot rapidly, without holding (mind) blank. The chicken and elephant came *at once*, on a very earnest request to my mind to 'come across.'" I have classified in this series two successes, five partial, and five failures: throwing out numbers twelve and fourteen, because Craig wrote: "Nothing except all the preceding ones come—too many at once—all past ones crowding in memory"; and again, "Nothing but everything in the preceding. Too many of them in my mind."

The anticipations run all through this series in a quite fascinating way. Thus, for number four Craig wrote: "Flower. This is a vivid one. Green spine—leaves like century plant." She drew Figure 68a:

Fig. 68a

And then again, for drawing number seven, she did more flowers, with this comment: "This is a *real* flower, I've seen it before. It's vivid and returns. Century plant? Now it turns into candlestick. See a candle" (Fig. 69a).

All this was wrong—so far. Number four was a table, and number seven was the rear half of a cow. But now we come to number eleven, the plant known as a "cat-tail," which seems to resemble rather surprisingly the lower of the two drawings in Figure 69a. My drawing is given as Figure 70, and the one Craig made for it is given as 70a.

Fig. 69a

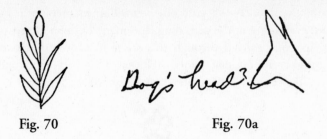

Fig. 70   Fig. 70a

Comment on the above read: "Very pointed. Am not able to see what. Dog's head?"

Drawing five was a large fish-hook; and this inspired the experimenter to a discourse, as follows: "Dog wagging—see tail in air busy wagging—jolly doggie—tail curled in air." And then: "Now I see a cow. I fear the elephant and chicken got me too sure of animals. But I see these."

Now, a big fish-hook looks not unlike a "tail curled in air." But when we come to number seven, we discover what Craig was apparently anticipating. It is the drawing of what I have referred to as "the rear half of a cow." It is badly done, with a cow's hoof, but I forgot what a cow's tail is like, and this tail that I drew would fit much better on a "jolly doggie," you must admit (Fig. 71):

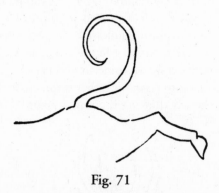

Fig. 71

Drawing number six was a sun, as children draw it, a circle with rays going out all round. Craig wrote: "Setting sun and bird in sky. Big bird on wing— seagull or wild goose." This I called a partial success. Number nine was the muzzle end of an old-style cannon, already reported in Figures 46, 46a.

I conclude the study of this partial series with drawing thirteen, to which was added the comment: "Think of a saucer, then of a cup. It's something in the kitchen. Too tired to see" (Figs. 72, 72a):

Fig. 72   Fig. 72a

In series fourteen, drawing three, Craig wrote: "Man running, can't draw it." She drew as follows (Fig. 73a):

Fig. 73a

Next came my drawing four, as follows (Fig. 73):

Fig. 73

In series thirty-five I drew a fire hydrant, and Craig wrote, "Peafowl," and added the following drawing, which certainly constitutes a partial success (Figs. 74, 74a):

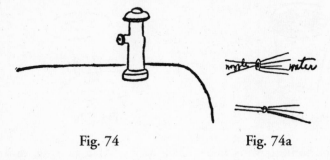

Fig. 74   Fig. 74a

My next drawing was the peafowl, as you see. For this Craig wrote: "Peafowl again," and apparently tried to draw the peafowl's neck, and a lot of those spots which I had forgotten are an appurtenance of peafowls (Figs. 75, 75a):

Fig. 75   Fig. 75a

In series twenty-nine I drew an elevated railway. If you turn it upside down, as I have done here, it looks like water and smokestacks. Anyhow, Craig drew a steamboat (Figs. 76, 76a):

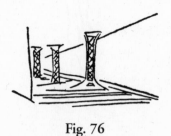

Fig. 76

Fig. 76a

And then came my next drawing—a steamboat! Craig wrote: "Smoke again," and drew the smoke and the stack (Figs. 77, 77a):

Fig. 77

Fig. 77a

She added two more drawings, which appear to be the wheel of the boat in the water, and the smoke (Figs. 77b, 77c):

Fig. 77b

Fig. 77c

In series thirty I drew a fish-hook with line, and you see it turned into a flower (Figs. 78, 78a):

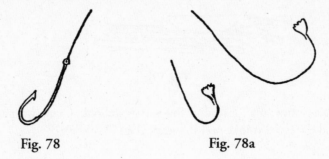

Fig. 78   Fig. 78a

Then came an obelisk, and Craig got it, but with novel effects, thus (Figs. 79, 79a):

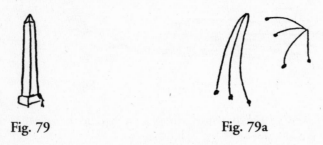

Fig. 79   Fig. 79a

Now why should an obelisk go on a jag, and have little circles at its base? The answer appears to be: it inherited the curves from the previous fish-hook, and the little circles from the next drawing. You will see that, having used up her supply of little circles, Craig did not get the next drawing so well (Figs. 80, 80a):

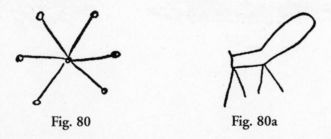

Fig. 80   Fig. 80a

In series twenty-two I first drew a bed, and Craig made two attempts to draw a potted plant. My second drawing was a maltese cross, and Craig turned it into a basket (Figs. 81, 81a):

Fig. 81   Fig. 81a

But she could not give up her plant. She added: "There is a flower basket in this lot, or potted plant."

The next drawing was a fleur-de-lis, which looks not unlike a potted plant or hanging basket (Fig. 82):

Fig. 82

In drawing four she got the elements of a door-knob pretty well, and added: "See head of bird, too—eagle beak." Drawing seven was a crane, with beak open.

| 16

I COULD GO THROUGH all thirty-five of the series, listing such "antic-ipations" as this: but I have given enough to show how the thing goes. Such occurrences make it hard for Craig because, when she has once drawn a certain object, she naturally resists the impulse to draw it again, thinking it is nothing but a memory. Thus, in series thirteen, my first drawing was a savage woman carrying a bundle on her head, and Craig drew the profile of a head with a long nose. My next drawing was the profile of a head, with a very conspicuous nose, and Craig wrote: "Face again, but [I] inhibit this. Then come two hands, and below"—and she draws what might be a cross section of a skull, side view.

Yet sometimes she overcomes this handicap triumphantly. Series twelve is marked: "Hastily done," and she adds the general comment: "Several times saw bristles on things of different shapes, some flowers, some bristled brushes. Saw flower, also more than once"—and then she appends a drawing of a four-leaf clover. As it happened, this series contained a three-leaf clover, and it contained another flower, and also a cactus-plant—more of one kind of thing than it was fair to put into one set of drawings. Nevertheless, Craig scored one of her successes with the cactus, setting it down as "fuzzy flower" (Figs. 83, 83a):

Fig. 83   Fig. 83a

Nor was she afraid to repeat herself when she came to another "fuzzy flower" in this series (Figs. 84, 84a):

Fig. 84   **Fig. 84a**

Frequently she will make a good drawing of an object, but name it badly. In that same series twelve I drew a hoe, and she got the shape of it, but wrote: "Maybe be scissors, may be spectacles with long stem ears" (Figs. 85, 85a):

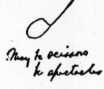

Fig. 85   **Fig. 85a**

Also in the same series these reindeer horns, which she calls "holly leaves." It is psychologically interesting to note that reindeer and holly trees were both associated with Christmas in Craig's childhood (Figs. 86, 86a):

Fig. 86   **Fig. 86a**

And in series eighteen, this fat baby bird of mine is hardly recognizable when called "flounder" (Figs. 87, 87a):

Fig. 87   Fig. 87a

This very dim stalk of celery, drawn by me, I must admit looks more like a fish-fork (Figs. 88, 88a):

Fig. 88   Fig. 88a

Craig's verbal description of the above reads: "Stone set in platinum; may be diamond, as points seem to be white light—at least it shines, not red shine of fire but white shine." How does a stalk of celery, which looks like a fish-fork, come to have a diamond set in it? You may understand the reason when you hear that three drawings later in the same series is a diamond set in a stick. Just why it occurred to me to set a diamond thus I cannot now recall, but the drawing is plain, and it led to a bit of fun. I had been to lunch with Charlie Chaplin that day, and had come home and told my wife about it; so here my sparkling diamond undergoes a transfiguration! "Chaplin," writes my wife, and adds: "I don't see why he has on a halo" (Figs 89, 89a):

Fig. 89   Fig. 89a

From the point of view of bad guessing, the most conspicuous series is number twenty. In this I have recorded four successes, seven partial, and one failure; yet there is hardly an object that is correctly named. Here are the three which I call successes; there may be dispute about any one of them, but it seems to me the essential elements have been got. You may be surprised at a necktie which "began to smoke"—but not when you see that the next drawing is a burning match! (Figs. 90, 90a, 91, 91a, 92, 92a):

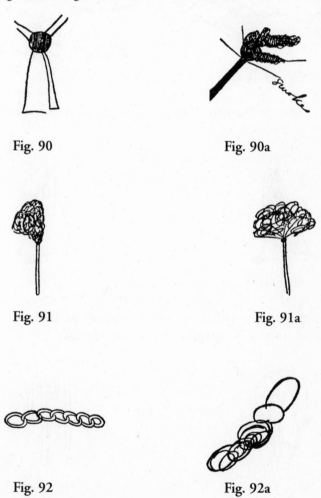

Fig. 90   Fig. 90a

Fig. 91   Fig. 91a

Fig. 92   Fig. 92a

As for the partial successes, I give six of them by way of samples. For the first, Craig's comment was: "The body is vague, but see there is a body." You will agree that my mountain landscape looks oddly like a body (Figs. 93, 93a):

Fig. 93   Fig. 93a

And the pedals of this harp make a charming pair of lady's feet (Figs. 94, 94a):

Fig. 94   Fig. 94a

This balloon is described in my wife's comment as: "Shines in sunlight, must be metal, a scythe hanging among vines or strings."

Fig. 95   Fig. 95a

This, which is called "front foot and leg of dog, though I don't see the dog," is really drawn more like the spigot of my drawing (Figs. 96, 96a):

Fig. 96   Fig. 96a

A butterfly's wings are "got" remarkably well (Figs. 97, 97a). And the trademarks on my little box are called "tiny stars, or sparks" (Figs. 98, 98a):

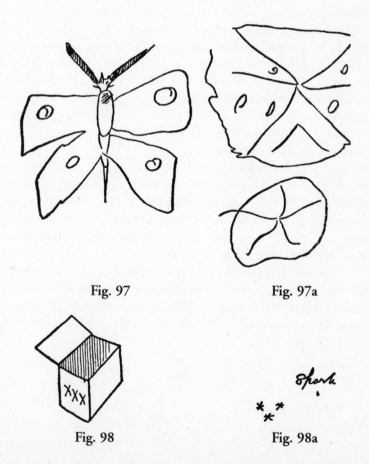

Fig. 97   Fig. 97a

Fig. 98   Fig. 98a

I 17

I HAVE REFERRED to the fact that my wife's drawings sometimes contain things which are not in mine, but which were in my mind while I was making them, or while she was "concentrating." One of the most curious of such cases came in series twenty-eight, which was after we had given up, as too great a nuisance, all precautions in the way of sealing the drawings in envelopes. I made eight drawings, and laid them face down on my wife's table, and then went out and took a walk while she did them. So, of course, it was easy for her to do what she pleased—and maybe she "peeked," the skeptic will say. But as it happens, she didn't get a single one right! Instead of reproducing my drawings, what she did was to reproduce my thoughts while I was walking up and down on the ocean front. It seems to me that in so doing, she provided a perfect answer to those who may attribute these results to any form of deception, whether conscious or unconscious.

There was a moon behind a bank of dark clouds, and it produced an unusual effect—a well-defined white cross in the sky. I watched it for nearly half an hour, and my continued thought was: "If this were an age of superstition, that would be a portent, and we should hear about it in history." It was so strange that I finally went home and called my wife out onto the street. I did not tell her why. I wanted to see her surprise, so I purposely gave no hint. I said: "Come out! Please come!" Finally she came, and her comment was: "I just drew that!" We went back into the house, and she handed me a drawing. I give it alongside my drawing of an Indian club, which Craig had held while doing hers. You may see exactly how much of her impulse came from that source (Figs. 99, 99a):

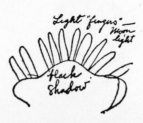

Fig. 99   Fig. 99a

The "comment" reads: "Light 'fingers'—moonlight." Also: "black shadow."

Let me add also that in the eight drawings I handed to Craig there was neither moon, cloud, cross, nor light. Two of these eight my wife failed to mark, and so I cannot identify them as belonging to this series; but we examined all eight at the time, and made sure of this point. Those which I now have are a flag, a bearded man, a chiffonier, a cannon, a dirt-scraper, and the Indian club, given above.

You will ask, perhaps, did Craig look out of the window. As it happened, this sky effect was invisible from any window, and I have her word that she had not moved from her couch. I should add that she is nervous, and keeps the curtains tightly drawn at night, and never goes out at night unless it is to be driven somewhere. It was early in March, with a cold wind off the sea, and I had to labor to persuade her to put a wrap over her dressing gown and step out into the middle of the street to look up at the sky.

| 18

THE CASUAL READER may be bored by too many of these drawings, but they are easy to skip, or to take in at a glance, and there may be students who will want to examine them carefully. So I will add a selection of the significant drawings, with only brief remarks. I begin with what I have called partial successes, and then add a few more of those I have called "complete."

Let us return to the early drawings, made by my secretary. On the automobile ride to Pasadena, there was an ash-can (Fig. 100):

Fig. 100

For the above my wife wrote: "I see a chain dangling from something—resembling little chimney pot on top of house."

And here is design for which the comment was: "These somehow belong together but won't get together" (Figs. 101, 101a):

Fig. 101 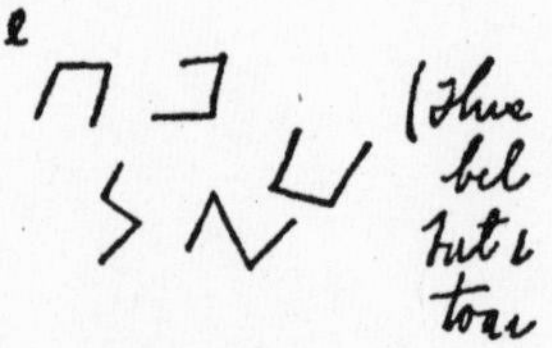   **Fig. 101a**

Here is a fan, with comment: "Inside seems irregular, as if cloth draped or crumpled" (Figs. 102, 102a):

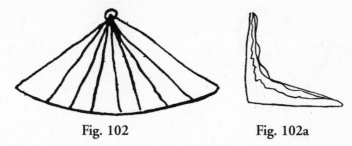

Fig. 102   Fig. 102a

Here is a one-half success (Figs. 103, 103a):

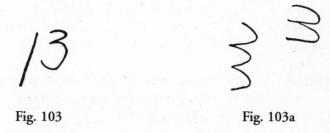

Fig. 103   Fig. 103a

Here is a broom, drawn by my secretary (Fig. 104), and several efforts to reproduce it (Figs. 104a, 104b):

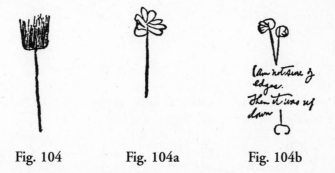

Fig. 104   Fig. 104a   Fig. 104b

The comments accompanying these drawings read: "All I'm sure of is a straight line with something curved at end of it; once it came" (here is drawing of the flower). "Then it doubled, or reappeared, I don't know which. (Am not sure of curly edges.) Then it was upside down."

The next drawing was a heart, and my wife got the upper half with what are apparently blood-drops added (Figs. 105, 105a):

Fig. 105   Fig. 105a

The above is interesting, as suggesting that whatever agency furnished the information knew more than it was telling. For if Craig's drawing, a pair of curves, constituted a crude letter N, or had no significance, why add the blood-drops, which were not in the original? On the other hand, if her subconscious mind knew it was a heart, why not give her the whole heart, and let her draw it?

So much for the drawings of my secretary; and now for my own early drawings. When I was a school boy, we used to represent human figures in this way; and, as you see, Craig got the essentials (Figs. 106, 106a):

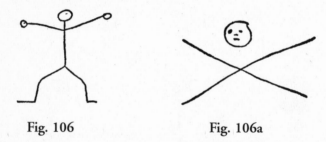

Fig. 106   Fig. 106a

Several weeks later, I drew a pair of such figures in action and the comment was: "It's a whirligig of some sort" (Figs. 107, 107a).

Fig. 107   Fig. 107a

After the following drawing, Craig asked me not to do any more hands, for the reason that she "got" this, but thought it was my own hand doing the drawing. She guessed something else, and wrote: "Turned into pig's head, then rabbit's" (Figs. 108, 108a):

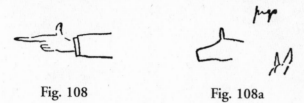

Fig. 108   Fig. 108a

Next, this bat, with very striking comment. "Looks like ear-shaped something," and again: "Looks like calla lily" (Figs. 109, 109a):

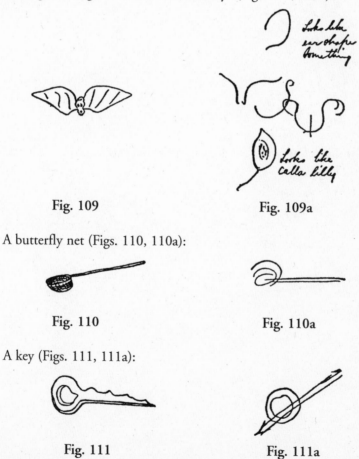

Fig. 109   Fig. 109a

A butterfly net (Figs. 110, 110a):

Fig. 110   Fig. 110a

A key (Figs. 111, 111a):

Fig. 111   Fig. 111a

This highly humorous sunrise (Figs. 112, 112a):

Fig. 112   Fig. 112a

A carnation which came after the preceding drawing, and apparently had been anticipated in the "sunrise" (Figs. 113, 113a):

Fig. 113   Fig. 113a

Note that this camp-stool, as I drew it, really does appear to be standing on water (Figs. 114, 114a):

Fig. 114   Fig. 114a

For this little waiter, who follows, no drawing was made by my wife. Her written comment was: "I see at once the profile of human face. Am interrupted by radio tune. Something makes me think of a cow. Now see two things sticking out like horns" (Fig. 115):

Fig. 115

The following had no comment (Figs. 116, 116a):

Fig. 116

Fig. 116a

Nor the next ones (Figs. 117, 117a):

Fig. 117

Fig. 117a

The comment on this caterpillar was: "Fork—then garden tool—lawn rake. Leaf." I might add that we have a lawn-rake made of bristly bamboo, which looks very much like my drawing (Figs. 118, 118a):

Fig. 118   Fig. 118a

In the following case I drew sixteen stars, and you may count and see that Craig got twelve of them, and made up the difference with a moon! (Figs. 119, 119a):

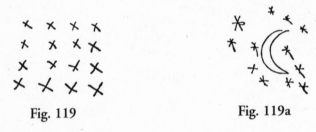

Fig. 119   Fig. 119a

Comment on the following: "Looks like a monkey wrench, but it may be a yardstick" (Figs. 120, 120a):

Fig. 120   Fig. 120a

In the next one, the curve of the worm is amusingly reproduced by the bird's neck. The comment added: "But it may be a snake." Craig says this is an example of how one part of the drawing comes to her, and then, in haste, her memory-trains and associations supply what they think should be the rest (Figs. 121, 121a):

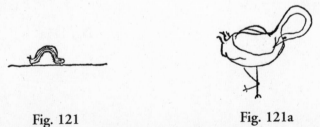

Fig. 121   Fig. 121a

The umbrella brings up Craig's reptile "complex" again. I assure you that in her garden, she turns sticks into snakes when they are far less snake-like than my drawing. Her comment was: "I feel that it is a snake crawling out of something— vivid feeling of snake, but it looks like a cat's tail" (Figs. 122, 122a):

Fig. 122   Fig. 122a

I drew a wall-hook to hang your coat on (Figs. 123, 123a):

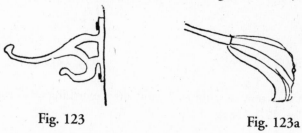

Fig. 123   Fig. 123a

A design, evidently felt as a design, though not well got (Figs. 124, 124a):

Fig. 124   Fig. 124a

A screw, with comment: "light-house or tower. Too fat at base." If Craig's drawing were made narrower at base, it would reproduce the screw very well. Note that in the right-hand "tower" the screw-like effect of the "setbacks" is kept (Figs. 125, 125a):

Fig. 125   Fig. 125a

Here is a love story which seems to go wrong, the hearts being turned to opposition (Figs. 126, 126a):

Fig. 126   Fig. 126a

Here is the flag, made simpler—"e pluribus unum!" (Figs. 127, 127a):

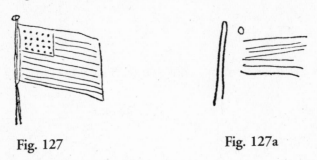

Fig. 127   Fig. 127a

Here is a cow, as seen by the cubists. Comment: "Something sending out long lines from it" (Figs. 128, 128a):

Fig. 128   Fig. 128a

Telegraph wires, apparently seen as waves in the ether (Figs. 129, 129a):

Fig. 129   Fig. 129a

Comment on the following: "Horns. Can't see what they are attached to" (Figs. 130, 130a):

Fig. 130   Fig. 130a

And here is a parrot turned into a leaf, with comment. "See veins and stem with sharp vivid bend in it"—which seems to indicate a sense of the parrot's beak (Figs. 131, 131a):

Fig. 131   Fig. 131a

▮ 19

THE BORDER-LINE between successes and failures is not easy to determine. Bear in mind that we are not conducting a drawing class, nor making tests of my wife's eyesight: we are trying to ascertain whether there does pass from my mind to hers, or from my drawing to her mind, a recognizable impulse of some sort. So, if she gets the essential feature of the drawing, we are entitled to call it evidence of telepathy. I think the fan with "crumpled cloth" (Fig. 102), and the umbrella handle that may be a "snake crawling out of something," but that "looks like a cat's tail" (Fig. 122), and the screw that was called a "tower" (Fig. 125)—all these are really successes. I will append a number of examples, about which there seems to me no room for dispute, and which I have called successes. The first is a sample of architecture (Figs. 132, 132a):

Fig. 132   Fig. 132a

And here is an hour-glass, with sand running through it. Not merely did Craig write "white sand," but she made the tree the same shape as the glass. I have turned the hour-glass upside down so that you can get the effect better. It should be obvious that "upsidedownness" has nothing to do with these tests, as Craig is as apt to be holding a drawing one way as another (Figs. 133, 133a):

white sand

Fig. 133   Fig. 133a

And these three circles, with comment: "Feel sure it is," written above the drawing (Figs. 134, 134a):

Fig. 134   Fig. 134a

As to the next comment, "Trumpet flower," let me explain that we have them in our garden, whereas we do not have any musical trumpets or horns (Figs. 135, 135a):

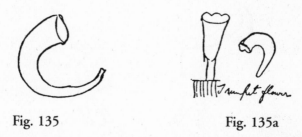

Fig. 135   Fig. 135a

This strange object from my pencil tried to be a conch-shell, but got a bad start, and was left unclassified. Craig made it "life bouy in water," which is good, except for the spelling. She insists upon my pointing out that shells also belong in water (Figs. 136, 136a):

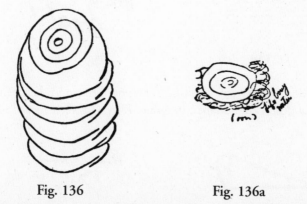

Fig. 136   Fig. 136a

This one, described in good country fashion, "Muley cow with tongue hanging out" (Fig. 137):

Fig. 137

This next one was described by the written word: "Goat" (Fig. 138):

Fig. 138

And this one is so striking that I give the words in facsimile (Figs. 139, 139a):

Fig. 139   Fig. 139a

For the following, my wife described a wrong thing, and then added: "Now a sudden new thing, cone-shaped or goblet-like. This feels like *it*" (Figs. 140, 140a):

Fig. 140   Fig. 140a

This was correctly named: "2 legs of something running" (Figs. 141, 141a):

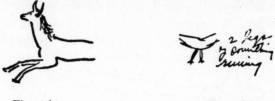

Fig. 141   Fig. 141a

This Alpine hat with feather seems to me no less a success because it is called "Chafing dish" (Figs. 142, 142a):

Fig. 142   Fig. 142a

Nor this wind-mill because the sails are left off (Figs. 143, 143a):

Fig. 143   Fig. 143a

These concentric circles are called "Horn (very curled), or shell" (Figs. 144, 144a):

Fig. 144   Fig. 144a

And here is a curious one, which came early in the tests. I call attention to the comment about the handle, which ran off the sheet of paper without any ending, just as she says. "Letter A with something long above it. Key or a sword, there seems to be no end to the handle. Think it's a key" (Figs. 145, 145a):

Fig. 145

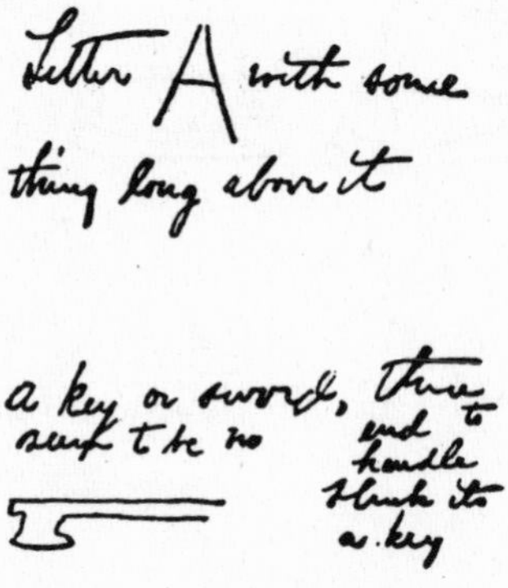

Letter A with some
thing long above it

a key or sword, there
seems to be no   end to
                   handle
                   think its
       ∑   a key

Fig. 145a

And finally, this still more astonishing one, to serve a climax. Let me explain that I am not so good an artist as this; I copied my drawing from some magazine (Figs. 146, 146a):

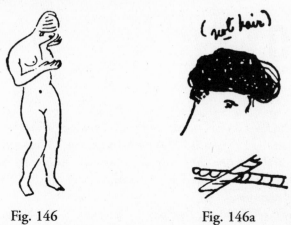

Fig. 146   Fig. 146a

You note that my wife "got," not merely the whole top of the drawing, but some impression of the arms, which are crossed in a peculiar way. I asked her about this case—the drawing having been made less than a month ago—and I find that she remembers it well. She saw what she thought was a turban wound about the head, and got the impression of color. She wrote the words "not hair" to make this clear. The rest of the comment written at the time was: "See back of head, ear, and swirling scarf tied around head."

20

I HAVE NOW GIVEN nearly all the 65 drawings which I call "successes," and about half the 155 which I call "partial successes." This, I think, is enough for any purpose. No one can seriously claim that such a set of coincidences could happen by chance, and so it becomes necessary to investigate other possible explanations.

First, a hoax. As covering that point, I prepared a set of affidavits as to the good faith of myself, my wife, her sister, and her sister's husband. These affidavits were all duly signed and witnessed; but friends, reading the manuscript, think they use up space to no purpose, and that the reader will ask no more than the statement that this book is a serious one, and that the manuscript was carefully read by all four of the persons mentioned above, and approved by them as representing the exact truth.

That a group of persons should enter into a conspiracy to perpetrate a hoax is conceivable. Whether or not it is conceivable of the group here quoted is something of which the reader is the judge. But this much is clear: any reader who, having read the above, still suspects us, will not be convinced by further protestations.

How about the possibility of fraud by one person? No one who knows Mary Craig Sinclair would suspect her; but you who do not know her have, naturally, the right to consider such an hypothesis. Can she be one of those women who enjoy being talked about? The broaching of this idea causes her to take the pencil away from her husband, and you now hear her own authentic voice, as follows:

"I happen to be a daughter of that once very living thing, 'the Old South,' and there are certain ideals which are in my blood. The avoidance of publicity is one of them. But even if I had ever had a desire for publicity, it would have been killed by my actual experiences as the wife of a social crusader. My home is besieged by an endless train of persons of every description, who travel over the place, knocking on doors and windows, and insisting upon having a hearing for their various programs for changing the nature of the universe. I have been driven to putting up barriers and fences around my garden, and threatening to flee to the Himalayas, and become a Yogic mistress, or whatever a Yogic 'master' of my sex is called.

"Jack London tried to solve this problem by putting a sign on the front door which read, 'Go to the back door,' and on the back door one which read, 'Go to the front door.' But when I tried this, one seeker of inspiration took his seat halfway between the two doors, and declared that he would remain there the rest of his life, or until his wishes were acceded to. Another hid himself in the swimming-pool, and rose up from its depths to confront me in the dusk, when, as it happened, I was alone on the place, and went out into the garden for a breath of air. A third announced that he had a million dollars to present to my husband in person, and would not be persuaded to depart until my brother invited him to go downtown to supper, and so got him into a car. Having faithfully fed the hungry millionaire, my brother drove him to the police-station, where, after a serious talking-to by the chief, he consented to carry his million dollars away. A fourth introduced himself by mail as having just been released from the psychopathic ward in Los Angeles, and intending to call upon us, for reasons not stated. A fifth announced himself by telephone, as intending to come at once and shoot my husband on sight. Yet another, seven feet tall and broad in proportion, announced that he had a revelation direct from God, and had come to have the manuscript revised. When politely asked as to its nature, he rose up, towering over my none too husky spouse and declaring that no human eye had ever beheld it, and no human eye would ever be permitted to behold it. Such experiences, as a continuing part of a woman's life, do not lead her to seek publicity; they tend rather to develop a persecution complex.

"Speaking seriously, I consider that I have every evidence of the effect of people's thoughts on each other. And my distrust of human nature, in its present stage of evolution, is so great, that the idea of having many persons concentrate their attention on me is an idea from which I shrink. I agree with Richet that the fact of telepathy is one of the most terrifying in existence; and nothing but a deep love of truth has induced me to let this very personal story be told in print."

Next, what about the possibility of unconscious fraud? This also is a question to be frankly met. All students of psychology know that the subconscious mind has dubious morals. One has only to watch his own dreams to discover this. A person in a trance is similar to one talking or walking in sleep, or a drunken man, or one under the influence of a drug. But in this case it must be noted that my wife has never been in a trance. In these mind-reading tests, no matter how intense the "concentration," there is always a part of her mind which knows what she is doing. If you speak to her, she is immediately "all there." When she has her mental pictures, she sits up and makes her drawing, and compares it with mine, and this is a completely conscious act.

Moreover, I point out that a great deal of the most impressive evidence does not depend upon Craig alone. The five drawings with her brother-in-law, Figures 1, 16, 17, 18, 19, constitute by themselves evidence of telepathy sufficient to convince any mind which is open to conviction. While it would have been possible for Craig and Bob to hoax Dollie and me, it could certainly not have been done without Bob's connivance. If you suggest that my wife and my brother-in-law may have been fooling me, I reply that there is a still greater mass of evidence which could not have been a hoax without my connivance. When I go into my study alone, a little sun-parlor at the front of a beach-house, with nothing but a couch, a chair and a table, I certainly know that I am alone; and when I make a drawing and hold it before my eyes for five or ten minutes, I certainly know whether any other person is seeing it. This covers the drawings presented as Figures 2, 20, and 21, with four others told about in the same series. It seems to me these seven cases by themselves are evidence of telepathy sufficient to convince any open mind.

Furthermore, there are the several score drawings which I made in my study and sealed up in envelopes, taking them to my wife and watching her lay them one by one upon her body and write down more or less accurately what was in them. I certainly know whether I was alone when I made the drawings, and whether I made the contents of the envelopes invisible, and whether my wife had any opportunity to open the envelopes before she made her drawings. Of course, I understand the familiar conjuring trick whereby you open one envelope, and hide it in your palm, and pretend to be describing the next one while really describing the one you have seen. But I would stake my life upon the certainty that my wife knows no sleight-of-hand, and anyhow, I made certain that she did not open the first one; I sat and watched her, and after each test she handed me the envelopes and drawings, one by one—the envelopes having previously been numbered by me. She would turn out the reading-light which was immediately over her head, but there was plenty of light from other parts of the room, enough so that I could look at drawings as they were shown to me. Often these tests were done in the daytime, and then all we did was to pull down the window-shades back of the couch.

It should be obvious that I stand to lose more than I stand to gain by publishing a book of this sort. Many have urged me not to take the risk. It is the part of prudence not to believe too many new and strange ideas. Some of my Socialist and materialist friends are going to say—without troubling to read what I have written: "Sinclair has gone in for occultism; he is turning into a mystic in his old age." It is true that I am fifty-one, but I think my mind is not entirely gone; and if what I publish here is mysticism, then I do not know how there can be such a thing as science about the human mind.

We have made repeated tests to see what happens; we have written down our observations as we go along; we have presented the evidence carefully and conscientiously, without theories; and what any scientist can do, or ask to have done, more than this, I cannot imagine. Those who throw out these results will not be scientists, but merely another set of dogmatists—of whom new crops are continually springing up, wearing new disguises and new labels. The plain truth is that in science, as in politics and religion, it is a lot easier to believe what you have been taught, than to set out for yourself and ascertain what happens.

Of course the thing would be more convincing if it were done in the presence of strangers. That brings up a question which is bound to be asked, so I will save time by answering it here. The first essential to success in these tests is a state of mind; and at present my wife is a sensitive woman, at the stage of life described as "glandular imbalance." She has never tried these experiments in the presence of a stranger, and has no idea whether she could get the necessary concentration. She learned from her experiments with her sick brother-in-law that the agent can send you pain and fear, as well as chairs and table-forks, and she would certainly not enter lightly into a condition of *rapport* with those whom she did not know and trust.

She insists that the way for you to be really certain is to follow her example. If you sat and watched her do it, you might go away with doubts, as she did after her experiments with Jan. But when you have done it yourself, then you *know*. One reason the thing has not been proven to the public is that people depend on professional mediums, many of whom are deliberate and conscious cheats. Others are vain and temperamental, difficult to manage; and research is hindered by their instability. That is why Craig set to work and learned to do it, and she believes that others can do the same, if they have the desire and the patience.

21

THE NEXT THING is to carry out our promise and tell you the technique. My wife has, among her notes, a mass of writing on this subject in the form of instructions to Bob, and others who were interested. I tried to condense it, but found I could not satisfy her, and in the end I realized that her point of view is correct. No one objects to repetition of phrases in a legal document, where the one essential is precision; and the same thing applies to descriptions of these complicated mental processes. This was the most difficult writing task she ever undertook, and the reason lies in its newness, and the complexity of the mind itself.

If you want to learn the art of conscious mind-reading, this will tell you how; and if you don't want to learn it, you can easily skip this section of the book. Here is Craig's statement:

"The first thing you have to do is to learn the trick of undivided attention, or concentration. By these terms I mean something quite different from what is ordinarily meant. One 'concentrates' on writing a chapter in a book, or on solving a problem in mathematics; but this is a complicated process of dividing one's attention, giving it to one detail after another, judging, balancing, making decisions. The kind of concentration I mean is putting the attention on *one* object, or one *uncomplicated* thought, such as joy, or peace, and holding it there steadily. It isn't thinking; it is inhibiting thought, except for one thought, or one object in thought.

"You have to inhibit the impulse to think things about the object, to examine it, or appraise it, or to allow memory-trains to attach themselves to it. The average person has never heard of such a form of concentration, and so has to learn how to do it. Simultaneously, he must learn to relax, for strangely enough, a part of concentration is complete relaxation.

"There seems to be a contradiction here, in the idea of simultaneous concentration and relaxation. I do not know whether this is due to a contradiction in the nature of the mind itself, or to our misunderstanding of its nature. Perhaps we each have several mental entities, or minds, and one of these can sleep (be blankly unconscious), while another supervises the situation, maintaining the first one's state of unconsciousness for a desired period, and then presenting to it some thought or picture agreed on in advance, thus restoring it to consciousness.

"Anyway, it is possible to be unconscious and conscious at the same time! Almost everyone has had the experience of knowing, while asleep, that he is having a bad dream and must awaken himself from it. Certainly some conscious entity is watching the dream, and knowing it is a dream; and yet the sleeper is 'unconscious.' Or perhaps there is no such thing as complete relaxation—until death.

"All I can say is this: when I practice this art which I have learned, with my mind concentrated on one simple thing, it is a relaxation as restful, as seemingly 'complete,' as when I am in that state called normal sleep. The attention is not allowed to be on the sensations of the body, or on anything but the one thing it is deliberately 'concentrated' on.

"Undivided concentration, then, means, for purposes of this experiment, a state of complete relaxation, under specified control. To concentrate in this undivided way you first give yourself a 'suggestion' to the effect that you will relax your mind and your body, making the body insensitive and the mind a blank, and yet reserving the power to 'break' the concentration in a short time. By making the body insensitive I mean simply to relax completely your mental hold of, or awareness of, all bodily sensation. After giving yourself this suggestion a few times, you proceed to relax both body and mind. Relax all mental interest in everything in the environment; inhibit all thoughts which try to wander into consciousness from the subconsciousness, or from wherever else thoughts come. This is clearly a more thorough affair than 'just relaxing.'

"Also, there is something else to it—the power of supervising the condition. You succeed presently in establishing a blank state of consciousness, yet you have the power to become instantly conscious, also; to realize when you are about to go into a state of sleep, in which you have not the power of instantly returning to consciousness. Also, you control, to a certain degree, what is to be presented to consciousness when you are ready to become conscious. For example, you want a message from the person who is sending you a message; you do not want a train of subconscious 'day dreams.'

"All this is work; and so far, it is a bore. But when you have learned to do it, it is an art worth knowing. You can use it, not only for such experiments as telepathy and clairvoyance, but for improving your bodily health. To relax thoroughly several times each day while holding on to a suggestion previously 'planted' in the subconsciousness is more beneficial to health than any other one measure I know.

"The way to relax is to 'let go.' 'Let go' of every tense muscle, every tense spot, in the body. Pain is tension. Pain can be inhibited by suggestion *followed by complete relaxation.* Drop your body, a dead-weight, from your conscious mind. Make your conscious mind a blank. It is the mind, conscious or subconscious, which holds the body tense. Give to the subconsciousness the suggestion of concentrating on one idea, and then completely relax consciousness. To make the conscious mind a blank it is necessary to 'let go' of the body; just as to 'let go' of the body requires 'letting go' of consciousness of the body. If, after you have practiced 'letting go' of the body, you find that your mind is not a blank, then you have not succeeded in getting your body rid of all tension. Work at it until you can let both mind and body relax completely.

"It may help you to start as follows: Relax the body as completely as possible. Then visualize a rose, or a violet—some pleasant, familiar thing which does not arouse emotional memory-trains. Gaze steadily, peacefully, at the chosen object—think only of it—try not to let any memories it may arouse enter your mind. Keep attention steady, just seeing the color, or the shape of the flower and nothing else. Do not think things about the flower. Just look at it. Select one thing about it to concentrate on, such as its shape, or its color, or the two combined in a visual image: 'pink and round.'

"If you find that you are made nervous by this effort, it is apt to be due to the fact that you are thinking things. Maybe the object you have chosen has some buried memories associated with it—something which arouses unconscious memories of past unhappy events. Roses may suggest a lost sweetheart, or a vanished garden where you once were happy and to which you long to return. If so, select some other flower to concentrate on. Flowers are usually the most restful, the things which are not so apt to be involved with distressing experiences. A bottle of ink might suggest the strain of mental work, a spoon might suggest medicine. So, find a peace-inspiring object to look at. When you have found it, just look at it, with undivided attention.

"If you succeed in doing this, you will find it hard not to drop asleep. But you must distinguish between this and the state you are to maintain. If you drop asleep, the sleep will be what is called auto-hypnotic sleep, and after you have learned to induce it, you will be able to concentrate on an idea, instead of the rose, and to carry this idea into the sleep with you as the idea to dominate the subconsciousness while you sleep. This idea, taken with you into sleep in this way, will often act in the subconsciousness with the same power as the idea suggested by a hypnotist. If you have ever seen hypnotism, you will know what this means. You can learn to carry an idea of the restoration of health into this auto-hypnotic sleep, to act powerfully during sleep. Of course this curative effect is not always achieved. Any idea introduced into the subconsciousness may meet a counter-suggestion which, if you are ill, already exists in the subconsciousness, and a conflict may ensue. Thus, time and perseverance may be necessary to success.

"But this is another matter, and not the state for telepathy—in which you must avoid dropping into a sleep. After you have practiced the exercise of concentrating on a flower—and avoiding sleep—you will be able to concentrate on holding the peculiar blank state of mind which must be achieved if you are to make successful experiments in telepathy. There may be strain to start with, but it is getting rid of strain, both physical and mental, which constitutes relaxation, or blankness, of the conscious mind. Practice will teach you what this state is, and after a while you can achieve it without strain.

"The next step: ask someone to draw a half-dozen simple designs for you on cards, or on slips of paper, and to fold them so that you cannot see the contents. They should be folded separately, so that you can handle one at a time. Place them on a table, or chair, beside your couch, or bed, in easy reach of your hand, so that you can pick them up, one at a time, while you are stretched out on the bed, or couch, beside them. It is best at first to experiment in the dark, or at least in a dimly lit room, as light stimulates the eyes and interferes with relaxation. If you experiment at night, have a table lamp within easy reach, so that you can turn the light off and on for each experiment without too much exertion, as you must keep your body and mind as passive as possible for these experiments. If you have no reading light near, use a candle. You must have also a writing pad and pencil beside you.

"After you have placed the drawings on the table, turn off the light and stretch your body full length on the couch. Close your eyes and relax your body. Relax completely. Make the mind a complete blank and hold it blank. Do not think of anything. Thoughts will come. Inhibit them. Refuse to think. Do this for several moments. It is essential to induce a passive state of mind and body. If the mind is not passive, it feels body sensations. If the body is not relaxed, its sensations interfere with the necessary mental passivity. Each reacts on the other.

"The next step, after having turned off the light and closed your eyes and relaxed mind and body full length on the couch, is to reach for the top drawing of the pile on the table. Hold it in your hand over your solar plexus. Hold it easily, without clutching it. Now, completely relaxed, hold your mind a blank again. Hold it so for a few moments, then give the mental order to the unconscious mind to tell you what is on the paper you hold in your hand. Keep the eyes closed and the body relaxed, and give the order silently, and with as little mental exertion as possible.

"However, it is necessary to give it clearly and positively, that is, with concentration on it. Say to the unconscious mind, 'I want the picture which is on this card, or paper, presented to my consciousness.' Say this with your mind concentrated on what you are saying. Repeat, as if talking directly to another self: 'I want to see what is on this card.' Then relax into blankness again and hold blankness a few moments, then try gently, without straining, to see whatever forms may appear on the void into which you look with closed eyes. Do not try to conjure up something to see; just wait expectantly and let something come.

"My experience is that fragments of forms appear first. For example, a curved line, or a straight one, or two lines of a triangle. But sometimes the complete object appears; swiftly, lightly, dimly-drawn, as on a moving picture film. These mental visions appear and disappear with lightning rapidity, never standing still unless quickly fixed by a deliberate effort of consciousness. They are never in heavy lines, but as if sketched delicately, in a slightly deeper shade of gray than that of the mental canvas. A person not used to such experiments may at first fail to observe them on the gray background of the mind, on which they appear and disappear so swiftly. Sometimes they are so vague that one gets only a notion of how they look before they vanish. Then one must 'recall' this first vision. Recall it by conscious effort, which is not the same thing as the method of passive waiting by which the vision was first induced. Instead, it is as if one had seen with open eyes a fragment of a real picture, and now closes his eyes and looks at the *memory* of it and tries to 'see' it clearly.

"It is necessary to recall this vision and make note of it, so as not to forget it. One is *sure* to forget it—indeed it is his duty to do so—in the process of the next step, which is one of blankness again. This blankness is, of course, a deliberate putting out of the conscious mind of all pictures, including the one just visioned. One must now order the subconscious not to present it to the conscious mind's picture-film again unless it is the right picture, *i.e.,* the one drawn on the card which is held in hand. Make the conscious mind blank again for a brief space. Then look again on the gray canvas of mind for a vision. This is to test whether the first vision came from subconscious guessing, or whether it came from the deeper mind—from some other source than that of the subconscious, which is so apt to offer a 'guess,' or false picture.

"Do this whole performance two or three times, and if the first vision persists in coming back, accept it. As soon as you have accepted it—that is, decided that this is the correct vision—turn on the light, and without looking at the card, or paper, which contains the real picture, pick up the writing pad and pencil and make a sketch of every detail of the vision-picture. This is a nuisance, as it interrupts concentration and the desired passivity. But it is absolutely necessary to record the vision in every detail, before one looks at the real picture, the one on the card he has been holding in hand. If one does not make a record of his vision in advance of looking at the card picture, he is certain to forget at least some part of it—maybe something which is essential. Worse yet, he is apt to fool himself; the mind is given to self-deception. As soon as it sees the real drawing, it not only forgets the vision, but it is apt to imagine that it visioned the picture it now sees on the card, which may or may not be true. Imagination is a far more active function than the average person realizes. This conscious-subconscious mind is 'a liar,' a weaver of fiction. It is the dream-mind, and also it is the mind of memory-trains.

"Do not omit fragments which seem to be out of place in a picture. These fragments may be the real things. If in doubt as to what the object of your vision is, do not try to guess. But if you have a 'hunch' that something you have seen is connected somehow with a watch, for example, or with an automobile, make a note of this 'hunch.' I use this popular word to indicate a real presentation from some true source, something deeper and more dependable than our own subconscious minds. I call this the 'deep mind' in order to have a name for it. I do not know what it is, of course—I am only judging from the behavior of the phenomena.

"Do not fail to record what seems to be a very stray fragment, for it may be a perfect vision of some portion of the real picture. Record everything, and then later you can compare it carefully with the real drawing. Of course, do not be fantastic in your conclusions. Do you think you have gotten a correct vision of an automobile because you saw a circle which resembled a wheel. However, I once saw a circle and felt that it was an automobile wheel—felt it so vividly that I became overwhelmed with curiosity to see if my 'feeling' was correct, and forthwith turned on the light and examined the real picture in my hand. I found that it was indeed the wheel of an automobile. But I do not do this kind of thing unless I have a very decided 'hunch,' as it tends to lead back to the natural impulse of the mind to 'guess'—and guessing is one of the things one has to strive to avoid. To a certain extent, one comes to know a difference between a guess and a 'hunch.'

"The details of this technique are not to be taken as trifles. The whole issue of success or failure depends on them. At least, this is so in my case. Perhaps a spontaneous sensitive, or one who has a better method, has no such difficulties. I am just an average conscious-minded person, who set out deliberately to find a way to test this tremendously important question of telepathy and clairvoyance, without having to depend on a 'medium,' who might be fooling himself, or me. It was by this method of careful attention to a technique of details that I have found it possible to get telepathic messages and to see pictures on hidden cards, and symbolic pictures of the contents of books.

"This technique takes time, and patience, and training in the art of concentration. But this patience is in itself an excellent thing to learn, especially for nervous and sick people. The uses of mental concentration are too various and tremendously beneficial to enumerate here. The average person has almost no power of concentration, as he will quickly discover by trying to hold his undivided attention on one simple object, such as a rose, or a bottle of ink, for just a few minutes. He will find that a thousand thoughts, usually association-trains connected with the rose, or the ink, will appear on his mental canvas, interrupting his concentration. He will find that his mind behaves exactly like a moving-picture film, or a fireworks display. It is the division of attention that uses up energy, if I am not mistaken.

"Of course this technique is not 'original.' I got it by selecting from hints here and there in my reading, and from my general study and observation of the behavior of the mind.

"Among the difficulties to be overcome—and this is one which is easily detected—is the appearing of visions of objects one has observed in the environment just before closing the eyes. When I close my eyes to make the next test, I invariably find that the last picture, and my own drawing of it, and also the electric light bulb which I have lighted in order to see the last picture—all these immediately appear on the horizon of my mind. It often takes quite a while to banish these memory-ghosts. And sometimes it is a mistake to banish them, as the picture you hold in your hand may be quite similar to the preceding one. If, therefore, a picture resembling the preceding continues obstinately to represent itself, I usually accept it, and often find that the preceding and present cards contain similar pictures.

"Another difficulty is the way things sometimes appear in fragments, or sections, of the whole picture. A straight line may appear, and it may be either only a portion of the whole, or it may be all there is on the card. Then I have to resist the efforts of my imagination to speculate as to what object this fragment may be part of. For instance, I see a series of points, and have the impulse to 'guess' a star. I must say no to this guesswork, unless the indescribable 'hunch' feeling assures me it is a star. I must tell myself it may be indeed a part of a star, but, on the other hand, it may be a complete picture of the drawing in hand, perhaps the letter W, or M, or it may be a part of a pennant, or what not. Then I must start over, and hold blank a while. Then repeat the request to the deep mind for the true picture. Now I may get a more complete picture, or maybe this fragment reappears alone, or maybe it repeats itself upsidedown, or doubled up in most any way.

"I start all over once more and now I may get a series of fragments which follow each other and jump together as do the comic cartoons which are drawn on the screen with pen and ink. For instance, two points appear, then another appears separately and jumps to the first two, and joins up with them, then two more. The result is a star, and this may be the true picture. It usually is. But sometimes this is the subconscious mind, or perhaps the conscious, trying to finish the object as it has 'guessed' it should be. This error of allowing the conscious or the subconscious mind to finish the object is one to be most careful about. As one experiments, he realizes more and more that these two minds, the conscious and the subconscious, are really one, subconsciousness being only a disorderly store-house of memories. The third, or 'deep mind' is apparently the one which gives us our psychic phenomena. Again I say, I do not know what this 'deep mind' is; I use the words merely to have a name for that 'other thing' which brings the message.

"The conscious mind, combined with the subconscious, not only wants to finish the picture, but decides sometimes to eliminate a detail which does not belong to what it has guessed should be there. For example, I will discuss the drawings which have been given as Figures 35, 35a, in this book. I 'visioned' what looked like a figure 5, except that at the top where there should be a small vertical line projecting toward the right, there was a flare of very long lines converging at one end. I consciously decided that the long lines were an exaggeration and multiplication of what should properly be at the top of a five, and that I should not accept them. Here was conscious mind making a false decision. But by obeying the rules I had laid down in advance, I was saved from this error of consciousness. I closed my eyes, gave a call for the true picture, and the lines appeared again, so I included them in my drawing. When I opened the envelope and looked at the picture inside, it was an oil derrick. So the flare of long lines was the real thing, while the figure 5 was the interloper, at least, so I now consciously decided. I thought that the figure 5 and the flare of lines were entirely separate mental images, one following the other so rapidly that they appeared to belong together.

"But again my conscious decision was in error. Several hours later, after I had put the whole matter out of my mind and had been attending to household duties, I suddenly remembered the paper jacket of a German edition of my husband's novel, *Oil!* which was on a shelf in the next room to the one in which I had made my experiments. Why did I suddenly remember this book? I had not noticed it for a long time—its jacket drawings were out of sight, as the book was wedged between many others on the book shelves in an inconspicuous place in the room. On one side of the jacket of this book was a picture of three oil derricks; on the other side was a large dollar mark, almost covering one entire side of the book. I had seen this jacket, had indeed taken special notice of it, at the time of its arrival from Germany. So here seems to have been a clear case of the subconscious mind at work during my experiment, adding to my true vision of an oil derrick, the subconsciously remembered dollar mark which looked like a figure 5, partly hidden by the oil derrick in my vision. Here was a grand mix-up of the false guesses of consciousness and subconsciousness, and the true presentations from the 'deep mind.'

"But this was not the end. This confusion in regard to the dollar mark went forward, in memory-trains to two other experiments. Several days later, I was trying a new set of drawings, and one of them caused in my mind a vision of the capital letter S. Instantly, two parallel straight lines crossed it, turning it into a dollar mark. Then it became an S again without the lines. Then the lines came back. This strange behavior of my vision continued. I was in a quandary as to which to accept, the S or the mark. Then there appeared an old-fashioned money-bag, such as I used to see in my father's bank as a child, full of small coins. It took its place in the vision beside the dollar mark. I decided with the usual erroneous consciousness that this money-bag was a hint from my real mind, so I accepted the dollar mark as correct. But it turned out not to be. When I looked at the drawing in hand it was a letter S. My subconsciousness had supplied the money-bag, and the two parallel lines.

"Several days later, in a vision with a third set of drawings, I saw a letter S, and then at once the bag of small change appeared, but there were no parallel lines on the S. This time the real drawing was a dollar mark! So, my subconsciousness, as soon as the dollar mark had appeared in subconsciousness, had meddled again; it had remembered the last experiment and the scolding I had given it for its guesswork so it now subtracted the parallel lines from the new vision to make it correct, according to the last experiment. It had remembered the last experiment only, forgetting the first one, of the oil derrick, just as I had ordered it to do on the occasion of the second experiment. So, it subtracted the two parallel lines, but it added the remembered bag of money, which I had included in my scolding. From this kind of interference by the subconsciousness, I realized that it is indeed no simple matter to get things into consciousness from the 'deep mind' without guesses and additions and subtractions made by the subconsciousness. Why the subconscious should meddle, I do not know. But it does. Its behavior is exactly like that of the conscious mind, which is also prone to guessing. All this sounds fantastic—to anyone who has not studied his mind. But I tell you how it seems to me.

"Maybe everything comes from the subconscious. Maybe there is no 'deep mind.' Maybe the subconscious gets its knowledge of what is on the drawing directly from the drawing, and is merely blundering around, adding details by guesswork to what it has seen incompletely. But I think that these experiments prove that this is not the case. I think a study of them shows that a true vision comes into the subconsciousness, not directly from the drawing, but from another mind which has some means of knowing, and sending to consciousness via the subconsciousness whatever I ask it for. Of course I cannot attempt to prove this here. It was one of the questions to which I was seeking an answer, and the result seems to point to the existence of a deeper mind, showing how its behavior is quite different from that of the subconscious.

"I wanted to find out if the true vision could in any way be distinguished from 'imagination,' or these busy guesses of the subconsciousness. To help myself in this matter, I first made an examination of exactly how these guesses come. I said to myself: every thought that ever comes to consciousness, excepting those due to direct outside stimulation, may proceed from some deeper source, and by subconscious memory-trains attaching to them, appear to be the work of subconsciousness. So I shut my eyes and made my mind blank, without calling on my mind to present any definite thing. I had no drawing in my hand. After a brief space of blankness, I relaxed the enforced blankness and waited, dreamily, for what might come. A picture soon came, with a whole memory-train. First a girl in a large garden hat, then a garden path and flowers bordering it, then a spade, a wheelbarrow, and so on—things associated in my memory with a girl in a garden hat. As to where the girl in the hat came from, I know not. As to why she should come instead of any other of billions of things seen by me during my life, I know not. I had not asked my mind for her. The question of why she came is interesting.

"But it was easy to account for the other things—the association-train. I learned from this experiment, and several repetitions of it, that something always came—a girl, or a steamship, or the fact that I had not attended to some household duty, or what not—and a train of associated ideas followed. I learned, in a more or less vague way, how these things behaved, and how I *felt* about them. This enabled me to notice, when later I got a true vision, that there was a difference between the way this true vision came and the way the 'idle' visions came. When the true visions came, there usually came with them a 'something' which I call a 'hunch.' There was, of course, always in my consciousness the question: is this the right thing, or not? When the true vision came, this question seemed to receive an answer, 'yes,' as if some intelligent entity was directly informing me.

"This was not always the case. At times no answer came, or at least, if it came, it was obscured by guesses. But usually it did, after I had watched for it, and a sort of thrill of triumph came with it, quite different from the quiet way in which the money-bag had appeared in answer to my uncertainty. The subconscious answers questions, and its answers are always false; its answers come quietly, like a thief in the night. But the 'other' mind, the 'deep mind,' answers questions, too, and these answers come, not quietly, but as if by 'inspiration,' whatever that is—with a rustling of wings, with gladness and conviction. These two minds seem different from each other. One lies and rambles; the other sings, and is truthful.

"But do not misunderstand me. I am not a religious convert. I am searching for knowledge, and recording what I find. Others on this search may have found these same things, but the conclusions they have drawn may not turn out to be the ones I shall draw.

"One or two other things of interest should perhaps be mentioned. First, I found that, in doing a series of several drawings, the percentage of successes was higher in the first three attempts. Then there began to be failures, alternating with successes. This may have been due to the fact that the memory-pictures of these first three experiments now constituted a difficulty. So much attention had to be given to inhibiting these memory-pictures, and in deciding whether or not they were to be inhibited. Or it may be due to some other cause, such as fatigue or boredom.

"The second detail is that during the earliest experiments, I developed a headache. I think this was due to the fact that I strained my closed eyes trying to see with them. I mean, of course, trying to see a vision, not the card in my hand. Using the eyes to see with is a habit, and habits are not easily overcome. I soon learned not to use my eyes, at least not in a strained way, and this was the end of the headaches. However, this use of the eyes in telepathy may perhaps mean more than a mere habit. The mental canvas on which these 'visions' are projected seems to be spread in the eyes, and it is the eyes which seem to see them—despite the fact that the room may be dark, the eyes closed, and the drawing on the paper be wrapped in thick covering and not within normal range of the eyes. But this may be due to the habit of associating all pictures with your eyes."

22

So much for the art of voluntary mind-reading. In conclusion I, the husband, attempt to say a few words about what these phenomena mean, and how they come about.

This attempt involves me in a verbal duel with my wife, which lasts into the small hours of morning. It involves the everlasting debate between the vitalists and the mechanists, which had best be left to Dr. Watson and Professor McDougall, and the others who are no more able than I am to look at the neurons of the brain in action, to see what happens. But I insist that until Craig and Dr. Watson, Professor Eddington, and Mrs. Eddy have found out positively whether the universe is all mind or all matter, I must go on speaking in the old-fashioned way, as if there were two worlds, the physical and the mental, two sets of phenomena which interact one upon the other continuously, even though the manner of this happening is beyond comprehension.

With this much apology, I obtain permission to put forth my humble guess as to the part played by mental concentration in the causing of telepathy, clairvoyance, and trance phenomena. It seems to me that the process of intense concentration may cause the nervous energy, or brain energy, whatever it is, to be withdrawn from some of the brain centers and transferred to others; and it may be this displacement and disturbance of balance which accounts for such phenomena as catalepsy, automatism, and somnambulism. Portions of the mind which are ordinarily below the level of consciousness are raised to more intense forms of activity. New levels of mind are tapped, new "personalities" or faculties are brought into action, and persons under hypnotism develop mental powers they do not consciously possess.

That it is intense concentration upon one suggestion—the narrowing of the attention to one focus—which produces the cataleptic trance is something which my wife set out to prove, and by going close to the borderline she feels that she did prove it. The rigidity began at the extremities and crept rapidly over the body. In spite of my protests, Craig insisted that she was going the whole way, and asked me to stand by and make some tests. I was to wait three minutes, and then lift her up by the feet. I did so, and found an extraordinary thing— the body was perfectly rigid, like a log of wood, except at the neck! When I lifted her by her feet, the neck bent, so that the head remained on the pillow, while the feet were raised at least a yard in the air. Later, when Craig had relaxed, she told me that she had known what was happening; there had been one point of consciousness left, and she had the belief that she could let that go in another moment, but was afraid to do so, because she might not come out again. For an instant, she had felt that strange terror one feels at the moment he ceases to struggle against the fumes of gas or ether, and plunges into oblivion. The difference is that, in the case of gas or ether, one cannot hold on to consciousness; but in the case of the cataleptic state, he can recall his receding consciousness. Craig, of course, had not concentrated with complete attention to one idea; one portion of her mind was concentrating upon achieving rigidity, while another was watching and protesting against oblivion.

Dr. Morton Prince wrote to Craig: "You are playing with powerful and dangerous forces." And so she dropped this form of experiment. But more should be known about these trances, which often occur spontaneously, and can be caused by fear—that is to say, an intense concentration on the idea of escape from danger, which produces a tension amounting to paralysis. In such cases there are a number of new dangers; one being that some doctor will try to restore you with drugs and wrong suggestions. Every suggestion of fear on the part of the onlookers must be avoided in case of trances, for the subconscious mind of the victim hears every word, and believes it; also telepathy has to be remembered. One must not only speak quietly and firmly, repeating that everything is all right, and that the person will come out safely; one must also *think* this. The trance may last a long time, but keep calm and sure of success, and keep the doctor and the undertaker away. The condition of catalepsy is more common than is realized, and it is unpleasant to think how many persons are embalmed while in this condition.

All this sounds disturbing, but it has nothing to do with our telepathy experiments, in which the state of concentration is not one of tension accompanied by the suggestion of rigidity, or of fear, but on the contrary is a state of relaxation, accompanied by the suggestion of control, or supervision. This matter of supervision has been carefully set forth by Craig in her statement. It is one of the mind's great mysteries: how, while thinking about nothing, you can not only remember to give a suggestion, but can also act upon it. Craig insists that we have three minds; and she has in this the backing of William McDougall, an Englishman, who was called the "dean" of American psychologists. McDougall talks about the various "monads" of the mind; so let us say that one "monad" gives an order to a second "monad" to become blank, after it has given an order to a third to present to the first a picture.

The psychic Jan gives such "auto-suggestions" to himself when he goes into a trance, and tells his trance mind to bring him out at a certain moment. How that trance mind can measure time as exactly as a clock is another of the mysteries; but that it happens is beyond doubt. My wife took Jan to a group of scientists in Boston, and several of them held watches and expressed their surprise at what Jan was able to do. It is obvious that when the psychic lets himself be buried six feet under the ground in an ordinary pinewood coffin, he is staking his life upon his certainty that he will not come out of the state of lethargy until after he has been dug up.

He also stakes it upon the hope that the physicians who have the test in charge will have sufficient sense to realize the importance of having him dug out at the time agreed. In one case they were several minutes late, and Jan nearly suffocated. I never saw one of these burials, because Craig obtained his promise not to do them after she knew him; but I have talked with several physicians who watched and directed all the details, and I have a moving-picture film of one.

23

MENTION TELEPATHY in company, and almost everyone has a story to tell. You can find a clairvoyant to tell you about yourself for a dollar—and maybe she is a fraud, but then again, maybe she is a person with a gift which she does not understand, and the police throw her into jail because they don't understand it either. I am sorry if I aid the mass of fraud which I know exists in this field, but there is no power of man which may not and will not be abused. The person who invented high explosives and made possible great tunnels and bridges, also made possible the destruction of the Louvain library. The person who makes a dynamo may electrocute himself.

In spite of all fraud, I am convinced that there are thousands of genuine clairvoyants and psychics. My friend Will Irwin told me recently how he spent a year or so collecting material and writing an exposure of fraud, "The Medium Game," published in *Collier's Weekly* some twenty years ago. At the end of his labors he went, on sudden impulse, into a "parlor" on Sixth Avenue, a cheap neighborhood of New York, and a fat old woman in a greasy wrapper took his dollar, and held his hand in hers, and told him things which he believed were known to no human being but Will Irwin.

"What is the use of it?" some will ask. I reply with another question: "What was the use of the lightning which Franklin brought down from the clouds on his kite-string?" No use that Franklin ever knew; yet today we make his lightning turn the wheels of industry, and move great railroad systems, and light a hundred million homes, and spread jazz music and cigarette advertising thousands of miles in every direction. It is an axiom of the scientist that every scrap of knowledge will be put to use sooner or later; get it, and let the uses wait. The discovery of the cause of bubonic plague was made possible because some foolish-minded entomologist had thought it worth-while to collect information about the fleas which prey upon the bodies of rats and ground squirrels.

I know a certain Wall Street operator who employed a "psychic" to sit in at his business conferences, and tell him if the other fellow was honest. I believe it didn't work very well; perhaps the circumstances were not favorable to concentration. Needless to say, Craig and I have no interest in such uses to be made of our knowledge. What telepathy means to my wife is this: it seems to indicate a common substratum of mind, underlying our individual minds, which we can learn to tap. Figure the conscious mind as a tree, and the subconscious mind as the roots of that tree: then what of the earth in which the tree grows, and from which it derives its sustenance? What currents run through that earth, affecting all the trees of the forest? If one tree falls, the earth is shaken—and may not the other trees feel the impulse?

In other words, we are apparently getting hints of a cosmic consciousness, or cosmic unconsciousness: some kind of mind-stuff which is common to us all, which we can bring into our individual consciousness. Why is it not sensible to think that there may be a universal mind-stuff, just as there is a universal bodystuff, of which we are made, and to which we return?

When Craig orders her mind, or some portion of it, or faculty of it, to get what is in Bob's mind, while Bob is forty miles away—and when her mind does that, what are we to picture as happening? If I am correct in my guess, that mind and body are two aspects of one reality, then we shall find some physical form of energy being manifested, just as we do when we communicate by sound waves. The human brain is a storage battery, capable of sending impulses over the nerves. Why may it not be capable of sending impulses by means of some other medium, known or unknown? Why may there not be such a thing as brain radio?

Certainly we know this, that every particle of energy in the universe affects to some slight extent every other particle. The problem of detecting such energy is merely one of getting a sufficiently sensitive device. Who can say that our thoughts are not causing vibrations? Who can set a limit to the distance they may travel, or to the receiving powers of another brain, in some way or other attuned thereto? Any truly scientific person will admit that this is a possibility, and that it is purely a question of experimenting, to find out if it does happen, and how.

Again, consider the problem of clairvoyance, suggested by Craig's ability to tell what is inside a book she holds in her hand without seeing it, or to reproduce drawings when no human mind knows what drawing she holds. How are we to figure that as happening? Shall we say that brain vibrations affect material things such as paper, and leave impressions which endure for a long time, possibly forever? Can these affect another brain, as in the case of a bit of radium giving off emanations? It seems to me correct to say that, theoretically, it is inevitable. Every particle of energy that has ever been manifested in the universe goes on producing its effects somewhere, somehow, and the universe is forever different because of that happening. The soil of Britain is still shaking with the tramp of Caesar's legions, two thousand years old. Who can say that some day we may not have instruments sensitive enough to detect such traces of energy? On the very day that I am reading the galley proofs of this book, I find in my morning paper an Associated Press dispatch, from which I clip a few paragraphs.

"A fundamental discovery in photography that takes the 'pictures' directly on cold, hard untreated metal without the usual photographer's medium of a sensitized plate was made public tonight at Cornell University. It reveals that seemingly impervious metal records on its surface unseen impressions from streams of electrons and that these marks can be brought into visibility by the right kind of a 'developer,' exactly as photographic images are brought out on sensitized paper . . .

"While studying sensitivity of photographic plates to electron rays it suddenly was realized that polished metal surfaces might be able to pick up impressions of these beams, and when tests were made they showed that not only could such records be made on metals, but the amazing fact appeared that some metals are almost as sensitive as photographic film, and for very low velocity electrons much more sensitive . . .

"This young physicist one day was looking at the rough spots produced on the metal target of an x-ray tube by electron bombardment. Such spots are commonplace, familiar sights to laboratory workers. It occurred to Dr. Carr that perhaps long before the electrons produced the rough place they made an invisible impression, which might be 'developed' in the same manner that the still invisible image on a photo is brought out by putting it into a developing bath. Carr shot the electron rays at gold plates and developed them with mercury vapor, he shot them at silver and developed with iodine, he used hydrochloric acid to develop zinc plates and iodine to develop copper."

And now, if x-rays leave a permanent record on metal, why might not brain-rays, or thought-rays, leave a record upon a piece of paper? Why might not such energies be reflected back to another brain, as light is reflected by a mirror? Or perhaps the record might stay as some other form of energy, turned back into brainrays or thought-rays by the percipient. We are familiar with this in the telephone, where sound vibrations are turned into electrical vibrations, and in this form transported across a continent and under an ocean, and then turned back into sound vibrations once again.

That mental activities do leave some kind of record on matter seems certain; at any rate, it is the basic concept of the materialistic psychologist. For what is memory, to the materialist, but some kind of record upon brain cells? He compares these cells to photoelectric cells, and imagines a lot of stored up records which we can consult. If now it should be found that such memory records are impressed, not merely upon living brain cells, but upon the molecules or electrons which compose any form of matter, what would be so incredible about that?

I have gone this far, in the effort to meet my materialist friends halfway. For my part, I have no metaphysics; I am content to say that I do not know what matter is, nor what mind is, nor how they interact. If you want to realize the inadequacies of the materialistic dogma, so far as concerns this special field, you may consult the work of Dr. Rudolph Tischner, a qualified scientist of Germany, whose book, *Telepathy and Clairvoyance,* is published in translation by Harcourt, Brace and Company. The last chapter, called "Theory," deals with the suggested explanations in more detail than I have the space for here.

24

APRIL 21, 1929. I am over at the office fixing up this manuscript to send to the publisher; and just as I have it nicely wrapped, it has to be opened again—for this is what has happened. Craig, with her anxiety complex, has had this thought: "Here is Upton committing himself in this public way, on a subject about which people know so little and suspect so much; and suppose this faculty, whatever it is, should be gone in these last few weeks, while I have been fussing over spring housecleaning! Suppose I should find I can never do it again!"

She has to make sure all over again. She has in her desk a fat envelope marked: "To try." A lot of old drawings, left-overs from different series that she has tried and failed on during the past several months; some that she herself has drawn for friends; some that she was interrupted while doing—a job lot, in short. She does not know how many, as she has stuck them in from time to time, and never looked into the envelope; but it is well filled. Now she takes out some drawings, with averted eyes, and lies down and tries them. The house is quiet, a good opportunity, so she does nine drawings, and there is only one complete failure in the lot.

One is a marvel—as good as any. It is a drawing I had made, a donkey's head and neck, with a wide collar. Craig writes: "Cow's head in 'stock'"—a "stock" being in Mississippi a wooden yoke made to keep cattle from jumping fences. She draws the head of the so-called "cow" and the "stock"; it is a perfect donkey's head, facing just as mine does.

And then there is a duck, about to eat a snail. Such a jolly duck, and such a wheely snail shell! Craig has made this drawing to amuse the little daughter of Bob and Dollie, who had a pet duck, called "Mary Ann," fed on snails. Craig made this drawing several months ago, to let the child "concentrate" on, and try telepathy like the grown-ups. And now, with this drawing under her hand, Craig writes: "See wheels. Think of children. Has to do with children." The drawing of the snail shell is plainly a lot of "wheels."

Now, of course, Craig had previously seen every one of these drawings, and so they were all in her subconscious mind. But these drawings had never been seen by her at the same time. They were put into the envelope, some at one time, some at another. Now she has taken out a few at random. What a jumble for any subconscious mind to keep track of! How is Craig's mind to know which drawings she has taken out, and which one she is holding under her hand?

Again we have something more than telepathy. For no human mind knows what drawings she has taken from that envelope. No human mind but her own even knows that she is trying an experiment. Either there is some superhuman mind, or else there is something that comes from the drawings, some way of "seeing," other than the way we know and use all the time. Make what you can of this, but don't laugh at it, for most certainly it happens.

25

OCTOBER 1929. At my wife's insistence, I have held up this book for six months, in order to think it over, and have the manuscript read by friends whose opinions we value. A score or more have read it, and made various suggestions, many of which I have accepted. Some of the reactions of these friends may be of interest to the reader.

The news that I was taking up "psychic" matters brought me letters both of curiosity and protest. My friend Isaac Goldberg of Boston reported the matter in the Haldeman-Julius publications under the title: "Sinclair Goes Spooky." I hope that when he has read this book, he will find another adjective. My friends, both radical and respectable, must realize that I have dealt here with facts, in as patient and thorough a manner as I have ever done in my life. It is foolish to be convinced without evidence, but it is equally foolish to refuse to be convinced by real evidence.

There came to me a letter of warning from a good comrade, T. H. Bell of Los Angeles, an elderly Scotchman who has grown up in the Socialist movement, and known the old fighters of the days when I was a child. He begged me not to jeopardize my reputation; so I thought he would be a good test for the manuscript, and asked him to read it. Some of his suggestions I accepted, and the work is the better for them. But Comrade Bell was not able to believe that Craig's drawings could have come by telepathy, for the reason that it would mean that he was "abandoning the fundamental notions" on which his "whole life has been based."

Comrade Bell brought many arguments against my thesis, and this was a service, because it enables me to answer my critics in advance. First, what is the value of my memory? Can I be sure that it does not "accommodate itself too easily to the statement Sinclair wishes to believe?" My answer is that few of the important cases in the book rest upon my memory; they rest upon records written down at once. They rest upon drawings which were made according to a plan devised in advance, and then duly filed in envelopes numbered and dated. Also, my memory has been checked by my wife's, who is a fanatic for accuracy, and has caused me torment, through a good part of our married life, by insisting upon going over my manuscripts and censoring every phrase. Also

Bob and Dollie and my secretary have read this narrative, and checked the statements dealing with them.

Next objection, that I am "a man without scientific training." The acceptance of that statement depends upon the definition of the word "scientific." If it includes the social sciences, then I have had twenty-five years of very rigid training. I have made investigations and published statements, literally by thousands, which were criminal libels unless they were true and exact; yet I have never had any kind of libel suit brought against me in my life. As to the scientific value of the particular experiments described in this book, the reader can do his own judging, for they have been described in detail. I don't see how scientific training could have increased our precautions. We have outlined our method to scientists, and none has suggested any change.

Next, the fact that in the past I have shown myself "naïve and credulous at times." No doubt I have; but I have learned by such experiences, and I am not so naïve and credulous as when I was younger. Neither do I see how these qualities can play much part in the present matter. I surely know the conditions under which I made my drawings, and whether I had them under my eyes while my wife was making her drawings in another room; I know about the ones I sealed in envelopes, and which were never out of my sight. As for my wife, she certainly has nothing of the qualities of naïveté and credulity. She was raised in a family of lawyers, and was given the training and skeptical point of view of a woman of the world. "Trust people, but watch them," was old Judge Kimbrough's maxim; and following it too closely has almost made a pessimist of his daughter.

Next, that Craig is "in poor health." That is true, but I do not see how it matters here. She has often been in pain, but it has never affected her judgment. She chose her own times for experimenting, when she felt in the mood, and her mind was always clear and keen for the job.

Next, "a husband and wife are a bad pair to make telepathic experiments. Living so much together, their common life does tend to make them think of the same thing at the same time." This is true; but how does it account for the half-dozen successes with a brother-in-law, twenty or thirty with a secretary, and many with Jan? How does it account for the covers and jackets of books in which I had no interest, but which had come to me by chance, and which Craig had never even glanced at, so far as she remembers?

It is true that in the early days most of our drawings were of obvious things which lay about the house, scissors, table forks, watches, chairs, telephones; so there was a better chance of guesswork. How much chance, was determined by my son and his wife, who, hearing that Craig and I were trying telepathy experiments, decided to try a few also—without knowing anything about the technique. They also drew scissors, tableforks, watches, chairs, telephones, and such common objects. The only trouble was that when David tried to reproduce Betty's drawings, he drew the chair where she had drawn the scissors, and drew the watch where she had drawn the table-fork, and so on. They did not get a single success.

I think that if you will go back and look over those drawings as a whole, you must admit that the objects were as varied as the imagination could make them. I do not see how any one could choose a set of objects less likely to be guessed than the series which I have numbered from four to twelve—a bird's nest full of eggs and surrounded by leaves, a spiked helmet, a desert palmtree, a star with eight double points, a coconut palm, a puppy chasing a string, a flying bat, a Chinese mandarin, and a boy's foot with a roller-skate on it. None of these objects has any relationship whatever to my life, or to Craig's, or to our common life. To say that a wife can guess such a series, because she knows her husband's mind so well, seems to me out of all reason.

Next, the point that some of the cases are not convincing by themselves. I am familiar with this method of argument, having encountered it with others of my books. Let me beg you to note that the cases are not taken by themselves, but are taken as a whole. I can think, for example, of several ways by which Craig might have known that I had put my little paper of written notes into the pocket of my gray coat, or that I had left some medical apparatus under the bathtub at the office. She might have seen these things, and then have forgotten it, and her subconscious mind might have brought back to her the location of the objects, but failed to remind her of the previous seeing. If such cases had stood alone, I would not have thought it worthwhile to write this book.

The same thing applies to Craig's production of German words. Having spent several weeks with me in Germany, and having known many Germans, she no doubt has German words in her subconscious mind. This also applies to certain dream cases. Any one who wants to can go through the book and pick out a score of cases which can be questioned on various grounds. Perhaps it would be wiser for me to cut out all except the strongest cases. But I rely upon your common sense, to realize that the strongest cases have caused me to write the book; and that the weaker ones are given for whatever additional light they may throw upon the problem.

If you want to deal fairly with the book, here is what you have to explain. How did it happen then at a certain agreed hour when Bob at Pasadena drew a table-fork and dated and signed the drawing, Craig in Long Beach wrote: "See a table fork, nothing else," and dated and signed her words? If you call this a coincidence, how are you going to account for the chair, and the watch, and the circle with the hole in the middle, and the sense of pain and fear, and the spreading black stain called blood, all reproduced under the same perfect conditions? I say that if you call all this coincidence, you are violating the laws of probability as we know them. I say that there are only two possible explanations—either telepathy, or that my wife and her brother-in-law were hoaxing me.

But if you want to assume a hoax, you have to face the fact that my wife a few days later was reproducing a series of drawings which I made and kept in front of my eyes in a separate room from her, in such a position that she could not see them if she wanted to. If I thought it worthwhile, I could draw you a diagram of the place where she sat and the place where I sat, and convince you that neither mirrors, nor a hole in the wall, not any other device would have enabled my wife to see my drawings, until I took them to her and compared them with her drawings. The only way you can account for that series of successes is to say that I am in on the hoax.

My good friend and comrade Tom Bell does not suggest that I am in it; but others may say it, so I will answer. Let me assure you, there is no reason in the world why I should take the field on behalf of the doctrine of telepathy—except my conviction that it has been proved. I don't belong to any church which teaches telepathy. I don't hold any doctrine which is helped by it. I don't make any money by advocating or practicing it. There is no more reason why I should be concerned to vindicate telepathy, than there is for my coming out in support of the Catholic doctrine of the Immaculate Conception, or the Mormon doctrine of Urim and Thummim, or the Koreshan doctrine that the earth is a hollow sphere and we live on the inside of it.

I assure you I am as cold-blooded about the thing as a man can be. In fact, I don't like to believe in telepathy, because I don't know what to make of it, and I don't know to what view of the universe it will lead me, and I would a whole lot rather give all my time to my muckraking job which I know by heart. I don't expect to sell especially large quantities of this book; I am sure that by giving the same amount of time and energy to other books I have in mind, I could earn several times as much money. In short, there isn't a thing in the world that leads me to this act except the conviction which has been forced upon me that telepathy is real, and that loyalty to the nature of the universe makes it necessary for me to say so.

My friend and publisher Charles Boni thinks that I should write this book without protestations; taking a dignified position, sure that my readers will trust me. But as it happens, I have read, not merely the literature of psychic research, but also the literature in opposition to it, and I know the arguments advanced by persons who are unwilling to change their "fundamental notions." It seems common sense to answer here the objections which are certain to be made.

I submitted this manuscript to the two leading psychologists of America, Morton Prince and William McDougall. Dr. Prince was taken by death before he found time to read it, but Professor McDougall read it, and has stated his reactions in the preface. In writing to me, he expressed the hope that my wife would be able to make some of these telepathy tests under the observation of well-known scientists. In replying, I assured him that my wife and I shared this hope; but whether it can ever be realized is a problem for the future. All Craig's work so far has depended upon a state of complete peace and relaxation. As she has pointed out, it is a matter of "undivided concentration," and even such disturbing things as light and noise are an interference. One friend who has tried to experiment lately at our instigation gave it up because of automobile horns in the street outside. She declared that these had never disturbed her before, but that the effort not to hear them when concentrating only caused her to concentrate on the horns, and so threatened to give her a case of "nerves."

Whether Craig would be able to get the necessary state of mind in the presence of strangers, skeptical or possibly hostile, is a problem yet to be solved. Unless we are going to beg the question, we have to assume that telepathy may be a reality; and if it be a reality, then certainly what is in the other person's mind makes a difference, and certainly it is a serious matter to ask a woman in delicate health to open her mind to the moods of strangers. Some day in the future Craig is going to make the test, but whether it succeeds or fails will not alter, so far as I am concerned, what has already happened in my presence.

Another of my friends who read the manuscript was Floyd Dell, and he thinks that readers of my books will wish to know to what extent, if any, my interest in the subject of telepathy is going to change my attitude to the struggle for social justice. To that I reply that I have been interested in psychic research for the past thirty-five years, ever since, as a youth, I met Minot J. Savage; but this has not kept me from believing ardently in the abolition of parasitism, exploitation, and war. While the telepathy experiments were going on I wrote *Boston*, a novel of some 325,000 words, in less than a year. While I am consulting with my friends about this manuscript, I am writing a novel, *Mountain City*, which I hope my Socialist friends will find of interest. The only discovery that can weaken my interest in the economic problem will be one which enables human beings to live without food, clothing, and shelter. But in the meantime, I see no reason why Socialists are required to be ignorant of psychology.

James Fuchs, another patient critic of my writings, thinks I appear naïve in this book, and should reveal some knowledge of the vast literature on the subject. My reason for not doing so is that very vastness; one would need several volumes to handle it. In the Proceedings of the American and British Societies for Psychical Research lies buried endless evidence on the subject; but scientific authority remains for the most part uninterested in that evidence, and would not be interested in my rehash of it. I have written this book to tell my readers and friends what I myself have seen with my own eyes. That is my job, and I leave the rest to others who are better qualified.

Fuchs reminds me that "umbilical sensory perception" is a well-known psychic phenomenon, and that Craig, in holding the drawings over her solar plexus, is repeating the method of Justinus Kerner (1786–1862), about whom you will find an article in the "Encyclopedia Britannica." Craig knew about that from various sources, and some of her experiments were designed to test the explanation. I made eight drawings and laid them face down on the table by her couch, perhaps three feet from her head. I put them there while she was out of the room, and I sat and watched, to be sure she did not ever touch them. She lay on the couch and made some notes and drawings which reproduced the essential features of half a dozen of my drawings—all at once! So, if Craig has an umbilical eye, she must also have one in the side of her head which can see through several thicknesses of paper.

My daughter-in-law at that time also made suggestions which I accepted. She spoke for the new generation of radicals, saying: "The book aroused a storm of metaphysical speculation in my mind, and I could wax eloquent with slight provocation." This is different from refusing to "abandon the fundamental notions on which my whole life has been based."

26

ONE INTERESTING POINT I observe: in any company where the subject of this manuscript is brought up, invariably some person declares that he or she has had such experiences. One lady, highly educated, assured me that she and her husband had developed telepathy to a point where it served them on a lonely ranch in the place of telegraph and telephone. Only a few days ago I met at luncheon Bruno Walter, orchestra leader, who had come from Germany to conduct concerts in the Hollywood Bowl. Mr. Walter narrated to me the incident which follows:

While conducting in some middle western city, he was a guest at a luncheon, and found himself becoming very ill. He explained matters to his host, who called a taxicab, but this cab did not arrive, and Mr. Walter, in great distress, took his hat and left the house, saying that he would look for a cab. Turning the corner of the street, he came upon his manager, driving a car, and hailed him. "A most fortunate accident!" exclaimed the sick man, but the manager assured him that it was no accident; about half an hour previously, the manager had been seized by an intense feeling that Mr. Walter was in trouble, and had been moved to get into his car and drive. He did not know where Mr. Walter had gone, but simply followed his impulse to drive in a certain direction.

Another incident, told me by Fremont Older, editor of the San Francisco *Call*, and a veteran fighter in the cause of social justice. Older had seen many demonstrations of telepathy, and was completely convinced of its reality. A friend of his, living on a ranch, employed a cook named Sam who had the gift, and agreed to give a demonstration for the Olders. Sam asked Older to get a book and wrap it in thick paper, and Sam would tell the name of the book and the author. Older went out to his car, but could find no book, only a folder of maps, which he wrapped in several thicknesses of paper. Sam put the package to his head, and after a minute or two said, "This is not a book, it is a map or something. Why don't you get me a regular book?" So Older went to his car again and found a book belonging to his wife, and wrapped it with care and tied it. Sam put it to his head, and began to spell letters, and finally stated as follows: "*Julia France and her Times*, by Gertrude Atherton, published by the

Macmillan Company." This was correct. Sam added: "I get another name. What has Ernest Hopkins got to do with this book?" Older and his wife were dumbfounded; for the name was that of a member of the newspaper staff who had been asked to review the book, but Mrs. Older had taken the copy from him because at the last moment she wanted something to read on her trip.

As this book is going to the printer, my attention is called to the fact that Dr. Carl Bruck of Berlin has published a book entitled *Experimentelle Telepathie*, in which he reports a series of tests closely resembling those here described. The main difference is that he used hypnotized subjects, four different young men, as the recipients of his telepathic messages. He made drawings at home, and locked them in a large portfolio, which he placed in an adjoining room from the subject, two or three yards distant through a wall. He himself sat in front of the hypnotized subject, and concentrated upon "sending" one of the drawings. Under these conditions, in a total of 111 experiments, one-third were successful. The Berlin correspondent of the *Scientific American* reported these tests in the issue of May 1924, where those interested may read the details, and inspect twelve of the drawings. The tests were conducted in the presence of various physicians and scientists; and I am interested in a recent comment on the matter by a German physician living in Mexico City: "Bruck's work has gone almost wholly unnoticed."

I say to scientific men, that such work deserves to be noticed. There is new knowledge here, close to the threshold, waiting for us; and we should not let ourselves be repelled by the seeming triviality of the phenomena, for it is well known that some of the greatest discoveries have come from the following up of just such trivial clues.

What did Benjamin Franklin have to go on when he brought the lightning down from the clouds on the string of a kite? Just a few hints, picked up in the course of the previous hundred years; a few traces of electricity noted by accident. The fact that you got a spark if you stroked a cat's fur; the fact that you got the same kind of a spark by rubbing amber, and a bigger one by storing the energy in a glass jar lined with tinfoil—that was all men had as promise of the miracles of our time, dynamos and superpower, telegraph and telephone, x-ray surgery, radio, wireless, television, and new miracles just outside our door. If now it be a fact that there is a reality behind the notions of telepathy and clairvoyance, to which so many investigators are bearing testimony all over the world, who can set limits to what it may mean to the future? What new powers of the human mind, what ability to explore the past and future, the farthest deeps of space, and those deeps of our own minds, no less vast and marvelous?

To set limits to such possibilities is not to be scientific, it is merely to be foolish. The true scientist sets no limits to human powers, he merely asks that we verify our facts. This my wife and I have tried to do, and I think that, so far as concerns telepathy at least, we can claim success. We present here a mass of real evidence, and we shall not be troubled by any amount of ridicule from the ignorant. I tell you—and because it is so important, I put it in capital letters: TELEPATHY HAPPENS!

ADDENDUM

The following was originally published as Part I of Bulletin XVI of the Boston Society for Psychic Research in April 1932. The figure numbers listed herein refer to the illustrations in *Mental Radio,* with the exception of Figures 147, 148, and 149 which appeared in the Bulletin only.

The author of the report was Dr. Walter Franklin Prince, Research Officer of the society. He was a doctor of divinity of the Methodist Episcopal Church and had been pastor of several churches. Later he retired and took up the work of the society. He died two years after this report appeared.

THE SINCLAIR EXPERIMENTS FOR TELEPATHY

ABOUT EIGHTEEN MONTHS AGO I first opened a new book by the novelist Upton Sinclair, entitled *Mental Radio,* then newly issued. In 239 pages it outlined the story of the discovery and development of what purported to be a supernormal faculty possessed by his wife, and rehearsed a large number of experiments in which she seemed to have achieved a large and convincing percentage of successes as a telepathic "percipient," the "agent" generally being Mr. Sinclair, but sometimes her brother-in-law or another person. I confess to misgivings as I began to read, first for the very reason that the writer is a novelist (unmindful of Wells and certain other writers of fiction who, nevertheless, have shown themselves capable of serious and even scientific thinking),[1] and secondly because I had suspected, rightly or wrongly, that once or twice in the past he had failed to discover the devices of certain clever professionals. To be sure, his wife was not a professional, and all the conditions could be under his own hand, but sometimes through sheer confidence people are deceived by their own relatives.

This, to be frank, was my initial attitude—one of cautious interrogation and alertness to find signs of credulity, failure to appreciate the possibilities of chance, or lack of data by which the calculus of chance coincidence could be determined. But as I read on and studied the reproductions of drawings it became more and more evident that something besides chance had operated, that the conditions of many of the experiments had been excellently devised, and that where the conditions were relaxed Mr. Sinclair had been quite aware of the fact and was candid enough to admit it. He stated that such relaxation did not increase the percentage of success, and it certainly so appeared from the examples given. He reported the total number of experiments, and estimated

---

[1] Oliver Wendell Holmes was a poet and novelist, but as the Encyclopedia Britannica says: "In 1843 he published his essay on the Contagiousness of Puerperal Fever, which stirred up a fierce controversy and brought upon him bitter personal abuse, but he maintained his position with dignity, temper and judgment, and in time was honored as the discoverer of a beneficent truth." It was about the same time that Semmelweiss was making similar observations, but he did not take preventive measures until 1847, and Lister came still later.

S. Weir Mitchell was one of the most prominent novelists of America at the close of the 19th century, but he was also conspicuous as a neurologist and member of many scientific societies.

The mentality of a man cannot be determined by his profession or by his prevailing occupation. Mendel, who influenced biology hardly less than did Darwin, was a monk and an abbot. Copernicus, who revolutionized solar astronomy, was canon of a cathedral, and astronomy was only his avocation.

A thing is as it acts. An automobile is a good automobile if it behaves as an automobile should. We shall see how Mr. Sinclair carried on his experiments and how he reported them. At times he pursued a defective method, but he was aware of the fact and reports it, while certain technically scientific investigators of telepathy and other matters have not seemed even to be aware of their mistakes.

the percentages of successes, partial successes, and failures. In 290 experiments, he made these percentages: successes, approximately 23 per cent; partial successes, 53 per cent; failures, 24 per cent. He admitted that judges probably would not agree upon exactly the same ratios. In fact I personally think that certain examples which he did not publish are better than a few which he did, but have not yet found reason to quarrel with his general estimates.

After considerable study of the book, becoming interested beyond any expectation, I wrote to Mr. Sinclair, stating that I had become favorably impressed, and making the somewhat audacious proposal that he should send me all the original materials for a fresh study by the individual standards and through the particular methods of a professional investigator. One can think of several reasons which might make the most honest and confident man hesitant to assent to such a proposal, coming from one whom he had never seen, and who might for all he knew have a set of prejudices which after all would cause him to make a lawyer's argument against the case. I was really surprised that the bundle of materials was sent as quickly as it could be gotten together.[2]

Among the objects in mind were: (1) To study the materials in their strict chronological order, day by day. The mode of presentation in *Mental Radio* was to give some of the most striking results first, then many more that were more or less classified according to subjects and aspects. This is effective for popular reading but not satisfactory to the serious student. (2) To see if there were signs, in any part of the results, of profiting from normal knowledge, whether consciously or subconsciously acquired, of what the "agent" had drawn. Mr. Sinclair took this theory into account and quite decidedly killed it, but it was my duty to try it out anew by my own processes, with the same rigor shown in relation to my own wife and my daughter in *The Psychic in the House*. Later, in summary fashion, these tests will be set forth. (3) To try out other theories to account for the ratios and degrees of correspondence between "original drawings" and "reproductions" in the Sinclair experiments, such as involuntary whispering and chance coincidence. (4) To make a large number of guessing tests on the basis of the Sinclair originals, both as a means of deciding whether the "mere coincidence" theory is tenable (as aforesaid) and, if it should prove otherwise, in order to make a rough measurement of the disparity between telepathic results and those of guessing. (5) In the event that there appeared to be no reasonable escape from conclusion that telepathy is displayed by the material, to ascertain (a) whether the telepathic faculty with Mrs. Sinclair was constant, vacillating, progressively constant, or what; (b) whether the telepathic impressions came to her in the form of ideas, images, names or in

---

[2] From earlier correspondence and other sources, Mr. Sinclair was quite aware that the man to whom he was sending the materials is hard-boiled enough to reject them and drop the whole case or report on it adversely if the results of examination were unsatisfactory.

more than one fashion; (c) whether any further hints as to the mental processes involved could be discerned or any particular pieces of information isolated which might be helpful in this field of study. (6) Finally, to urge readers to institute experiments of their own, and to give amateurs some directions as to procedure. If many could be persuaded to start "games" of this character with their friends, doubtless favorable subjects could be discovered or developed. Attention being called to these persons, series of tests could be made with them under conditions against which none of the old objections could be offered.[3]

The Sinclair experiments are treated first in this Bulletin, since they are its chief subject. The drier Historical Notes, presenting a sketch of the first steps in methodical research relating to alleged Thought-Transference, with summaries of some of the classic series of tests particularly such as are based upon drawings, are relegated to Part Two. The more earnest and methodical students of such matters will prefer to read that first.

Mr. Upton Sinclair, about fifty-two years old when his book *Mental Radio* was issued, is, as everyone is supposed to know, one of the leading novelists of the United States. His stories are all, or nearly all, characterized by an intense purpose. To those who claim that art should be exercised only for art's sake this may be obnoxious. But from the point of view of this examination of his book purporting to prove telepathy, the fact that his novels also attempt to prove something, on the basis of studies made by him, is quite in his favor.[4] Whether he has in fact proved the thesis of his respective tales is not within our province to determine; we do propose rigidly to analyze and review his claims to have proved telepathy.

Mr. Sinclair is a Socialist, and a very active and prominent one; he has been Socialist candidate for Congress in New Jersey and later in California, besides having been Socialist candidate for the United States Senate and for governor in the latter-named state. Political prejudices or predilections should be strictly excluded from the minds of readers of the book or this review of it.[5] It is another gratifying indication that Mr. Sinclair was not deterred from publishing *Mental Radio* by the solicitations or irony of influential friends in his political group, for the scientific spirit is in part compounded of courage, honesty and candor.

Mrs. Sinclair, née Mary Craig Kimbrough, somewhere about forty-five years old when the experiments afterwards published took place, is the daughter of a retired judge, bank president, and planter of Mississippi.

The reader may judge of the quality of her mentality by reading Appendix 1. That is, in part, the reason that it is printed. It is a piece of writing by Mrs.

---

[3] In some cases it might be necessary to increase rigidity of the conditions gradually, as friendly confidence and ease of the percipient became better established. It is futile to ignore the fact that nervous excitement and mental unrest are unfavorable to success.

[4] For example, in 1906 Mr. Sinclair assisted the Government in the investigation of the Chicago stockyards.

[5] [Historical reference deleted.]

Sinclair shortened according to permission given. Almost immediately after my suggestion that the experimental materials should be sent for examination, they were bundled up and sent, together with some stray scraps, among which was this unfinished piece of manuscript which, as it proved, the Sinclairs did not know had been included. In spots the composition may be a bit diffuse and repetitious, but the woman really thinks and reasons, which is more than many do.

There is in it a sincerity, earnestness, and intensity of desire to know, which can hardly be counterfeited. Its writer fairly rivals Descartes in her determination to find some salient and secure spot from which to start in her quest. But in a manner she goes back farther than Descartes, at least she splits his ultimate in two. She is satisfied with "I am," not because "I think," but because "I am conscious of thinking"; but she does not so readily grant the "*I* think." She wants to know, "Am *I* doing all the thinking I am conscious of?"

In fact, the document is so intense in its eagerness to penetrate the secret of personality in relation to its cosmic environment that it is almost febrile. At least in its first pages there is something pathological. To paint life with such dark colors and to dwell so upon its "discouragements" is not an indication of perfect health.

And yet it is certain that the writer is not self-absorbed. The painful reactions of the kind which she has experienced, the torture produced in her by the existence of so much in life that seems unmeaning and disapppointing, she supposes to be quite general with her fellow-men and so feels a great pity for them. Whereas, in my belief, while more are complaining than are happy or contented, it is common to fret because of income taxes, and inability to wear such fine clothes as those of Mrs. Jones, and cold weather and squalling cats, and such sordid matters, but uncommon to be agonized by the desire to fathom the mysteries of the human spirit.

The main points of what Mr. Sinclair tells us of the characteristics of his wife are to be discerned in this revealing manuscript. He says, "She has nothing of the qualities of naïveté and credulity. She was raised in a family of lawyers and was given the training and skeptical point of view of a woman of the world. 'Trust people, but watch them,' was old Judge Kimbrough's maxim, and following it too closely has almost made a pessimist of his daughter. In the course of the last five or six years Craig has acquired a fair-sized library of books on the mind, both orthodox scientific, and 'crank.' She has sat up half the night studying, marking passages and making notes, seeking to reconcile various doctrines, to know what the mind is, and how it works, and what can be done with it." This began with a breakdown of health when she was about forty years old. "A story of suffering needless to go into; suffice it that she had many ills to experiment upon, and mental control became suddenly a matter of life and death." This breakdown, it is said, resulted directly from "her custom of carrying the troubles of all who were near her." She is intensely sympathetic, we are told. "The griefs of other people overwhelm Craig like a suffocation."[6]

The book relates several spontaneous experiences of Mrs. Sinclair when she was young and which, taken together, strongly indicate telepathy. Her husband rightly remarks that it is the number of such incidents which is impressive; one or two might well be coincidence. Still the coincidence of being suddenly impressed that Mr. B., whose home was three hundred miles away, was at her home where he had never been, and turning back from a drive and finding him there, even taken by itself, is a very striking one. Mr. Sinclair himself is witness to the fact that she suddenly, for no known reason became very much worried about Jack London, insisting that he was in mental distress, whereas it proved that London committed suicide at about that time.

Such incidents indicate that her experimental successes were not solely the result of the method which she explains at length, but that she had an inborn gift from early childhood. Her interest in that gift seems to have been much stimulated by her acquaintance with "Jan," the "young hypnotist" of Appendix 1, whose advent is probably not in that narrative placed in chronological order. She became convinced that he showed evidence of telepathy, and tried in turn to ascertain what he was thinking or what he was doing when absent, and became convinced that many times she had been successful. Also, "Craig has been able to establish exactly the same *rapport* with her husband," who relates instances. These were "written down at the time." So few even intelligent people do make immediate record of such things that we would have suspected, even if he had not informed us on another page, that he has made a considerable study of the literature of psychic research.

One of these incidents we shall particularly notice here, and that because Mr. Sinclair himself has either not noticed all of its evidential value, or has not fully called attention to it. [Refer to Figs. 14a and 14b and experiment.]

Probably Mr. Sinclair thought it would be sufficiently obvious to the reader that the first drawing is as similar in shape to a clover blossom as a person

---

[6] If there are those who think there is no value in knowing something of the make-up of the chief witnesses in this case, I emphatically do not agree with them. That such knowledge is not absolutely determinative is, of course, true.

We are investigating a field of phenomena by all the methods which are practicable. The larger part of the phenomena are sporadic and spontaneous, and can hardly be expected to occur in a laboratory. There are many cases where a man has experienced but one apparition in his lifetime, and that at or close to the time when the person imaged died. Will any director of a laboratory consent to keep people under surveillance for a lifetime, to test if such an experience will take place in a laboratory, and can any persons be found who will consent to spend a lifetime? And if under such conditions an apparition should be experienced and it should prove beyond doubt that the person imaged died at that moment, even though the apparitional experience occurred in a laboratory, in no sense would or could laboratory tests be applied to it. The authentication of the incident would be the testimonies of the scientific gentlemen present, to the effect that the story of the apparition was related to them and written down before the death of the person was known, with, perhaps, details of how the person who experienced the apparition looked and acted at the time. But the testimonies of witnesses outside of the laboratory are evidence of precisely as much weight, provided that their mentality and reputation for veracity are equal.

With favorable subjects experiments for telepathy can sometimes be and sometimes have been carried on with all the rigidity of method and the scrupulosity of a laboratory, or, if there remain doubts and objections on grounds seemingly almost of as "occult" a nature as telepathy itself, doubtless in time to come methods will be devised to meet these doubts and objections. But subjects of singularly calm and poised nature will be required. It seems to be a fact with which we have to deal, however regrettable, that with most persons who under friendly and unstrained conditions at times strongly evidence telepathic powers, suddenly to place them in a room containing strange apparatus, and before a committee of strangers, some perhaps cold and stern in appearance, others whose amiable demeanor nevertheless betrays an amused scepticism, is to make it improbable that they can exhibit telepathy at all. It will have to be recognized as a scientific datum that a state of mental tranquillity and passivity is generally requisite for such manifestations. Nor is this peculiar to psychical manifestations; the principle applies more or less to a variety of psychological manifestations and powers. Mark Twain could reel off witty utterances when he was mentally at ease, but had he been surrounded by a solemn-visaged group of psychologists with his wrists harnessed to a sphygmometer, and placed in face of an apparatus for recording graphs and a stenographer with poised pencil, it is very certain that his reactions would not have been those of brilliant and original humor. So I have seen a prominent violinist, invited to play at a reception, try to keep on amidst the waxing murmur of conversation, and finally falter and almost break down.

In this laboratory-fixation age it is well to remember that certain even of the physical sciences quite or mostly elude laboratory experimentation. Take astronomy, a great and promising but difficult and problematical field of research. No sun of all the millions, no planet, no planetary satellite, no comet, no tiniest of the asteroids can be brought into a laboratory. Once in a while a meteoric stone reaches the earth, and this can be analyzed, but no laboratory can control or predict time or place of its falling. It is necessary to devise agencies, telescopes, spectroscopes and so on, which in a sense, go out and bring back data about the subjects of this science, and to develop methods of mathematical deduction by which to reach conclusions which are accepted by most people on authority only, since to most people the mathematics is quite unintelligible.

Astronomy, perhaps entitled to be called the most ancient of sciences, is one of the most difficult. A multitude of theories to account for its multitudinous phenomena have been supplanted by others; within the memory of persons now living many opinions once firmly held have been discarded or at least called in question. This is not in the least to the discredit of the science, but it is a fact. Today there are many contradictions of opinion among astronomers. While an article by a scientific man was printing in the Scientific American expressing the common view that in a little while, about a minion million years, the earth will become too cold for anybody to live on it, another scientist was announcing to the world his reasons for questioning that conclusion. Even facts of a declared visual character are called in question. Professor Percival Lowell to his death in 1916 supported Schiaparelli's announced discovery of canals on Mars, described them as he saw them through the telescope, and declared that they must be or [of] artificial origin. It is said that there are astronomers who can see the canals but who question that they are artificial. And it is certain that there are astronomers who deny that there are any canals at all, and who claim that what seem to be canals to some are optical illusions or sheer hallucinations. (Is not astronomy getting to look like psychic research?)

But in spite of all its shifting and reconstruction of theories, its assertions and counter-assertions, the complexity and enormous difficulty of its numerous problems, and the exceedingly subtle methods by which, in a great measure, these problems must be studied, no one is so foolish as to think that astronomical investigation should not be pursued, or that there does not lie before it a great field for the pursuit of truth.

To a very large extent psychic research is analogous with astronomy. It, the youngest of the sciences (by few as yet acknowledged to be a science), has a very difficult field, lying as far apart from the ordinary life of most men as the multitudinous realities of infinite space lie outside the range of thought of ordinary men; its problems are many, theories are shifting and contradictory, certain facts are both affirmed and denied, and, what is more to the point for our present purpose, only to a limited extent can its problems be taken into the laboratory, but for the most part techniques and logical methods have to be devised to fit the nature of the facts with which we deal. In astronomy, most of the subjects of study can be found in place at any time; the great drawback is that they are so fearfully distant as to be sensed very slightly. On the other hand, with certain exceptions, either of kind or degree, the subjects of psychical study cannot be found in place whenever wanted but appear occasionally, yet when they do appear often do so with a nearness and clearness which spares the witnesses the necessity of those cautious qualifying phrases so common in articles dealing with astronomy.

In order at length to turn the attention of scientific men to a quarter of reality to which most of them are now voluntarily blind, we must continue to do what some people condemn as "old stuff," and that is to multiply the number of intelligent and reputable witnesses by teaching people how to observe and how to record, and by ridding them of the cowardice which now keeps at least five out of six potential witnesses of such standing silent.

having no gift for drawing would be likely to make it, in addition to the corre-spondence of color. But it should also be remarked that the second drawing is like the flower-head of the American aloe, as one may see by comparing it with the cut shown in the article entitled "Agave," in the *Encyclopedia Britannica*. The article provokingly fails to tell us what are the colors of the flower, but the cut shows that it is at least much lighter above than below.

Another incident is remarkable for its apparent revelation of subconscious mechanisms. Seemingly here Mrs. Sinclair not only got an impression of what her husband had drawn, but it was modified by something he was then reading, and that by the aid of memories from childhood. His drawing repre-sented a football, "neatly laced up" (Fig. 15). Hers (Fig. 15a) shows a band of exactly the same shape of a figure not so very far from that of a football, but with an extension suggesting the head of an animal, and a line suggesting a leg. And she wrote "Belly-band on calf."!

"Wishing to solve the mystery!" But why should the lady have felt that there was any mystery in her drawing and script, any more than in the generality of her results? But she evidently did, or she would not have asked the question. It is one of the most interesting features of this experiment that she seemed to feel that something else than the original drawing or her husband's thoughts about it was influencing her impression, and suspected that this something was his contemporaneous reading.

Sometimes the apparent telepathy was exercised in a dream, especially during its latter stage, while the lady was gradually emerging into full consciousness.[7]

THE SINCLAIR-IRWIN LONG-DISTANCE GROUP OF EXPERIMENTS

On July 8, 1928, the first formal set of experiments with drawings began, by arrangement between Mrs. Sinclair and the husband of her younger sister; Robert L. Irwin, "a young American businessman, priding himself on having no 'crank' ideas." The arrangement was that at a stated hour Mr. Irwin should seat himself in his home in Pasadena, make a drawing, and then fix his mind upon the drawing from fifteen to twenty minutes. At the same hour in her home at Long Beach, twenty-five or thirty miles distant as the crow flies, Mrs. Sinclair proposed to lie on a couch, in semi-darkness and with closed eyes, compose her mind according to the rules she had by this time evolved, and after coming to a decision, make a drawing corresponding with her mental impression. It appears that there was one such experiment on July 8, two on the 9th, two on the 10th, and one each on the 11th and 13th.

---

[7] It is so judged from such expressions as "Or maybe she has been asleep and comes out with the tail end of a dream, and has written down what appears to be a lot of rubbish but turns out to be a reproduc-tion of something her husband has been reading or writing at that very moment"; "Says my wife, 'There are some notes of a dream I just had.' "

We have here, then, a set of seven experiments under ideal conditions. Since something like thirty miles separated the parties, there could be no contact, no "involuntary whispering" that would carry that far and no conceivable other source of information or material for surmise.

1. On July 8, Irwin drew a chair with horizontal bars at the back (Fig. 16). Mrs. Sinclair drew first a chair with horizontal bars (Fig. 16a), then a chair with vertical ones. And she distinctly set down on the same paper her sense of greater satisfaction with her first drawing, her feeling that the second was not as "Bob" had drawn it, and her feeling that the second may really express the foot of his bed. She also set down that his drawing was on "green paper." Here is a remarkable combination of impressions: (a) his drawing on *green paper,* (b) seen as a *chair* "on his paper," (c) his chair with *horizontal bars,* (d) her chair with vertical bars *perhaps derived from "his bedfoot."* Even had there been, as there was not, a pre-understanding that some object familiar in daily life was to be drawn, to hit exactly the same one would be very unlikely. To do this and also to get the unusual color of the paper he drew on is remarkable. To get all the enumerated particulars exactly correct is incalculably beyond chance expectation. For he drew a chair, on green paper, with horizontal bars, then gazed at the chair through the vertical bars of his bed!

[Refer to Figs. 16 and 16a and experiment.]

She added that she sees a star and straight lines, and draws the star and the lines, horizontal like those of the chair.

There are several partial correspondences besides those we have enumerated. Bob did sit at the northeast corner of the dining-room table. He faced a sideboard (but apparently did not take anything out of it) where were silver (not glass) candlesticks; there is a star on the back of the chair; whether any white object was in front of him as he sat at the table, before lying down on the bed, is not reported. But it is to be presumed that Mrs. Sinclair was familiar with his room and furniture, and these particulars add comparatively little. Once she got the chair, subconscious memory might supply the star; but it would not give any clue to the green paper or to his looking through vertical bars.

2. On July 9, at the stated hour, Bob drew a watch (Fig. 17).[8] First Mrs. Sinclair drew a chair, but cancelled it with the words then written down, "but do not feel it is correct." Then she drew Figure 17a.

This is not a success, but the flower which is not a flower, the petals, which are not petals and should be more uniform, the "metal," the "wire" (adumbration of the hands?), the "glass circle," the bridging across the extremities of the "petals" as if from an urge toward making a circle, the black center corresponding with the center post of a watch, taken together are very suggestive. Other impressions resulted in the addition of an ellipse, a drinking-glass and a glass pitcher, and Bob did have in front of him a glass

---

[8] The words "Bob drew watch," etc., were added by Mrs. Sinclair after she had read his statement.

bowl of goldfish, which may have furnished a telepathic hint, but this is doubtfully evidential.

3. Another experiment was scheduled for the same day. Bob made an elaborate drawing of a telephone receiver, transmitter, dial, cord and all. The top part, the transmitter, as drawn, is strikingly like a round, black, glass ink-bottle, seen with mouth facing the spectator. Mrs. Sinclair made four drawings. The first looks like such an ink-bottle seen from the side, and she writes, "Ink bottle?" The second drawing shows a twisted line attached to a triangle, reminding one of the twisted telephone cord attached to a sharp angle of the base, and the third repeats the twisting line. The fourth inverted is considerably like the base of the telephone. The correspondences are very suggestive.

4. On the 10th, Bob drew, on the back of the paper having the telephone drawing (he should not have done this), which he of course saw anew, what is probably intended to represent a square frame containing a picture, both very black. The percipient first drew two lines forming an angle and placed in relation to it about as the dial of the telephone is placed in relation to the angle of the telephone base, a black disc. Her next and last drawing was a circle containing about a dozen round spots, as the circular dial of the telephone contains eight spots.

5. On the 10th, also, Bob drew a pair of scissors (Fig. 18), and the percipient made two attempts which, taken together, certainly do sense its parts (Figs. 18a and 18b).

6. On the 11th, Bob, whose health had been in bad shape for several years, made a circle with a compass of course producing a hole in the center of it. And this is what Mrs. Sinclair got (Fig. 19a). There is a circle—in fact, a number of them concentrically arranged—and there is a central dot corresponding to the mark made by the compass leg. But other impressions came to Mrs. Sinclair, accompanied by poignant emotions, and she seemed to see and tried to draw a spreading stain of blood. She wrote her feeling and her conviction: "All this dark like a stain—feel it is blood; that Bob is ill, more than usual." She did not draw, but directly told her husband, "I wanted to draw a little hill." And why all this? It transpired that while Bob was making the circle he was in a state of distress, for, he afterwards testified, "I discovered that I had a hemorrhoid, and couldn't put my mind on anything but the thought, 'My God, my lungs—my kidneys—and now this!'" It is hardly necessary, perhaps, to point out that a hemorrhoid is like a little hill and that one is very likely to bring on hemorrhage,[9] so that this possibility was probably in Bob's mind.

Had Mrs. Sinclair been in a laboratory with one professor of psychology or of physics, and her brother-in-law in another laboratory with another, not all the apparatus of both laboratories nor all the ingenuity of both professors

---

[9] "Ulceration and bleeding are also common symptoms, hence the term 'bleeding piles.'" *Encyclopedia Britannica.*

could have made the conditions more rigid, or tested the essence of the matter farther. There would simply have been the testimony of four persons, two at each end, and that is exactly what there is. Bob's affliction was of sudden occurrence, and the particular terms of Mrs. Sinclair's impressions could not have been produced by any hint of knowledge. His willingness in the interest of psychic research, in order that this remarkable demonstration of telepathy should not be lost, to put aside squeamishness, is a rebuke to the human violets who shrink, for no intelligible reason from allowing evidence to be used which relates to them.

7. On the 13th, Bob drew a table fork (Fig. 1), and Mrs. Sinclair, at the same hour, many miles away, drew nothing but wrote, "See a table fork. Nothing else." (Fig. 1a).

These seven experiments[10] are all that were undertaken between Mrs. Sinclair and her brother-in-law. This is unfortunate, for it certainly appears from this short but remarkable series as though they were remarkably suited to each other, for reasons we cannot yet fathom, for long-distance experiments. But "he found them a strain," and since his health was so poor and strains were most undesirable, we cannot blame him for discontinuing them.

One pauses to consider the words "he found them a strain." May it be that when experiments reveal thought-transference the agent generally does feel a strain beyond that involved in merely gazing at an object and wishing (or willing, or what you please) that the percipient may get the idea of it. If so, it would seem to imply, not necessarily some energy proceeding outwardly, but at any rate some process going on within which causes the special exhaustion. But no statistics bearing on this question have been gathered from successful agents. It is one of the many sorts of data which must be accumulated in the future.

Mr. Irwin and his wife made corroborating affidavits, as follows:

To whom it may concern:

   Robert L. Irwin, having been duly sworn, declares that he has read the portion of manuscript by Upton Sinclair dealing with his experiments in telepathy with Mary Craig Sinclair, and that the statements made therein having to do with himself are true according to his clear recollection. The drawings attributed to him were produced by him in the manner described, and are recognized by him in their photographic reproductions. The experiments were conducted in good faith, and the results may be accepted as valid.

                                        [Signed] ROBERT L. IRWIN.

To whom it may concern:

   Dollie Kimbrough Irwin, having been duly sworn, declares that she has read the portion of manuscript by Upton Sinclair dealing with

---

[10] [Deleted.]

experiments in telepathy by her sister, Mary Craig Sinclair, and having to do with her husband, Robert L. Irwin; that she was present when the drawings were made and the tests conducted, and also when the completed drawings were produced and compared. The statements made in the manuscript are true according to her clear recollection, and the experiments were made in good faith and with manifest seriousness.

[Signed] DOLLIE KIMBROUGH IRWIN.

These statements were severally

"Subscribed and sworn to before me this 26th day of July, 1929, [Signed] LAURA UNANGST, Notary Public in and for the County of Denver, Colorado."

THE SINCLAIR-SINCLAIR GROUP OF JULY 14–29, 1928

We are in two passages told precisely the conditions of this group of experiments. Since her brother-in-law felt obliged to withdraw from participation, Mrs. Sinclair asked her husband to make some drawings.

1. July 14. Mr. Sinclair made the above drawing (Fig. 2), a very imperfectly constructed six-pointed star. Mrs. Sinclair, reclining 30 feet away, with a closed door between, produced five drawings (Fig. 2a).[11] Immediately after the agent's and percipient's drawings had been compared, the lady stated that just before starting to concentrate she had been looking at her drawing of many concentric circles made on the previous day in the concluding test of the Sinclair-Irwin group. This was bad method, but we can hardly regret it, as the sequel is illuminating. At first she got a tangle of circles: "This turned sideways [thus assuming the shape of one of the star-points], then took the shape of an arrowhead [confused notion of the star-point, one would conjecture], and then of a letter A [another attempt to interpret the dawning impression], and finally evolved into a complete star." The star so nearly reproduces the oddities of the original star, its peculiar shape and the direction which its greatest length takes, that had it been produced in one of the unguarded series, one would have been tempted to think that the percipient "peeked." But the original was actually made, as well as gazed at, behind a closed door, so that there is no possible basis for imagining any such accident or any inadvertence on the part of either experimenter.

2. July 14. In his room Mr. Sinclair drew the grinning face of Figure 21, and then Mrs. Sinclair drew in hers Figure 21a. Two eyes in his, one "eye" in hers.

---

[11] "I explain that in these particular drawings the lines have been traced over in heavier pencil; the reason being that Craig wanted a carbon copy, and went over the lines in order to make it. This had the effect of making them heavier than they originally were, and it made the whirly lines in Craig's first drawing more numerous than they should be. She did this in the case of two or three of the early drawings, wishing to send a report to a friend. I pointed out to her how this would weaken their value as evidence, so she never did it again."

Look at the agent's drawing upside down (how can we or he be sure that he did not momentarily chance to look at it reversed and retain the impression?), and note the parallels. At the top of his two eyes—at the top of hers one "eye"; midway in his two small angles indicating the nose—somewhat above midway in hers, three similarly small angles unclosed at the apexes; at the bottom of his a crescent-shaped figure to indicate a mouth, with lines to denote teeth—at the bottom of hers a like crescent, minus any interior lines. Had the percipient drawn what would be instantly recognizable as a face, though a face of very different lines, it would be pronounced a success. But such a fact would be very much more likely as a guess than a misinterpreted, almost identical crescent (she thought it probably a "moon"), so similar little marks, angularly related (she "supposed it must be a star"), and an "eye," all placed as in the original.

3. July 17. Mr. Sinclair, lying on a couch in one room, drew and then gazed at a drawing which can easily be described; it is a broad ellipse with its major axis horizontal, like an egg lying on its side, and a smaller and similar one in contact over it. Mrs. Sinclair, lying on a couch in another room, first drew a broad ellipse (not quite closed at one end), with major axis horizontal, and beside it and not quite touching, a somewhat smaller circle not quite closed at one end. Then she got an impression represented in a second drawing, four ellipses of equal size, *two of them in contact with each other.*

4. July 20. Under the same conditions Mr. Sinclair drew two heavy lines like a capital T. Mrs. Sinclair drew what is like an interrogation point with misplaced dot, then a reversed S with two dots enclosed, then an upright cross composed of lines of equal length, and finally such a cross circumscribed by a tangential square. Though, as Mr. Sinclair remarks, the cross is the T of the original with its vertical line prolonged, I should call this experiment barely suggestive.

5. July 20. Under the same conditions Mr. Sinclair drew a long-handled fork with three short tines. Mrs. Sinclair, to use the language of her own record, "kept seeing horns," and she attempted to draw them. She also "thought once it was an animal's head with horns, and the head was on a long stick—a trophy mounted like this. . . ." But her drawing was like a long-handled fork with two short tines combining to make a curve very close to that of the two outer tines of the original.

6. July 20. Under the same conditions Mr. Sinclair drew a cup with a handle. Mrs. Sinclair twice drew a figure resembling the handle of the original, then the same with an enclosed dot, then lines parallel and at an angle. She felt confused and dissatisfied. It is possible that her first impression was derived from the cup, but we can hardly urge this evidentially.

7. July 21. Under the same conditions Mr. Sinclair drew a man's face in profile (Fig. 20). Mrs. Sinclair wrote: "Saw Upton's face—saw two half circles. Then they came together, making full circle. But I felt uncertain as to whether they belonged

together or not. Then suddenly saw Upton's profile float across vision." Well, Mr. Sinclair is a man, hence his face is a man's face, and it was seen in profile like the original drawing.

Thus far there is no gap in the record of this group. There were experiments on July 27 and 29, but apparently two or more papers are missing. It is certain that on the 29th, under the same conditions, Mr. Sinclair drew a smoking cigarette and wrote beneath it, "My thought, 'cigarette with curls for smoke,'" and that Mrs. Sinclair drew a variety of curving lines and wrote, "I can't draw it, but curls of some sort." So it appears that on this date there was a suggestive result, but as there is doubt whether one or two other experiments may not have been tried, the papers of which were not all preserved, we had better regard the group as closed with No. 7.

So far as concerns the question solely whether Mrs. Sinclair has shown telepathic powers, I would be willing to rest the case right here, after but fourteen experiments under the conditions which have been stated.[12] Every intelligent reader who really applies his mind to them must see the extreme unlikelihood that the results of those fourteen experiments, taking them as they stand, successes, partial successes, suggestive and failures, are the products of chance. And any one who has had hundreds of experiments in guessing, as I have done, will know that there is no likelihood of getting out of many thousands of guesses anything like the number and grades of excellence in correspondence found in these fourteen consecutive tests for telepathy.

We cannot take space to comment on all the tests made, the papers of which were sent us, and we here pass over three on as many dates, one a success though not a perfect one, two failures.

The Series of January 28, 1929

Mr. Sinclair asked his secretary "to make simple geometrical designs, letters and figures, thinking that these would be easier to recognize and reproduce." It seems a little strange that when things were going on so well, he should have wanted a change, though any experiment is interesting. It is by no means certain, and I very much doubt from these and earlier printed experiments, that the assumption is a correct one. It may well be that geometrical diagrams, letters of the alphabet and such like fail to interest the agent and afford him a lively mental representation, as do pictures of miscellaneous objects. And if I understand rightly, another change of method was also initiated, and that was for Mrs. Sinclair to try to get the drawings not while the maker of them was gazing intently at them, but after they had left his hands. This certainly was often the case later on.

---

[12] Of course, there would be theoretical possibility that the four persons involved joined in a conspiracy to deceive, and there would be the same theoretical possibility if four psychologists from the *sanctum sanctorum* of a laboratory announced similar results.

I wrote and asked Mr. Sinclair if Mrs. Sinclair was told the fact that this and several other series of original drawings consisted of geometrical drawings, letters and figures, and he said that she was not so told, that he would have regarded this as a vitiation of the experiments. It would certainly increase the chance of getting drawings right by guess, but it would hardly have ruined the experiments. In fact, some people think that the most scientific experiments are those in which the range of chance guess is limited to an extent known to the percipient, as when the problem is to determine which of the 52 cards of a pack is being looked at, or which of only ten known diagrams. This opinion is probably based on the fact that then the ratio of success to chance expectation can be exactly calculated, though why it should be more satisfactory to know that the chance of a correct guess is exactly 1 in 10 than it is not to be able to tell exactly what the chance is but to be sure at least that it cannot be 1 in 100, I do not know.

Unless I had carefully recorded at the time that there was no chance of the percipient having a hint that the drawings were now for a time to consist of geometrical designs, letters and figures, I would not dare to be certain of it after several years have passed. If Mrs. Sinclair had no inkling, the change in the general character of her drawings is a fact of great interest. But we will take cognizance only of whatever resemblance may or may not be found between the several reproductions and their originals.

The first series of drawings by the secretary were seven in number, and, says Mr. Sinclair, "They brought only partial successes; Craig would get elements of the drawing, but would not know how to put them together . . . There is some element right in every one." Let us see.

1. *Agent's* drawing, a script B; *Percipient's* drawing, a figure very like a script 3, practically the B without its vertical line.

2. *Agt.*, a script S; *Per.*, a script J. As made, each has two balloon-like parts joined at the small ends, certain details of course different.

3. *Agt.*, a hexagon; *Per.*, two lines forming an acute angle, like two sides of the hexagon, also a capital E with a line drawn down at an acute angle to the left from the upper extremity of the vertical line.

4. *Agt.*, script M made with a peculiar twist in its first line; *Per.*, almost precisely that first line with its twist.

5. *Agt.*, a thin, long, quadrilateral, like a shingle; *Per.*, (1st drawing) what would be almost exactly the same quadrilateral, narrow and long, but its shorter sides are wanting, and (2nd drawing) a closely similar quadrilateral, with another and longer one attached to its side at a sharp angle.

6. *Agt.*, an interrogation point; *Per.*, a figure hard to describe, a round dot with curves springing from it like concentric 3's, and two parallel lines shooting to the left. The points which attract notice are the dot, like that of the original, and the curves similar to that of the interrogation point.

7. *Agt.*, script E; *Per.*, same minus the "curls."

Several of the above are not impressive taken alone; taken together, the greater or less approaches to the several originals defeat chance, though how much no man can measure. Counter-tests by guessing will come the nearest to measuring.

The Series of January 28–29, 1929

This series also has to do with drawings made by Mr. Sinclair's secretary.

1. *Agent's* drawing, a diamond or rhombus (Fig. 32); *Percipient's* drawing, the two halves of a rhombus, "wandering about," as Mr. Sinclair says (Fig. 32a); if connected they would make a rhombus closely similar to the original.

2. *Agt.*, a script capital Y; *Per.*, a print capital Y. (Figs. 33 and 33a.)

3. The *Agent's* drawing, a bottle of milk with "certified" written on it, was suggested by his knowledge that Mrs. Sinclair to a considerable extent lives on milk and is particular about its quality; *Per.*, an ellipse much like the top of the bottle, a straight line depending therefrom, and the script "Round white foamy stuff on top like soapsuds or froth." And foam is characteristic of her milk, as she drinks it sour and whipped (Figs. 34 and 34a). Here the percipient failed to get much as to shape, but got considerable in the way of associated ideas.

4. *Agt.*, an oil derrick (Fig. 35); *Per.*, got what will be seen in Figure 35a. There are long lines diverging like the long lines of the oil derrick, but at a slant, and with a 5 or perhaps a 9 at the top which has no counterpart in the original. This is not a very satisfactory reproduction, but the general shape and long downward lines are suggestive.

5. *Agt.*, something like a poplar leaf; *Per.*, three scrawls like letters [or] parts of letters. A failure.

6. *Agt.*, three small ellipses attached to a stem; *Per.*, script "See what looks like spider's web," but drawing shows a bunch of elliptic figures.

7. *Agt.*, apparently an apple with stem; *Per.*, (1) what looks like a tall script V, (2) the same less tall, (3) one so low and broad that it is nearly equivalent to the top of the apple minus the stem.

8. *Agt.*, a house from whose chimney proceeds smoke represented by a spiral line; (Fig. 36); *Per.*, (1) a double spiral cut by a straight line, same slant as in the original, (2) single spiral of nearly the same slant, (3) what looks like a battlement, the crenels or openings of which are like the windows of the house minus the upper sides (Fig. 36a). The rectangular openings are three in number, the rectangular openings in the house (two windows and a door) are also there.

9. *Agt.*, an open fan (Fig. 102); *Per.*, a drawing represented by Figure 102a, accompanied by the script, "Inside seems irregular, as if cloth draped or crumpled." Two words, "cloth," and "draped," suggest what takes place as one begins to shut a fan, though the drawing is an incorrect representation.

10. *Agt.,* the figures 13 (Fig. 103); *Per.,* (1) what would be a 3 but for a supernumerary curve, (2) a 3 (Fig. 103a).

11. *Agt.,* a conventional heart (Fig. 105); *Per.,* practically the upper part of such a heart, with three spots which may or may not represent blood-drops, according to Mr. Sinclair's conjecture (Fig. 105a). We can hardly contend, as an evidential point, that this is the meaning of the round spots. Some obscure subconscious recollection of expressions like "My heart bleeds," expressing suffering, may have come out in the drawing, though in that case one wonders why the whole heart was not drawn. But it may be that the three marks proceeding in the direction of the right side of the original came from a feeling that something should lie in that direction.

12. *Agt.,* a broom (Fig. 104); *Per.,* several attempts all more or less resembling the original (Figs. 104a, 104b), and a valuable script: "All I'm sure of is a straight line with something curved at the end of it [and this description, *all that she was sure of,* is so far correct]; once it came [here see the drawing at the left]—then it doubled, or reappeared, I don't know which [referring to the upper right drawing] (am not sure of the curly edges) [and she was justified in her doubt. Probably the curly edges resulted from the intermingling of her surmise that the curved something at the end of a line might be a flower]. Then it was upside down."

The Series of February 8, 1929

Tests with drawings in carefully sealed envelopes.

1. *Agt.,* a coiled snake (Fig. 45); *Per.,* no drawing, but this script: "See something like kitten with tail and saucer of milk. Now it leaps into action and runs away to outdoors. Turns to fleeing animal outdoors. Great activity among outdoor creatures. Know it's some outdoor thing, not indoor object—see trees, and a frightened bird on the wing (turned sidewise). It's outdoor thing, but none of above seems to be it."

This is much more interesting than if there had been the perfect success of writing the word "snake," because we seem to get inklings of the internal process. "Saucer of milk"—observe that the serpent's coil plus the unattached ellipse in the center (due to Mr. Sinclair's confessed bad drawing) really does look like a saucer. "Something like a kitten with a tail"—why mention tail? Most kittens have tails. But a tail sticks up back of the saucer. Later neither kitten, trees nor frightened bird is *it,* yet something is causing great commotion among outdoor creatures. It is an outdoor thing, therefore not a kitten, but evidently something alive. The scene is very appropriate to the appearance of a snake. Mr. Sinclair tells us that his wife's childhood was in part spent where there were many poisonous snakes, and that fear of them was bred in her. As he conjectures, it is very likely that dawning in the subconsciousness, not fully emerging in the conscious, the subject of the drawing stirred up imagery from childhood. I surmise that, if the truth, which she may not consciously remember, could be known, she saw while a child a kitten fleeing from a snake.

2. *Agt.*, a daisy (Fig. 59); *Per.*, got what is very like the petals around the disc of the daisy, also two stems, also various curving lines more or less like the daisy leaves or vegetation at least (Fig. 59a).

3. *Agt.*, an axe, seemingly a battle-axe, with AX printed (Fig. 145); *Per.*, as in Figure 145a. Note the parallels: (a) "letter A [right as far as it goes], (b) with something long (c) above it"; (d) "there seems to be no end to the handle"; (e) the drawing much resembles the original, in fact one type of ancient battle-axe was very much of the same shape. Although she finally guessed that it was a key, yet a suspicion of military use enters in the conjecture "a sword," which is perhaps all the more striking since the drawing bears little resemblance to a sword.

4. *Agt.*, a crab (Fig. 48); *Per.*, drew as in Figures 48a, 48b, and wrote "Wings, or fingers—wing effect, but no feathers, things like fingers instead of feathers. Then many little dots which all disappear, and leave two of them, O O, as eyes of something." And again, "streamers flying from something." The reader will judge for himself whether the drawings do not suggest the crab's nippers, and one of them the joint adjoining. "Wing effect but no feathers, things like fingers"—especially he lower pair in Mr. Sinclair's remarkable crab *do* look like fingers. "Many dots"; well the original has four. Then she sees but two of them and they are "O O, eyes of something." True enough, two of the "dots" in the crab are O O, and they are eyes.

5. *Agt.*, a man in a sledge driving a dog-team (Fig. 60). *Per.* by accident opened this drawing, so of course could not experiment with it. But after she had made her drawings for No. 2 she wrote, "Maybe snow scene on hill with a sled." On the back of No. 3, which was so brilliant a success, she wrote, "I get a feeling again of a snow scene to come in this series—a sled in the snow." It is unfortunate that an accident prevented her trying No. 5 when she had actually reached it, but she certainly got it by anticipation.

6. *Agt.*, a tobacco pipe with smoke issuing therefrom (Fig. 37); *Per.* first drew an ellipse and wrote "Now it begins to spin, round and round, and is attached to a stick"; (2) next she made the conventional "curl" which usually means smoke; (3) then she made another curl of smoke and pushed the open end of an ellipse into it,[13] joined a line to the ellipse just about where the stem of a pipe meets the bowl and at the end of the line made a small circle, which certainly is not found in the original but may express the feeling that there is a circular opening (Fig. 37a).

7. *Agt.*, a house with smoking chimney; *Per.*, two figures, each very like the frame of a window lacking the upper side, or like the crenels or openings in the battlement of Figure 36a, but longer. In connection with that drawing

---

[13] The cut does not show that the end is open like a pipe, but it is plainly so in the pencil drawing.

(Experiment of January 28–29) we made the remark (which may have seemed fanciful) that the number of these openings or uncompleted rectangles was the same as that of the windows and door in the original drawing. Here the uncompleted two rectangles equal in number the one window plus the one door of the house. She also wrote "There is something above this—can't see what it is part of." True, the roof and chimney are above the window and door.

The Series of February 10, 1929

1. *Agt.,* a bat (Fig. 109); *Per.,* as in Fig. 109a. The drawing at the top is accompanied by the remark "Looks like ear-shaped something." And certainly each of the bat's wings does resemble an ear in shape. The middle left drawing gets the idea that there are two symmetrical and diverging curves, but fails to complete them; space is left between them which in the agent's drawing is occupied by the body. The middle right figure again has symmetrical diverging curves, with a further approach toward shaping the wings. This time they are incorrectly joined at the bottom, but the perpendicular line between betrays an inkling that something belongs there. Imperfect as all these attempts are, they contain hints which it is difficult to attribute to chance. The agent, looking at his drawing, would of necessity have his attention focus first on one part of it and then upon another, and the percipient's drawings seem as though they caught his several moments of wandering attention.

2. *Agt.,* a hand with pointing finger, and thumb held vertically (Fig. 108); *Per.,* (1) a drawing not reproduced here of a negro's head with a finger-like projection drawn vertically from his skull, (2) then script "Turned into a pig's head, (3) then a rabbit's," as in Figure 108a. In one sense the *percipient's* drawings are all failures; that is, none of them would be recognized as a hand. But in all three a feeling seems to express itself that there is *something* sticking up. This is the more remarkable in Drawing 1, since such an excrescence does not belong on a head. Drawing 2 gets rid of the face, and the thumb of the original becomes a peculiarly thumb-like ear.

3. For this experiment see the "line-and-circle men" and their evidentially suggestive sequel (Figs. 144, 144a).

4. *Agt.,* a rudely drawn caterpillar (Fig. 118); *Per.,* script: "Fork—then garden tool—lawn rake. Leaf," and drawing representing a leaf which has a certain fantastic resemblance to the caterpillar (Fig. 118a). Mr. Sinclair makes the illuminating remark that he owned "a lawnrake made of bristly bamboo, which looks very much like my drawing."

5. *Agt.,* a smoking volcano (Fig. 25); *Per.,* what she called a "Big black beetle with horns" (Fig. 25a). But the body of the beetle closely matches the smoke of the volcano, while the antennae or "horns" nearly correspond to the outline of the mountain.

A Series of February 15, 1929[14]

Let us now inspect a complete and long series of February 15, 1929. It contains no such brilliant success as in Experiment 4 of February 20, but out of thirteen experiments there is but one absolute failure, the first. In this the agent drew a rat, the percipient two crossed objects like keys.

2. In Figure 147, the agent's drawing represents a door with lattice on the upper half; it is made up of perpendicular and horizontal lines only. The percipient's drawing (Fig. 147a) consists of four perpendicular lines finishing at the top in curves like fishhooks, and these lines are crossed by three horizontal lines. There is in the crossed lines a suggestion of the agent's drawing, a resemblance greater than to any other of the thirteen.

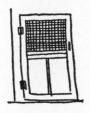

Fig. 147   Fig. 147a

3. The agent's next drawing (Fig. 93) represents a sun over hills. Mrs. Sinclair first seems to have got the notion of a sun, which was right (Fig. 93a). Then she made another circle and put features in it, as will be seen suggested in the agent's drawing (actually, in the original drawing, the features are plainly to be seen). Then she got the idea of something stretching out below it with curving lines, interpreted it to be a body, so probably, from mere inference, clapped her sun with features on to it.

4. Agent's Figure 97 is a butterfly but the percipient did not get the idea of a butterfly (Fig. 97a). However, the divergent lines and the spots, five instead of four, and similarly placed, do seem to bear a relation to it.

5. In Figure 96a, Mrs. Sinclair's drawing resembles a part of her husband's (Fig. 96), although she misinterpreted her mental picture. What she thought to be the leg of an animal, and which she drew twice, was judged by the way it bends to be a front one, but the knee of the leg roughly corresponds with the elbow of the pipe. Note that she seems to have got the bulge at the end of the pipe, translating it into a "foot," naturally at the end of the leg.

6. In Figures 98 and 98a, compare the three "sparks" with the three crosses on the box.

7. The shape of Figure 94a is like that of Figure 94 reversed, and there is a suggestion of the strings, while the feet represent the pedals of the harp.

---

[14] "A Series" since there was another of the same date at a different hour.

8. The percipient in the case of Figure 95a did not get the picture of the whole balloon bag of the agent (Fig. 95), but she did of half of it, with a strong suggestion of the cords.

Fig. 148   Fig. 148a

9. In Figure 148a, bad as the percipient's drawings are regarded as reproductions of Figure 148, yet they do contain suggestions of it. In her left upper drawing we may suppose that an impression of the leaf-stem (but badly twisted) was expressed with a leaf-lobe directly below the stem, together with an idea of the veining, that in the right upper one the stem is corrected, and that in the lower drawing a notion of the veining alone is conveyed. Exactly so would the attention of the agent, when drawing the leaf or afterward looking at or thinking of it, pass from and to, or at least stress, one part of the leaf after another.

10. The agent drew a necktie (Fig. 90). The percipient first drew what much resembled the necktie, even to the shaded knot (not given here), and almost exactly like Figure 90a aside from the "smoke." Next she wrote "Then it began to smoke," and drew as in Figure 90a. One would suppose that the knobby extremity and the diverging lines suggested a burning match.

11. But no, the alteration appears to have been an anticipation of the agent's next drawing, already prepared (Fig. 91)! In this case Mrs. Sinclair achieved a complete success (Fig. 91a), though she distrusted it, writing beside the drawing, "Must be memory of the last one."

12. In Figure 92a the percipient got the first two links of the agent's chain (Fig. 92) fairly well. The succeeding ones are suggested by a series of partially superposed ovals, owing to misinterpretation of her impressions. She wrote: "An egg-shaped thing smoking? Anyway, curls of something coming out of end of egg." Note that her combined "egg" and "curls" describe a curve similar to that of the chain, and one not far from the same length.

13. The last experiment of this date resulted in two percipient drawings (Fig. 149a), similar but with differences as noted below. Presumably the "arm" of the upper drawing is a reflection of the neck of the violin (Fig. 149), the "hand" of its bridge, the "strings" of the violin strings, while the

"something" very imperfectly stands for the body of the instrument. The bracelet (?) on the arm may result from an obscure impression of *something* curving in that region, really the volute termination above the keys. The lower drawing stops with the strings, but makes them more nearly parallel, like those of the violin.

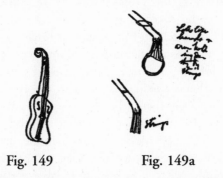

Fig. 149   Fig. 149a

No exact mathematics can be applied to such experiments as these. But, considering the multitude of objects and shapes which must have been familiar to both experimenters, do you believe that there was 1 chance in 16 of the successes in Experiments 10, 11 and 12? Or more than 1 chance in 4 for Experiments 5, 6 and 7? Or more than an average of 1 in 2 for such small degree of success as is discoverable in the rest, excluding the failure of the first? Multiply accordingly, and divide the product, let us say, by 2 for this failure. The result, on what I think a moderate basis, is 1 chance in 16,777,216. Figure any other way you like, but be reasonable.

Or substitute the first above percipient drawing for that in any and every one of the above twelve pairs. Then take the next drawing and match it with the other originals. And thus with the others, if your patience holds out to the end of 132 exchanges. Have you found a single one which will suit as well as in its actual position?

COUNTER-TESTS WHICH PROVE THE VAST DISPARITY BETWEEN THE RESULTS OBTAINED IN THE SERIES OF FEBRUARY 15TH AND THOSE OBTAINED BY GUESSING

It is proposed at this point to interrupt the review of Mr. Sinclair's report of his experiments for telepathy by a test applied to the series which has just been exhibited. In the light of the test, as it proves, the evidential weight of both the earlier series and those which will come later ought to be better appreciated. The only way to explain (?) such results is to hazard the conjecture that they were due to the possibilities of chance guessing. Well then, let us have a lot of guessing done on the basis of the same originals and see what we get and how it compares.[15]

It seems almost incredible that any intelligent person would hold, or suggest it possible, that the several degrees of resemblance between twelve of the thirteen originals in this series and the reproductions could have come about by chance guessing. Surely, no one possessing an average quality of logical and mathematical faculty, if he takes time to consider, will be guilty of so monstrous a *faux pas* of the intellect. But experience teaches that some, even of excellent academic or professional standing, to whom the notion of the possibility of telepathy has long been obnoxious, are indeed capable of dismissing an exhibit such as this after a passing glance, with the exclamation, "Merely chance coincidence." It is well, then, to make a large number of experiments in order to test the chances of chance-coincidence to produce such a result. Perhaps, after that is done, even those most convinced that chance cannot account for such correspondences as we have seen will be astonished to find the extent to which results where telepathy has played a part and results of mere guessing differ.

Ten ladies offered themselves for experimentation. Of course the likelihood was very small that any one of them would show a trace of telepathic faculty. As it proved, there developed no reason to suspect its possession by a single one of them. And it is certain that no one who disbelieves that *any one* gets impressions by telepathy will complain of our conclusion that the ten ladies did nothing more than guess.

If they did nothing more than to guess, it made no difference what method we employed, so long as the ladies were given no inkling of the original drawings. Nevertheless, the exact replicas of Mr. Sinclair's thirteen drawings of February 15th were separately sealed in numbered envelopes, and the lady was asked to hold the envelopes, one by one, in her hand, and to draw what came into her mind visually or by concept, choosing from such impressions according to vividness, recurrence or by whatever criterion seemed to her most congenial. She was told to take all the time she wished and was then left alone. Thus the conditions of the Sinclair experiments were imitated as closely as possible. The time occupied by the ladies for the series varied from half an hour to nearly an hour

---

[15] If it be objected that we are not told exactly what the conditions of the series of February 15th were, though assured that all series were carried out with scrupulous honesty, that is true. But it is also true that the results of this series were not better than some where we do know that the conditions were excellent, and that this series contains no successes of such astounding significance as three in the Sinclair-Irwin Group, when many miles separated the experimenters. I would have been quite willing to have employed for the guessing tests the originals in that group, plus those of February 17th, done under excellently satisfactory conditions. (To be sure, the parties were in the same room, but it will be shown later that, even granting all which the egregious "unconscious whispering" theory claims, it could not account for the results actually obtained.) In fact, the Sinclair-Irwin Group was avoided for the test for the very reason that it is an exceptionally good one. That of February 15th was selected because I wanted a series of a considerable number of experiments, an unbroken one produced at one time, and one which exhibited results of a more nearly average character.

and a half. Every woman would have been pleased, naturally, if her results had been such as to give grounds for suspecting telepathy, but the results of the ladies differed in quality only by narrow degrees, and, as said, there was not the slightest reason to suppose that with any of them there was anything but chance in play.

It is, of course, not practicable to reproduce their 130 drawings in this Bulletin. But they are to be mounted, the ten for each original drawing on a separate sheet together with a copy of the Sinclair original and reproduction, and the thirteen sheets will be preserved by the Boston Society for Psychic Research as a permanent exhibit which any visitor may inspect and judge for himself.

As has been seen, we classified the Sinclair reproductions of this series as Successes, Partial Successes, Suggestive and Failures. This is a rough method, and others might increase or decrease the number assigned to any of these classes, except the last. There can be no question that there is but one entire failure. But however faulty our standard of rating, it is the same standard which is applied to the drawings of the ten ladies.

Not only did I use the utmost care in rating the drawings of the ten ladies, but I asked my secretary, Miss Hoffmann, a lady of education and keen intelligence, to do the same. Her rating of the guessing sets was as absolutely independent of mine as mine was independent of hers.

Our mutually independent estimates were surprisingly alike. According to both, there were among the 130 trials (by 10 women) not a single Success, only 1 (Miss H) or 2 (W. F. P.) deserving to be entitled to Partial Success, 7 Suggestive, 5 Slightly Suggestive and 116 (W. F. P.) or 117 (Miss H) Failure. Compare with the Sinclair set, 3 Success, 5 Partial Success, 4 Suggestive, 1 Failure, out of a total of but 13.

Before the foregoing judging was done, I had Miss Hoffmann guess the whole set, twice a day, until another ten sets were produced, based upon the same Sinclair series. Our wholly independent estimates of the total results of these additional 130 experiments in guessing proved again to be surprisingly alike. Neither found a single Success, 1 (W. F. P.) or no (Miss H) reproduction deserved to be called a Partial Success, 5 (W. F. P.) or 7 (Miss H) were rated Suggestive, 8 (W. F. P.) or 7 (Miss H) as Slightly Suggestive and 116 as Failures.

We will now tabulate the two groups (the sets of the 10 ladies and Miss H's 10 sets), taken together (260 experiments in guessing).

W. F. P.'s Estimate		Miss H's Estimate	
S.	0	S.	0
P. S.	3	P. S.	1
Sug.	12	Sug.	14
S. Sug.	13	S. Sug.	12
F.	232	F.	233

If we calculate the averages for the twenty sets of experiments, we can more directly compare with the Sinclair results.

AVERAGE OF THE 20 GUESSING TESTS

Sinclair Set		W. F. P's Estimate		Miss H's Estimate	
S.	3	S.	0	S.	0
P. S.	5	P. S.	3/20	P. S.	1/20
Sug.	4	Sug.	3/5	Sug.	7/10
S. Sug.	0	S. Sug.	13/20	S. Sug.	3/5
F.	1	F.	11 3/5	F.	11 13/20

But there is perhaps a surer way of making comparisons. It is sometimes difficult to draw the line between a Success and a Partial Success, a Partial Success and a Suggestive, a Suggestive and a Slightly Suggestive. But when the drawings represent not simple diagrams, but objects animate and inanimate, and a reproduction by Mrs. Sinclair is placed beside a like-numbered one in any of the twenty guessing sets, it is very seldom that one cannot be certain whether one is better as compared with the common original, and within fair limits how much better. And the proof of this statement is found in the fact that when two persons passed upon the twenty sets of guessing reproductions, comparing them with the 1 set of Sinclair reproductions, to determine, case for case, in 260, which were more nearly like the originals, and to what degree, their rating was almost identical, although they worked in entire and absolute mutual independence of each other.

In the following table, Si. = Sinclair drawing, G. = a Guessing drawing, v.m.b. = very much better, m.b. = much better, b. = better.

W. F. P. found the guessing reproduction of experiment one to be bad to a degree equal with the Mrs. Sinclair failure, in sixteen instances. Miss Hoffmann found it equally bad also in sixteen instances, and deemed another reproduction equally to possess some tiniest resemblance to the original in 1 instance. Aside from these we have:

IN THE 20 SETS (10 LADIES AND MISS H'S 10)

W. F. P's Estimate			Miss H's Estimate		
Si.v.m.b.	222		Si.v.m.b.	222	
Si.m.b.	11		Si.m.b.	13	
Si.b.	7		Si.b.	4	
G.v.m.b.		2	G.v.m.b.		2
G.b.		2	G.b.		2
	240	4		239	4

It is almost incredible that two human beings could come to so close an agreement, unless one had some clue to the opinions of the other, but it is even so, no smallest hint passed in either direction. The fact is that in very few instances can there be the slightest hesitancy in deciding which is nearer the common original, the Sinclair or the guessing reproduction.

If there is any reproduction of the Sinclair series whose resemblance to the original might seem illusory it is that coupling with the leaf of a tree or plant (Figs. 148, 148a). But of the twenty guesses of that original not one is so near; in eighteen instances (W. F. P.) or at least fifteen (Miss H) Mrs. Sinclair's is very much the better, in one (W. F. P.) to three (Miss H) it is much better, and in one (W. F. P.) or two (Miss H) it is better.

Perhaps some persons would think that such resemblance as there is between the butterfly and Mrs. Sinclair's reproduction (Figs. 97, 97a) is too faint to count, or at least is accidental. But, by the independent judgment of two persons, not a single one of the corresponding guessing reproductions is as near the original or anything like so near.

Or one might sneer at calling Mrs. Sinclair's reproduction of Figure 147 "Suggestive." Only five vertical lines, wrongly curving at the top, crossed by three lines,

The Best of the Twenty Guessing-Sets

to stand for a "door with hinges, lower sash," and wire screen covering the upper half! But not a single one of the twenty guesses approaches so much resemblance. Miss H says that of nineteen of these, and W. F. P. of sixteen, "Si.v. m.b." Miss H says of 1, W. F. P. of two, "Si.m.b.," while W. F. P. at least is sure of his remaining two, "Si.b."

In the light of such tests as those just now made, even such degrees of resemblance as we have found in the very weakest numbers of the thirteen in this

Sinclair series take on deep significance. And the whole mass of our counter-experiments clearly indicates that the reproductions by Mrs. Sinclair in that series are prodigiously beyond the reach of chance guessing.

As already remarked, it is hardly practicable to reproduce here the 260 drawings resulting from twenty sets of attempts to guess what the thirteen originals (the same as those in the Sinclair series of February 15th) were. But above is shown Mrs. P—n's set of guesses, the one which made the nearest, though so distant, approach to success. Let the reader compare her drawings, one by one, with the reproductions of Mrs. Sinclair, and judge for himself both which were nearer the originals they had in common, and by how much.

A Series of February 17, 1929[16]

The conditions under which this series of experiments was conducted were excellent, and will be given partly in Mr. Sinclair's words and partly, for greater conciseness, abridged from his statement, aided by an examination of the materials.

(a) The original drawings were made by Mr. Sinclair when he was alone in his study. (b) They were made on green paper. (c) Each drawing was enclosed "in a separate sheet of green paper." (d) Each drawing with its enclosing sheet was folded once, making four thicknesses. (e) And each pair of sheets, that with the drawing and the blank outside one, was put in an envelope [Experiment shows that not even when held up to a strong light can a drawing made and enclosed in such paper and placed in an envelope be seen at all]. (f) The envelope was sealed. (g) The nine sealed envelopes were laid on the table by Mrs. Sinclair's couch. (h) Her procedure was to put an envelope, and each in turn as the tests proceeded, over her solar plexus, and when she had made her decision, to sit up and draw upon a paper pad. (i) Meanwhile, at her own insistence, Mr. Sinclair watched her throughout. (j) "Never did she see my drawing," he declares, "until hers was completed and her descriptive words written." (k) "I spoke no word and made no comment until after this was done." He adds: "The drawings represented here are in every case exactly what I drew, and the corresponding drawing is exactly what my wife drew, with no change or addition whatsoever."

1. *Agt.,* a geographical globe; *Per.,* an obscure drawing most probably representing the head and neck of some animal. Failure.[17]

---

[16] "A series" because there were other experiments at another hour of the same day.

[17] The general assumption is that Mrs. Sinclair got her successful results by telepathy. But could Mr. Sinclair remember just in what order his drawings came, so to be thinking of each just when his wife was holding that particular one? Unfortunately he did not record whether he laid them down in the order of their production.

We have judged Experiment 1 to be a failure. And yet it is not fanciful to say that if the drawing of the globe is looked at from its left side there is considerable resemblance between the very incorrectly drawn South America and Isthmus of Panama on the one hand, and the "animal's" head and neck on the other. If clairvoyance were involved, there would be no necessary guarantee that the drawing would be sensed—to a degree—right side up. Nor do we know how the envelope was held.

2. *Agt.*, a wall-hook (Fig. 123); *Per.*, the drawing of Figure 123a, which resembles the original to a certain limited degree, having a narrow extension to the left though not curving, and broadening to the right with a suggestion of curving at the bottom.

3. *Agt.*, a monkey hanging from a bough and grasping at another (Fig. 24); *Per.*, drew as in Figures 24a, 24b (except that in the former the cut fails to give all of the pencil drawing. Instead of four curving lines hanging from the flower or whatever it is, the ends of each pair should be united by a curve) and it seems as though elements of the original were caught but misplaced. Each figure is of the shape of the under branch in the original drawing, but with the slant of the monkey; there are two as-it-were arms reaching down instead of one; and while the drawings do not suggest any animal, the script begins "Buffalo or lion. Tiger," and concludes with the conviction that there is at least some "wild animal."

4. *Agt.*, man and woman standing together; *Per.*, two drawings, one almost exactly the shape of the woman's skirt, with two black spots below and touching its bottom line, exactly as the feet of the woman appear below her skirt; the other drawing similar but less like the original.

5. *Agt.*, an animal shape, probably intended for a goat (certain species, as the Angora, have long horns which resemble those of the drawing, and goats generally have a short tail) (Fig. 138); *Per.*, no drawing, but the single word "Goat."

6. *Agt.*, a mandolin, its neck drawn with several parallel lines, the body of the instrument composed of four curving lines with three straight ones for the strings; *Per.*, what may perhaps be intended for a flower, but its long stem indicated by several parallel lines and its blossom drawn with curving and straight lines constitute a strong resemblance, and entitle it to be regarded a partial success.

7. *Agt.*, a nearly round bag with a dollar mark on it, pursed and drawn up on top, as by a string; *Per.*, (1) a circle with a vertical line protruding from its upper edge, (2) a cup-like figure with a line from its bottom to above its upper edge.

8. *Agt.*, a Lima bean (?); *Per.*, a head wearing a turban, which in shape is conspicuously like the bean.

9. *Agt.*, a nest containing seven eggs and surrounded by leaves (Fig. 4); *Per.*, a drawing which she interpreted as "Inside of rock well with vines climbing on outside," but which presents features startlingly like the original (Fig. 4a).

There is the outer rim, like that of the nest, and which would probably have completed the circle if the top of the paper had not been reached. There are the "stones," for some unknown reason obscured in the cut but some of them in the center showing more plainly and more regularly ovoid in the pencil drawing, resembling the eggs of the original. And there are not only surrounding leaves as in the original, but they are leaves of similar shape.

The Series of February 20, 1929

There were four experimental tests made this day, the same when the remarkable case of spontaneous telepathy occurred, in which Mrs. Sinclair sensed that her husband was reading about flowers and described them by drawings and script (p. 25).

In the 1st, Mr. Sinclair drew a fire hydrant (Fig. 74); Mrs. Sinclair drew as in Figure 74a. This was certainly a partial success, as the drawings compare. And for aught we know it may in fact have been a still better success, since Mr. Sinclair in looking at his drawing may well have imagined water bursting forth from the spout of the hydrant. Oddly, Mrs. Sinclair first wrote "Peafowl," and then drew what had nothing to do with a peafowl. This is one of the many cases where it seems as though Mrs. Sinclair had glimpses ahead in a series.

For the agent's second drawing was a peacock (Fig. 75). And the percipient not only said "peafowl again," which constitutes a complete success, but she also drew what it seems likely are impressions of the peacock's long neck and of the "eyes" or spots of his wings (Fig. 75a).

The agent's third drawing was of an hourglass, with sand running from its upper to its lower part (Fig. 133). The resemblance in shape of the percipient's tree (Fig. 133a) to the upper half of the hourglass is evident, its trunk may represent the slender line of flowing sand, and "white" sand is placed relatively like the sand in the lower part of the hourglass. The percipient's results seem to be partly from the lines of the original drawing, but also from Mr. Sinclair's thoughts about the sand.

Mr. Sinclair's fourth drawing represents an animal (dog?) running after a ball attached to a string (Fig. 9). Mrs. Sinclair's drawing shows (a) an animal, (b) also running, (c) in the same direction, (d) having a short tail as in the original, (e) the tail represented by two diverging lines, (f) a line extending from its nose, but touching the nose, while there is a space between in the original, (g) the line running left and at about the same angle from the horizontal. Beside the script which appears in the cut (Fig. 9a) Mrs. Sinclair wrote "Long thing like rope flung out in front of him."

I should say that the addition of that "rope" drawn in front of the animal at that angle made chance guessing of the combination at least ten times as unlikely, and, on the basis of my hundreds of experiments in guessing, I should not *expect* in ten thousand such experiments on the basis of the same original drawing one reproduction as good in the summation of its correspondences.

The Series of March 11, 1929

1. *Agt.*, a fountain which, were it taken alone, might be taken for a tree, standing in what superficially appears like a long shallow tub-like structure (Fig. 53); *Per.*, a long, shallow tub, with two tree-like objects above it and on its rim, (2) a drawing, the upper portion of which parts in the center and leans

to either side, as does the fountain. The tree or plant-like objects are both said to "shine," which does not so well comport with a tree or plant as with a fountain sparkling in the sunshine (Fig. 53a).

2. *Agt.,* a melon on an inclined plane, having a stem and leaf on the stem; *Per.,* three drawings: (1) what suggests the leaf and stem of the original twice over, (2) an unnameable figure, but slanting like the original, (3) what looks like some kind of fruit with stem, also slanting like the original.

3. *Agt.,* the figure 6 followed by the mark indicating per cent, not single-line drawn but having breadth as if cut out of cardboard; *Per.,* the letter F, a failure except for the curious parallel that this also is formed as if made with strips of cardboard.

4. *Agt.,* a fish-hook (Fig. 78); *Per.,* (1) a figure very much like the fish-hook except that the barb is transformed into a tiny flower (Fig. 78a).

5. *Agt.,* an obelisk (Fig. 79); *Per.,* two drawings, the first of which shows the three long lines of the obelisk but with a slight curvature (Fig. 79a)[18]

6. *Agt.,* as in Figure 80; *Per.,* as in Figure 80a. Only point of resemblance the two angles formed by the legs of the reclining seat.

7. *Agt.,* what was probably intended to represent a German *Pickelhaube* (Fig. 5); *Per.,* what the accompanying script called a "Knight's helmet"; very similar (Fig. 5a).

8. *Agt.,* a row of five pillars (shown with a rather extraordinary perspective slant), each mainly indicated by three or four vertical parallel lines, an entablature above (Fig. 132); *Per.,* four pillar-like objects constructed of vertical parallel lines, three to five, the presumed pillars having no entablature but in themselves and additional lines showing the same slant as in the original. The presumed

---

[18] Mr. Sinclair says, "Now why should an obelisk go on a jag, and have little circles at its base? The answer appears to be: it inherited the curves from the previous fish-hook, and the little circles from the next drawing."

It is psychologically likely that a drawing just before made or even looked at sometimes unfortunately influences a succeeding drawing. The most interesting apparent example of this is Figure 2a made just after Mrs. Sinclair had been looking at the several concentric circles of her last reproduction in the Sinclair-Irwin Group. First she got a whirl of circles, then the whirl assumed the shape of a triangle, then came two angles differently characterized, and finally the angles multiplied and constituted a star duplicating the original. And a careful study makes it impossible to doubt that there were anticipations. Some are too striking to be likely as accidents in the same series, and in some cases Mrs. Sinclair announced ahead that such-and-such an object would be found among the originals, and was right. Indeed, in cases where a set of originals was not viewed by the agent one by one, as the tests were proceeding, but were submitted in a heap together, it is a wonder that as a general rule the correspondences were found in due order, and we are hardly able to explain it. I do not, however, count any feature theoretically left over from the previous drawing as evidential, but only as an interesting glimpse into the mental processes. Neither does Mr. Sinclair, as I understand him. Nor do I reckon any "anticipation" as evidential, unless it was announced in advance, and then only in a reduced degree. And Mr. Sinclair's principles of estimation were nearly the same. For he says (the italics mine):

"Manifestly, if I grant the right to more than one guess, I am increasing the chances of guesswork, and correspondingly reducing the significance of the totals. What I have done is this: where such cases have occurred, I have called them total failures, except in a few cases, where the description was so detailed and exact as to be overwhelming—as in the case of this 'Happy Hooligan.' Even so, I have not called it a complete success, only a partial success. In order to be classified as a complete success, my wife's drawing must have been made for the particular drawing of mine which she had in her hand at that time; and throughout this account, the reader is to understand that every drawing presented was made in connection with the particular drawing printed alongside it—except in cases where I expressly state otherwise."

pillars are likewise nearly equally spaced, but are of unequal heights, indicating that the percipient's impression was a visual one and that she had no clear idea what she was drawing (Fig. 132a).

9. *Agt.*, presumably a palm tree (Fig. 8); *Per.*, two objects hard to name, but each in a general way curiously like the original, even to the bend in what is presumably the trunk, though it is not the same bend (Fig. 8a).

The Series of March 16, 1929

There were seven tests on this date.

1. *Agt.*, a burning lamp (Fig. 40); *Per.*, as in Figure 40a, whether the drawing represents a tube from which flame proceeds, or the wick and that part of the lamp which is within the chimney, at any rate the same lines which conventionally signify light appear as in the original. Accompanying script says "flame and sparks."

2. *Agt.*, a butterfly net (Fig. 110); *Per.*, the handle of the net is duplicated, and the general shape of the net is pretty well shown (Fig. 110a).

3. *Agt.*, a carnation with four near-angles along its upper edge (Fig. 113); *Per.*, four triangles in a row with a hint of lines below (Fig. 113a).

4. *Agt.*, a trench mortar (Fig. 42); *Per.*, a figure considerably like but shorter than the trench mortar, and likewise pointing upward, a stem-like extension like the axle in the original but on the other side, whiffs of smoke emerging (Fig. 42a). Here the impressions received seem partly visual, partly ideational.

5. *Agt.*, a telegraph pole and four wires proceeding horizontally from it in two directions (Fig. 129); *Per.*, something like a pole, and five lines proceeding from it in one direction (Fig. 129a).

6. *Agt.*, two hearts side by side, transfixed horizontally by an arrow (Fig. 126); *Per.*, two balloon-like shapes side by side, transfixed horizontally by a line (Fig. 126a).

7. *Agt.*, a frieze (Fig. 124); *Per.*, what looks like a detail of a different design yet one which also consists of parallel lines enclosing narrow tracts which run in different directions (Fig. 124a). Even so much of distant resemblance would not occur anything like once in ten times by chance.

Miscellaneous Examples

February 23, 1929. The agent drew a steamboat with incorrectly designed stern paddle wheel (Fig. 77). The percipient's results are very interesting (Figs. 77a, 77b, 77c). There is smoke, so labeled, by itself, then the smoke stack with smoke issuing from it, then the paddle wheel in the water, its paddles more correctly placed externally to the rim, then what may mean smoke containing cinders. The cut of the paddle wheel has left out the axle-end, very distinctly indicated in the original pencil drawing.

February 17, 1929. The agent drew an Alpine hat with a feather (Fig. 142). Of the shapes drawn by the percipient (Fig. 142a) the one on the right may very possibly be related to the rim and the band of the hat, the top left one is very suggestive of the feather, and the bottom one, though called in the script a "chafing dish," is very like the hat. All this suggests that the attention of the agent was directed first to one part, then to another and another of his drawing.

February 29, 1929. The agent drew a very intricate and unusual cross, one with eight arms, notched at the ends (see Figs. 7, 7a). The percipient also drew a circle of notched arms, but seven in number. One would suppose that when she began she had no idea where the drawing would end, or it would be more regular.

Through all the experiments of the period covered by the book *Mental Radio,* and enough more to make 300, there is no other agent drawing resembling this. And nowhere is there another percipient drawing like it. Granting that the percipient should make such a drawing once, which was by no means certain (nothing like it appears among the 564 Guess-drawings reported in this Bulletin), then the chance of its coinciding in place with the eight-armed cross of the agent would be 1 in 300.

February 17, 1929. The agent drew an open umbrella, with curved handle (Fig. 122). The percipient wrote, "I feel that it is a snake crawling out of something—vivid feeling of snake, but it looks like a cat's tail." And in her drawing (Fig. 122a) we have the curved umbrella handle, but it has sprouted a tongue and an eye; the ellipse of the umbrella rim is retained but it is a smaller one; otherwise the "something" is shaped wrongly.

We have cited instances where Mrs. Sinclair proved that she got an inkling of some drawing in a series before reaching it, by writing down at the moment her conviction. In *Mental Radio* our attention is called to a number of instances of seeming anticipations even where Mrs. Sinclair was not so conscious of them, or at least did not write down her expectation that some particular thing was coming. Here is an instance not mentioned in the book. The next agent's drawing after the umbrella was a snake. Had it not been for the dawning consciousness of *that* snake, the umbrella handle might not have undergone metamorphosis.[19]

February ?, 1929. The agent made an American flag, with pole surmounted by a ball (Fig. 127). The percipient failed to get the stars but she got the stripes and the pole, and the ball, which last has wandered from its place, although the neighborhood in which it should be is sensed (Fig. 127a).

March ?, 1929. Mrs. Sinclair wrote "Muley cow with tongue hanging out." And this is the drawing her husband had made (Fig. 137). In 260 experiments in guessing, the originals being replicas of Mr. Sinclair's drawings on February 15, there was not one success. We would have said that Mrs. Sinclair had a success in this case had she merely said "Cow." But she did better than this, for

---

[19] When she reached the snake original, the percipient made no drawing, but wrote "Man running fast." If the reader will turn back to Experiment 1 of February 8th, where the original was a snake, he will again find the cat's tail and living things fleeing. I more than ever suspect that buried in her subconsciousness is the memory of some incident wherein a snake and a cat and something else in flight figure.

she got the particular "tongue hanging out," which certainly increases the value tenfold. I venture to say that not one time in twenty will a picture of a cow show her with her tongue hanging out.

Pursuing the tests past the period until more than 300 have been had, we find that Mr. Sinclair drew a cow's head three times. Once the percipient's response was technically a failure; it resembled horns, or rather antlers. The second time she got a chicken's face, again strictly a failure, but at least something with animal life. The third time was the "cow with tongue hanging out."

And there were three other times that Mrs. Sinclair either drew a cow's head or wrote "cow" or "calf." For the first see Figures 15, 15a. In the second instance the agent had drawn a face, not that of a cow but of a man. The third was a brilliant success, not in name but in form. The agent had drawn what was doubtless intended for a donkey with a harness band across its neck. In the reproduction the donkey's long ears were metamorphosed to resemble horns, and across the cow's neck is a band, which the lady interpreted in the following script: "Cow's head in stock."

March 2, 1929. The agent drew six concentric circles (Fig. 144). As in the case of the balloon (see Figs. 95, 95a), the percipient seemed to "see" only part of the original. She also draws concentric circles, but omits about a quarter of each (Fig. 144a).

We can allow space but for one more exhibit, and this because of its seeming suggestiveness (Figs. 56, 56a). Of course, when we move away from correspondences in visual form or direct correspondences in idea we enter a region where the possibilities of chance relation are considerable. Nevertheless, literature abounds in associations between fleeing foxes on the one hand and guns and sounding horns on the other. It seems likely enough, therefore (though I would not bring forward this case as *proof*), that the sensing of the original drawing found a path for emergence through association ideas.

There are many more tests described and illustrated in Mr. Sinclair's book. What we have given has been, save for a few exceptions, according to selected and entire groups or series on particular dates.

PERCIPIENT SEQUELAE TO CERTAIN CATEGORIES OF AGENT DRAWINGS

Mr. Sinclair remarks that "when in these drawing tests there has been anything [that is, in his drawings] indicating fire or smoke she has 'got' it, with only one or two failures out of more than a dozen cases." This would mean a much larger ratio of success for the drawings so characterized than that for the total number of drawings. Mr. Sinclair accounts for this by the fact that his wife, owing to terrifying incidents in her childhood, is exceedingly sensitive to the thought of fire and given to taking unusual precautions. Readers will probably agree that this is a plausible and sensible theory. I propose to tabulate all such tests, including the original drawings significant of light.

ORIGINAL DRAWINGS INDICATING FIRE OR SMOKE

1928
    1. July 29. O[20] smoking cigarette—R: Various curved lines, and "I can't draw it, but curls of some sort."

1929
    2. Jan. 28. O: House with smoking chimney—R: Curls as of smoke. (See Figs. 36, 36a.)

    3. Feb. ?. O: Lighted lamp—R: Pipe, and "Pipe with fire in it."

    4. Feb.8. O: Pipe with smoke—R: Drawing similar to a pipe, with smoke. (See Figs. 37, 37a.)

    5. Feb. 8. O: House with smoking chimney—R: *Failure.*

    6. Feb.?. O: Pipe with smoke—R: Written, "Smoke stack."

    7. Feb. 10. O: Smoking mountain—R: (No *thought* of smoke but) Drawing very like O. (See Figs. 25, 25a.)

    8. Feb. 15. O: Smoking match—R: Smoking match. (See Figs. 91, 91a.)

    9. Feb. 23. O: Steamboat with smoking stack—R: Draws smoke, "Smoke again," and draws figure like stack with smoke. (See Figs. 77, 77a, 77b, 77c.)

    10. Mar. 16. O: Lighted lamp—R: Drawing somewhat like the part of a lamp within the chimney, and "Flame and sparks." (See Figs. 40, 40a.)

ORIGINAL DRAWINGS NOT INDICATING
BUT SIGNIFICANT OF FIRE OR SMOKE

1929
    11. Feb. ?. O: Pipe—R: *Failure* (But a smoking pipe in same series of 8).

    12. Feb. 2. O: Candelabrum—R: Base of candelabrum correctly drawn.

    13. Feb. 10. O: Fire-rocket (felt unable to draw it bursting)—R: Six drawings labelled "light," several like swirling rocket, and words "whirling light lines."

    14. Feb. 11. O: Muzzle of end of cannon, mouth indicated by double circle—R: Drawing of "half circle double lines—light inside—light is fire busy whirling or flaming."

    15. Feb. 16. O: Gable and chimney—R: Chimney with smoke.

---

[20] O—original drawing. R—reproduction. Quoted matter was written by Mrs. S as a part of her result.

16. Mar. 7. O: Cannon—R: "Black Napoleon hat and red military coats."[21]
17. Mar. 16. O: Trench mortar, with wheels and axle—R: Drawing similar to mortar and axle, plus smoke. (See Figs. 42, 42a.)

ORIGINAL DRAWINGS SIGNIFICANT OF LIGHT

1929
18. Feb. ? O: Electric light bulb—R: Drawing and script very suggestive; but nothing about *light.*
19. Feb. 10. O: Electric light bulb—R: two drawings somewhat like O in shape; nothing about *light.*
20. Feb. 11. O: Sun—R: "Setting sun and bird in sky."
21. Feb. 15. O: Sun over hills—R: Sun over a "body." (See Figs. 93, 93a.)

ORIGINALS REPRESENTING FORMS OF ANIMAL LIFE

In some cases, after the agent had drawn an animal, a bird, or some other creature possessing animal life, the percipient's drawing was successful, partly successful or at least suggestive in shape; in many instances it was a flat failure. But as examination proceeded it began to appear that a number of the failures represented some other form of the animal kingdom, however diverse. A careful canvass was made, including the material in hand produced subsequent to that in the Sinclair book, embracing in all 388 experiments; drawings of human beings, animals, birds, fishes, insects, and parts of bodies, as a hand or a leg, were included.

The Agent drew 103 such out of 388.

The Percipient drew 98 such out of 388.

There were found to be 39 correspondences;[22] that is, in 39 cases, where the agent drew some animal form or part thereof, the percipient also drew some animal form or part thereof. If out of a total of 388, the agent makes 103 drawings of this character, chance would give about 26 correspondences, so

---

[21] Statistically this must be rated a failure. But it is quite possible that in fact there is an underlying real connection. Perhaps Mrs. S had read the life of Napoleon, and had been aware that he was by education primarily an artillerist, and that the increased and peculiar use of artillery was the chief distinctive feature of his campaigns. If so, it is quite possible that the idea of cannon, struggling for emergence in her mind, by association of ideas got sidetracked to Napoleon, and became expressed in "Black Napoleon hat and red military coat." I have not discovered what the uniform of Napoleon's artillerists was; his infantry, at any rate, wore coats brilliantly faced with red.

[22] Let it be understood that there were reproductions rated as Suggestive, Partial Successes or even Successes, where there was no such "correspondence." That is to say, the reproduction might not recognizably represent any living thing, might even be indeterminable as to its nature, and yet so notably imitate the leading features of the original (though omitting something necessary for identification) as to give it one grade or another of ranking otherwise than Failure.

defined, among the 98 reproductions. In fact, there are 39, another proof, by a peculiar test, that something more than chance is in operation.

Now let us make another test, this time including the material only up to the close of the period covered by the book, and not insisting, as we have done above, on strict recognition of reproductions, but stating precisely how they compare with the originals in form.

WHERE THE ORIGINAL DRAWINGS
REPRESENT VEGETABLE FORMS

1929

Feb. 2. O: Plant with 18 spots for flowers (?)—R: 9 similar spots and writing "Many dots."

Feb. 6. O: Daisy—R: 8 small assembled figures shaped like petals of daisy, and other figures indicating vegetation.

Feb. 11. O: Cat-tail—R: Three angular protrusions somewhat like cat-tail leaves, and "Dog's head?"

Feb. 12. O: Flower with stalk—R: Flower resembling O; no stalk.

Feb. 15. O: Stalk of celery—R: Flower and stalk somewhat resembling O.

Feb. 15. O: Leaf—R: Indeterminate drawings, but with features like O.

Feb. 16. O: Acorn—R: Drawing looks like an acorn, whatever is meant by it.

Feb. 16. O: Flower and leaves—R: *Absolute failure.*

Feb. 17. O: Lima bean—R: Man's head, but his large turban is curiously shaped like O.

Feb. 17. O: Leaves around nest of eggs—R: Same shape of leaves around what much resembles the nest of eggs.

Feb. ?. O: Fleur-de-lis—R: *Failure.*

Feb. 20. O: "Red" flower[23]—R: "Red" flower. (See Fig. 14a.)

Feb. 22. O: Odd tree—R: Similar odd tree.

Feb. 24. O: Branch of tree with thorns—R: Apparently branch of tree, not thorned.

Mar. 11. O: Melon, with stalk and leaf—R: Indeterminate vegetable or flower, with stalk, and what looks like two leaves similiar to the leaf in O.

Mar. 11. O: Palm tree—R: 2 indeterminate figures, curiously like O.

Mar.?. O: Dead tree with pointed limbs—R: 3 "horns," somewhat suggestive.

Mar. ?. O: Bouquet of "pink" roses, and leaves—R: An odd half flower-like figure, marked "green" exteriorly and "pink" inside.

Mar. 16. O: Carnation—R: Similar exterior four sharp angles; no other resemblance.

---

[23] Here the original was not a drawing but a "red flower" that Mr. Sinclair was simultaneously reading about.

ALL THE ORIGINAL DRAWINGS REPRESENTING CROSSES

1929

1. Feb. ?. O: Swastika cross (Fig. 101)—R: 3 drawing which together give 3 of the 4 rectangular quarters of the swastika cross, and the directions in which they open; 2 drawings, each of which practically represents a half of the cross, but one of these reversed (Fig. 101a).
2. Feb. 6. O: Swastika cross—R: *Failure.*
3. Feb. ?. O: Pattée cross (Fig. 81)—R: A figure, four of which rightly placed make the cross; but by adding a bail (because of inference?) it is made a basket (Fig. 81a).
4. Feb. 10. O: Eight-armed crosses (Fig. 64)—R: Script, "See spider, or some sort of legged pest." (Note that the Arachnida are eight-legged.)
5. Feb. 15. O: Three four-armed crosses on a box—R: Three six-armed crosses. (See Figs. 98, 98a.)
6. Mar. ?. O: Eight-armed cross with notched ends (Fig. 7)—R: Seven-armed cross with notched ends (Fig. 7a).

ORIGINALS REPRESENTING THE SUN

In the course of 300 experiments, extending a little beyond the period reported by the book, there were but two of these.

The first was on February 11, 1929. The agent made a sun as children draw it, a circle with rays surrounding it. The percipient made no drawing but wrote "Setting sun and bird in the sky. Big bird on the wing—sea gull or wild goose." Mr. Sinclair calls this a partial success, and surely it is.

The second was on February 15, more than fifty experiments having intervened. The agent drew a sun over hills, the percipient a circle with rays around it actually labelled "a sun," over a "body." (See Figs. 93, 93a.) This also was a partial success.

Thus both times out of 300 experiments when Mr. Sinclair made a sun, his wife "got it" and drew one also.

But twice, also, Mrs. Sinclair drew what was meant for the upper half of a sun at the horizon when there was no sun in the original. In one of these instances the original did have something, not a sun, considerably like the reproduction, and there was a certain degree of resemblance in the other. But let these count as failures. We will allow the reader to figure out the chances of two of Mrs. Sinclair's four suns, in the course of 300 experiments, being drawn at the same time when Mr. Sinclair drew his two suns.

"LINE-AND-CIRCLE-MEN" ORIGINALS

On February 6, 1929, Mr. Sinclair made a line-and-circle man; that is, one drawn in schoolboy fashion (Fig. 106). The percipient got the head circle, adding dots for features, and her crossing lines, properly placed below the circle, roughly represent the spread of arms and legs (Fig. 106a).

On February 10th, thirty experiments having intervened, the agent made two such men, facing each other in boxing attitudes (Fig. 107). It will be seen that just two vertical lines, longer than any of the others, enter into their composition. The longest lines in what the percipient drew are also two and vertical. And she got a confused notion of the legs and arms, each with its angle for knee or elbow. She failed to get any circles (Fig. 107a).

All through the period covered by the book, and past it until the 300th experiment, there is no other line-and-circle man original. The percipient in the same number of experiments made one drawing in which head and body are represented by a circle and an ellipse, and the rest of the man by single lines. And she made one fairly well drawn head with hair, the rest of the figure represented by single lines.

A STUDY IN "ANTICIPATIONS"

The Series of February 11, 1929

We have been pursuing the rigorous rule of estimating a percipient drawing by its correspondence or lack of correspondence with the agent drawing then in hand. Only when Mrs. Sinclair announced in advance that a described drawing would come in a series, and it actually came, have we given weight to an anticipation. Such an instance was that of the snow and sled drawing of February 8th. This is not by any means to say that other "anticipations" have not had weight, as a matter of fact. In some of the instances exhibited in *Mental Radio* the original drawings represented objects of such character that it was extremely unlikely that there should be a near correspondence among the half dozen or dozen reproductions constituting the whole series, or in fifty guesses.

Again, there could be a series with so many of these correspondences out of order that one is mathematically[24] and logically compelled to acknowledge that there was anticipation. Such a series is that of February 11, 1929.

1. *Agt.*, a molar tooth; *Per.*, an ellipse containing 19 tiny circles. This is emphatically a failure compared with the contemporaneous original drawing. However, see No. 12. Before the drawing was made, the percipient wrote "First see rooster. Then elephant."

2. And now *Agt.'s* drawing was an elephant, as far back as but lacking hind legs.

---

[24] Mathematically, that is, on the basis of a large number of counted experiments in guessing.

And *Per.* wrote "Elephant comes again. I try to suppress it, and see lines, and a spike sticking some way into something." And she draws two vertical lines, related to each other in ribbon fashion, what looks like a pin with circle for head, crossing the band through a slit indicated by two short vertical lines, and below the "spike" two widely separated vertical lines. The "spike" crosses what I have called a ribbon exactly as the elephant's tusk crosses his trunk, the round eye of the elephant has moved slightly to form the head of the "spike," and the vertical lines below may stand for a feeling that *something* (really the front legs) should be below. We have some warrant for our interpretation from the words "Elephant comes again. I try to suppress it." Had she not tried to suppress it (because of the erroneous notion that it is but a memory of the elephant impression of Experiment 1), it is fair to assume that she would have tried to draw an elephant. She "tried to suppress" the animal, but his eye and "spike," which was really "sticking into something," but not in the manner drawn, seem to have persisted. (See Figs. 66, 66a.)

3. And now *Agt. did* draw a rooster. Both elephant and rooster, with which she was impressed at Experiment 1, had come by the time Experiment 3 had been reached. This is rather too much for "chance coincidence," especially as the Sinclairs do not have an elephant among their domestic pets. But this is not all. As *Per.* not only announced an elephant in advance but got details of the elephant when that animal actually was in hand as the original, so not only was a rooster announced in advance but when the original is a rooster, *Per.* gets correspondences. She writes "I don't know what, see a bunch, or tuft clearly. Also a crooked arm on a body. But don't feel that I'm right." What she drew was remarkably like the rear three-quarters of the rooster, the "tuft" representing its tail, "the crooked arm" its two legs in conjunction. (See Figs. 67, 67a.)

4. *Agt.*, a table; *Per.*, "Flower. This is a very vivid one. Green-spine-leaves like century plant," and a corresponding drawing with tall flowering spike in the center. (See Fig. 68a.) A flat failure, but wait for Experiments 7 and 11.

5. *Agt.*, a fish-hook; *Per.*, no drawing but script: "Dog wagging tail—see tail in air busy wagging—jolly doggie—tail curled in the air." Well, a fish-hook is somewhat like a tail curled in the air. But script followed: "Now I see a cow. I fear the elephant and chicken got me too sure of animals. But I see these." A tail curled in the air—a dog or a cow! Wait for No. 7.

6. *Agt.*, a sun represented by a large circle surrounded by rays; *Per.*, "Setting sun and bird in the sky. Big bird on wing—sea gull or wild goose." Obviously this is a partial success.

7. *Agt.*, what was intended for the rear half of a cow, with tail curled almost exactly like a fish-hook. Remember that in No. 5 *Per.* had an impression of a dog with "tail curled in the air" and a later impression of a cow. As a matter of fact, Mr. Sinclair's cow does not have a cow's tail but one made in the fashion of a hound's tail. *Per.* in this No. 7 experiment makes a drawing like that of No. 4, except that the central spike is not so long, and writes "This is a *real* flower. I've

seen it before. It's vivid and returns. Century plant? Now it turns into a candle-stick. See a candle." And she drew what she probably meant for a five-armed candlestick, with one candle in the center. But it is much like the plant called "cat-tail," except that the leaves diverge too widely. (See Fig. 69a.)

8. *Agt.*, a long line with seven short evenly-spaced lines running from it at right angles—probably meant for a rake-head; *Per.*, what is probably intended for two sticks of wood, fire proceeding from one of them, and smoke above. Script: "Fire and smoke—flame." Also, "Must be campfire as I now see an Indian warrior near it in a war dress—feathered headpiece, etc." There is a certain amount of resemblance between the rake-head and the stick of wood with the more or less straight lines springing from one side of it. (See Fig. 43a). And one remembers that an Indian headdress, of the type which hangs down the back, consists of feathers on one side and directed outwardly from the band to which they are attached. But these are only suggested possibilities of connec-tion, and are doubtful. There is even another possible connection, for it may be that "Fire and smoke" was influenced by the cannon of the following original.

9. *Agt.*, the forward part of an old-style cannon, a double-line ellipse marking its mouth seen in perspective; *Per.*, the half of a double-line ellipse with a curving tangle as of smoke, labeled "Fire," and outside the script: "Half circle, double lines—light inside—light is fire busy whirling or flaming." Partly right and very suggestive. (See Fig. 44a.)

10. *Agt.*, three concentric triangles; *Per.*, two wheels and over them the suggestion of some vehicle-body—only a line and two angles. Failure.

11. *Agt.*, a "cat-tail," its leaves by no means correctly drawn, but there is no doubt of its identity; *Per.*, a drawing doubtfully marked "Dog's head," its ears, if such they are, also its muzzle, long and pointed, much resembling the upper halves of Mr. Sinclair's cat-tail leaves. But remember Mrs. Sinclair's "century plant" of No. 2 with its somewhat similar leaves and its central spike; remember especially the "candlestick" of No. 7, which so much resembles a cat-tail. (See Figs. 69a, 70, 70a.)

12. *Agt.*, ten small circles arranged in rows, pyramidal fashion; *Per.* wrote only "Nothing except all the preceding ones come—too many at once—all past ones crowding in memory." I wish she had stated which past one, if any, crowded most, and which came first. For it happens that her drawing for No. 2, so different from the impressions "a rooster" and "an elephant," set down at the same time, also consisted of little circles, also in rows, but more in number and enclosed within an elliptical line.

13. *Agt.*, a drinking-glass with double elliptic line at the top and small ellipse indicating the bottom; *Per.*, double elliptic line above, same below with indefinite lines rising from the latter. The script is more significant: "Think of a saucer, then of a cup. It's something in the kitchen. Too tired to see." Pretty close. (See Figs. 72, 72a.)

The occurrence of so many correspondences, direct and oblique, among thirteen consecutive experiments constituting the entire series performed at one time, and these by mere accidental coincidence, is practically unthinkable.

LATER EXPERIMENTS BY
PROFESSOR WILLIAM McDOUGALL

In the main, this review has dealt only with the period covered by *Mental Radio*, although it has exhibited some experiments not illustrated or even mentioned therein. A few of the special tabulations have also included a part or all of the later tests made by Mr. and Mrs. Sinclair, to the number of more than a hundred, the materials of which are in my hands. When the tabulations have reached so far, the fact has been stated.

But it may be well to say something about tests made by Professor William McDougall during a sojourn in California, July–August, 1930. He examined the proofs of previous work and consented to write an introduction to *Mental Radio*, saying: "A refusal would imply on my part a lack either of courage or of due sense of scientific responsibility. It is the duty of men of science to give whatever encouragement and sympathetic support may be possible to all amateurs who find themselves in a position to observe and carefully and honestly to study such phenomena. Mrs. Sinclair would seem to be one of the rare persons who have telepathic power in a marked degree and perhaps other supernormal powers. "The experiments in telepathy, as reported in the pages of this book, were so remarkably successful as to rank among the very best hitherto reported. The degree of success and the conditions of experiment were such that we can reject them as conclusive evidence of some mode of communication not at present explicable in accepted scientific terms only by assuming that Mr. and Mrs. Sinclair either are grossly stupid, incompetent, and careless persons or have deliberately entered upon a conspiracy to deceive the public in a most heartless and reprehensible fashion." As we have seen, the circle of conspirators would have to be enlarged to admit Mr. and Mrs. Irwin, for they vouched for an extraordinarily successful series of experiments at long distance. And it would have to be enlarged to include Professor McDougall himself, since he sent me the materials of his experiments, whose results, though inferior to many of the series of 1928 and 1929, yet show a ratio and quality of correspondence vastly beyond chance expectation. Remember that the 260 Guessing tests resulted in not one drawing which, being compared with the original, could possibly be regarded as a Success, and this by the independent verdicts of two judges. Of course, this does not mean that another set of 260 guesses would not show one Success or more than one, but it does show the great improbability that a particular drawing made by guess will correspond with the particular original enough so that it is possible to call it a Success.

The 260 guess-drawings, according to one of the judges, showed 3 Partial Successes, 1 according to the other. Then say there was no Success and but 3 Partial Successes, and it is still unlikely that a particular drawing made in any short guess series will correspond with the particular original to the extent of being worthy of the title Success or Partial Success. On the basis of those 260 guesses we would be warranted in assuming that there would be about one-third of a likelihood of getting either a Success or a Partial Success in a series of twenty-five. But another series of 260 guesses might be more fortunate, so call it an expectation of getting one. Professor McDougall had twenty-five experiments with Mrs. Sinclair.

On July 19th, "five cards drawn or chosen and sealed in envelope and thick paper at Santa Monica and presented in turn sealed to Mrs. S. at Long Beach." Reproductions 1, 3 and 4 were failures. But agent's No. 2 was a "prairie schooner" showing two wheels with spokes and a long black line crossing the wheels at their hubs and standing for both the bottom of the vehicle-body and the shafts in front, while the percipient drew (1) a wheel with spokes and a long black line running from the hub, and (2) a wheel-like shape without spokes, but the line extending far in one direction and passing through the hub and beyond the wheel a short way in the other direction, as in the original. Here we have a distinct Partial Success. Agent's No. 5 was a postal-card picture of a part of Oxford, the most conspicuous feature in which is the tower of Magdalen College with pinnacles and high, narrow windows. The percipient made a drawing which anyone would recognize as a tower, with bristling short lines projecting upward from the top suggesting pinna-cles, and high, narrow windows. The proportions of height and width are approximately correct. Below the lower window level are two parallel horizontal lines, which call attention to such lines in the original. This was drawn, however, while the percipient was holding agent's No. 4, his No. 5, the tower, still being in his pocket. It looks like an anticipation. But when she arrived at No. 5 she wrote "Turret of a castle and trees," and now she is right for the very original in hand, which does display, besides a river, a bridge and buildings, the conspicuous tower, and trees prominent in the picture. She added "Sword," "Scissors," and "Key," which may possibly be erroneous impressions from the pinnacles. So we have here a striking result, worthy to be called a Success. I have again taken pains to go through all the originals and all the reproductions, 413 of each, and find that but once besides did an original represent a tower. It was the Eiffel Tower, and all will remember its tall, slender, and tapering shape.

The percipient's drawing represented a long, slender, and tapering cone—a Partial Success. And but once besides, among all 413 drawings, did the percip-ient present a tower. This was on the following August 16th, when, apparently as an experiment, the drawings were "done in a hurry" and no record made of the order. If compared with a particular one of the originals, the "tower top" is a Partial Success, but it probably was a Failure. So here we have the factors: out of 418 agent drawings two represent towers, and one results in a percipient Success, the other in a Partial Success; out of 418 percipient drawings two represent towers, and one is a Success, the other a Failure.

On July 20th Professor McDougall made five drawings "at one end of a long room, while Mrs. Sinclair tried to reproduce them at the other end." The agent made what is supposed to be a stork, each foot furnished with three toes. The percipient made two long legs with three-toed feet, the legs extending from a curved line like the under side of a bird. Above and isolated is what looks like a crest, which the stork does not have. Partial Success. The 4th agent drawing is of a ringed target and a feathered arrow sticking in it, the barb not visible. The percipient drawing is practically the feathered part of the shaft. Partial Success. The 5th agent drawing shows a drum-like object with elliptical top, from the center of which a tube or spout projects vertically, with water rising from the spout, parting and falling to right and to left so that it looks something like a tree. The percipient drew (1) an ellipse, (2) an ellipse, (3) something like a very round teapot, with elliptic top and spout at an angle of 45 degrees, (4) something like the vertical trunk of a tree surmounted by a ball of foliage. Success; there are too many suggestive partial parallels to allow this to be doubted.

July 26th there were five experiments, all drawn by Professor McDougall except one, that being a postal-card picture of trees, bushes and the yucca in bloom. Agent's No. 2 was a wheel with spokes and tire nicely drawn. Percipient made three circles in a row with something like the connecting rod of a locomotive across them. This is at least Suggestive. Directly before the yucca picture, the percipient described plants with flowers, but the description did not fit the original next to come, nor did the impression of flowers persist when the yucca was at hand, so I do not allow this to count at all. There were no other successes in any degree.

Then followed experiments, one a day, with Professor McDougall drawing at Santa Monica, Mrs. Sinclair drawing at the same time at Pasadena, thirty miles distant.

July 30th. A failure.

August 2nd. Original drawing: a coffee-pot, its spout at the right of peculiar shape, somewhat like the profile of a boat's stern. The percipient's drawing was principally made up of a vertical line like the edge of the coffee-pot, and turned to the right from its upper extremity a projection curiously like the coffee-pot's spout. To the left of the vertical line seven dots. It may be a mere coincidence that in the original there are several, but not seven, dark spots in the drawing, placed relatively about as far from the right edge of the coffee-pot as the dots are from the vertical line in the percipient drawing. The drawing is Suggestive, at least.

August 10th. Original drawing a teapot, and percipient's drawing, a palm frond, was relatively to it, a failure.

August 11th. Agent drew a faucet. Percipient wrote "Teapot," which is a failure. But agent had drawn a teapot the previous day—did percipient get a deferred telepathic impression?

August 13th. Agent drew a palm tree and percipient's result was a failure. But, records agent, "Had it in mind to draw the palm in patio several days before. Mrs. S. seemed to get it August 10th." No agent should have in mind to draw one thing when he actually draws another. If the result is from telepathy, not clairvoyance, a percipient is at least as likely to get that on which the agent's mind has dwelt. On the whole it would perhaps be fair to count this as a Success.

August 16th. Agent drew a flower-pot and in it a plant with sword-shaped leaves, somewhat like a century plant. Percipient first drew what one might take to be a stalk with five straight, short leafless branches, but with the script "Velvet bow with band." She added, "Then saw" and drew a plant—no pot—with leaves exactly of the form of the leaves in the original, and added, "I have too many leaves in the above." Right: she had eleven leaves, the original had seven. This certainly is at least a Partial Success.

August 17th, August 18th, and August 19th each yielded a Failure.

Now let us take account of stock. On the basis of our 260 experiments in guessing we would have about one-third of an expectation of finding in the McDougall experiments one Partial Success, but as another series of 260 guesses might be more fortunate we proposed to reckon a full likelihood of getting one Success or Partial Success, on the theory that Mrs. Sinclair was guessing also. But we have found 3 Successes and 4 Partial Successes (not counting a possible "anticipation," and 2 instances of Suggestive). It is not mathematics, it is not logic, it is not common-sense to conclude that we have not, even in this series of Professor McDougall, although it does not equal some which have been exhibited, something for which chance is wholly unable to account.

It is not at all difficult to account for the fact that Professor McDougall's results were not quite up to the average of Mrs. Sinclair's work during the period covered by *Mental Radio,* both quantity and quality taken into consideration. In the first place, it has for many years been evident that something depends upon the degree of *rapport* between agent and percipient; in other words, that some persons are better suited than others to act as agents in relation to a particular percipient. Thus, we are told in the book (p. 27) that among the friends of Mrs. Sinclair there was one peculiarly adapted in this respect—Mrs. Kate Crane-Gartz. I venture to relate my own very limited experience, as fact, not scientifically guaranteed. I have had reason to suppose that I was getting telepathic messages only with two persons. One was with my wife the first time I ever experimented with her, and then I got most of the objects she was thinking of, more or less satisfactorily, in about eight trials. But I never again had *any* measurable success with her, though I tried repeatedly. The other person I was for a time in sympathetic relations with, and there occurred a number of incidents which convinced me that I was acting as a spontaneous percipient. The most striking category of these is the same which Mr. Sinclair describes when he says: "My wife will say to me, 'Mrs. Gartz is going to phone,' and in a minute or two the phone will ring." Repeatedly, when I had no particular reason to think that the lady to whom I refer would phone me, and when I was occupied with work, I would suddenly, as by a jerk, look at the phone, expecting it to ring, and in a few moments it would do so. I have even gone to the phone, almost without thinking, and stood there for half a minute or so before it did so. This period lasted for perhaps three or four months only, then faded out. Never at any other time, nor with any other person, not even with my daughter between whom and me there is the most cordial sympathy, has there been evidence of this kind sufficiently striking and repetitious to arrest serious attention. So it may well be that Professor McDougall, however amiable and fairminded he is, not having been long known to the percipient and being invested with the awe of a psychologist of extended reputation, was not so well adapted to be an agent in relation to her as her husband or her brother-in-law.

But again, while at times Mrs. Sinclair to the last of her experimentation analyzed by me got excellent results, I find that, whether because she was wearied, or too much occupied by other things, or more anxious and less spontaneous, or for whatever reason, did not in the later months do so well on the average as during the earlier months. The poorest stretch of the period after the material covered by the book was that from August 1 to August 23, 1929, inclusive. There were 27 experiments, of which, according to my reckoning, 2 were Successes, 1 a Partial Success, 3 Suggestive, 2 Slightly Suggestive and 19 Failures in a series of 27 experiments. The poorest stretch of experiments during the book period was that ending with the series of February 17, 1929, nevertheless shown on account of its significance. Here there were 4 Successes, 8 Partial Successes, 4 Suggestive, 1 Slightly Suggestive and 10 Failures out of the same total number of 27. So, after all, while the McDougall results did not reach the highest level of the later period, they did not by any means mark the lowest level. They greatly transcend the expectation of chance, and, with the exception of five experiments only, were achieved when agent and percipient were either thirty miles apart or at the two ends of a long room.

ATTEMPTS TO EXPLAIN OTHERWISE THAN BY TELEPATHY

Would Chance Coincidence Explain?
It has already been proved by experiments in guessing that even the comparatively poor Dessoir results were far beyond the reach of chance. And it has been shown by experiments in guessing that the Sinclair results were much

farther beyond the reach of chance. Such countertests may be repeated by any reader *ad libitum*.

Would the Kindred Ideas of Relatives Explain?

It makes one feel foolish to add anything more about the curious "throb" to the effect that what is taken for telepathy between husbands and wives is really coincidence brought about by their community of thought and tendency to think about the same things. It should be evident that even if a husband and wife knew only one hundred objects in common, that astonishing fact of limitation would not imply that the lady would be likely to think of a particular one of these, say No. 92, at the particular time that her spouse chose it. For once it may be well to show just how narrow and connubial a range of drawings a husband may submit to his wife. (See Appendix II.)

Would Conscious or Subconscious Fraud on the Part of the Percipient Explain?

We must squarely face every possible theory, and this is one. Mr. Sinclair himself dealt with it. We must do so more thoroughly, in spite of Mrs. Sinclair's testimony to remarkable telepathic experiences in her earlier years (*Mental Radio*, pp. 12-13), in spite of her husband's testimony about her actually setting down in writing what "Jan" was doing at a distance before she got from him the substantially corresponding facts and getting in dreams or by "concentration" facts concerning himself at a distance (pp. 17-23), in spite of Mrs. Sinclair's reputation for practicality and non-credulity (pp. 14, 125), honor and conscientiousness (p. 44), her impressing her husband as being "a fanatic for accuracy" (p. 124), the grave reasons which caused her to institute these experiments (p. 13; Appendix 1), her intense desire to be sure, and to satisfy every misgiving of her own (p. 122), her urgency that her husband should watch her work (p. 44), her variations in the methods of experimentation to see what effect they would have (pp. 36-38, 39-40, 122-123, etc.), her reluctance that her husband should publish his book until still more experiments were had (pp. 14, 122), and the great pains she takes to describe her method of development and "preparation" in order to encourage others to experiment (pp. 104–114). All these considerations are cumulatively almost overwhelming, yet we proceed in disregard of them.

But the seven experiments with "Bob" were at long distance, and the conditions guaranteed by "Bob" and his wife.

The seven experiments of July 24–29, 1928, were conducted with the agent in one room and the percipient in another, thirty feet away, with a closed door between. That is to say, Mr. Sinclair, in one room, would call out "All right" when ready to draw; his wife, lying in another room, would call "All right" when she had completed her drawing, and then the two drawings were compared. He declares that there was no possible way by which Mrs. Sinclair could have seen his drawing. So that any charge of fraud would have to include him.

The nine experiments of February 17, 1929, were thus conducted. The original drawings were made by the agent, Mr. Sinclair, while alone in his study, on green paper, enclosed in a sheet of green paper, the whole folded, making four thicknesses absolutely impervious to sight (as established in the office of the B.S.P.R.), put in an envelope, the envelope sealed, and the 9 envelopes put on a table by the percipient's couch. She took each in turn and placed it over her solar plexus, kept it there until her decision was made, then sat up and made her drawing. All the while her husband sat near, but absolutely speechless until her drawing was done, when the wrappings were taken from the original drawing and it was immediately compared with the reproduction. If the experiments were at night, the reading light immediately over the percipient's head was extinguished, since she found that somewhat subdued illumination favored passivity, but there remained sufficient light in the room for comparison of the drawings, and every movement of the woman was distinctly visible. If in the daytime, the window shades back of the couch were lowered, but again every object was distinctly visible. Under precisely these conditions, step by step, no professional magician could have obtained knowledge of the original drawing before making his own.[25]

As we have seen, nine of Professor McDougall's experiments, later than the period of the book and reaching results defying the doctrine of chance, were made with thirty miles between the parties, and ten of them with the parties at opposite ends of a long room. Five more were done with McDougall at least watching his sealed envelopes. It will probably not be suggested that he was in a conspiracy to deceive the public, but in these cases fraud could hardly have been practiced by the percipient alone.

Already we have forty-seven experiments, sixteen with an intervening distance of above thirty miles, seven with agent and percipient in different rooms, and ten with agent and percipient at the two ends of a room; fourteen with agent near the percipient but closely watching her and his sealed opaque envelopes.

But since Mr. Sinclair says that "several score drawings" were drawn in his study, sealed in envelopes made impervious to sight, and watched by him as one by one his wife laid them on her body and set down her impressions, the total number of experiments, guarded to this or a greater extent, aside from the later ones by McDougall, could hardly have fallen short of 120.

Later, since Mr. Sinclair was very busy writing his novel *Boston* and disliked the interruptions, he ceased (about midway of the whole lot, he tells us) to enclose his drawings in envelopes and to watch his wife's work. Had this been the case throughout, any report based on such "experiments" would not, scientifically speaking, be worth the paper it was written on. As it is, I should be quite willing to rest the whole case on the 120 or more guarded experiments

---

[25] Unless by "involuntary whispering," a theory to be attended to later.

covered by the last two paragraphs. More than that, I would be willing to rest it upon the thirty-three experiments conducted with the participants separated by the length of a room, thirty feet and a closed door, or thirty miles.

But the logic of the situation is entirely against the assumption that fraud was used any more after it became easily possible than before, when it would have been possible only by the connivance of various conspirators. Let us see.

1. If advantage were to be taken of the relaxation of precautions it would plainly be but for one purpose, to increase the number or the excellence of favorable results, or both. But neither the number nor the excellence of favorable results was enhanced. On the contrary, not at once, but by a general though irregular decline, the results deteriorated. The last 120 experiments of the period covered by the book brought about half again as many complete Failures as the first 120 had done. Mr. Sinclair reminds us that "Series No. 6 which was carefully sealed up, produced 4 complete Successes, 5 Partial Successes, and no Failures; whereas Series 21, which was not put in envelopes at all, produced no complete Successes, 3 Partial Successes and 6 Failures." The declension, which has been noted in experiments with other persons, continued, in irregular fashion, after the period of the book. We have already noted that the worst consecutive run of 27 experiments during the last period yielded 19 Failures, while the worst consecutive run of experiments during the period of the book yielded but 10 Failures. Nor is there ever again, after precautions were relaxed, a single consecutive run of seven experiments with quite such astounding results as those of the first seven experiments of all, with "Bob," at some thirty miles distance in an air-line. Hence the percipient took no advantage of the relaxation of conditions, or she did so to make her work poorer on the average than it had been, which is against human nature and practically inconceivable.

2. It was almost silly to go further after fixing the fact that the opening up of opportunities for improving results by clandestine means was followed not by improvement but deterioration of results. But an examination was made to see whether the drawings underwent *any* modification such as would rather be expected from the introduction of a new causative factor. None; they continued to express in seemingly the same proportions, some the shape, some the idea. Still in many cases they were unrecognizable as any namable object, yet when compared with the original, showed more or less of its marked characteristics.

3. We even went so far as to compare the most of the later drawings with what could be seen of them folded and in envelopes, but unenclosed in opaque paper, when held up to the light. To be sure, Mrs. Sinclair had been accustomed to subdue the light, to lie with closed eyes in such a position that only the ceiling would have been visible had they been open, and to hold the envelope, or after the envelope itself was discarded, the paper in her hand lying on her solar plexus, all of which is an arrangement ill-adapted to "peeking." And, to be sure, Mr. Sinclair would have been considerably surprised had he

come in and found a different situation. But our experiments were meant to test whether, on the supposition that she did alter her procedure, her drawings were such as would have been explained by what was seen, even accidentally, through the folded paper held up to the light. Certainly, in that case, there would have been signs of the selection of heavy lines which showed through clearly, and some evidence of the effects from the paper being doubled. The result of the tests was negative.

It is concluded, mainly on the basis of Section 1 above, but assisted by Sections 2 and 3 were assistance necessary, that Mrs. Sinclair was as honest when unwatched as when watched, since, had fraud been used, it would have left traces. But, let me reiterate, I am favorable to any proposition to take into account only the guarded experiments, or even those guarded to an extent beyond cavil.

Would Involuntary Whispering Explain?

F. C. C. Hansen and Alfred Lehmann, Danish psychologists, in 1895 published a pamphlet of 60 pages entitled *Über Unwillkürliches Flüstern (On Involuntary Whispering)*. This brochure reported experiments by the authors which, they claimed, showed that the apparent success in telepathic transmissions of numbers achieved under the control of representatives of the S. P. R. and published in its *Proceedings* (Vols. VI and VIII) might not have been due to telepathy, but to involuntary whispering with closed lips. Messrs. Hansen and Lehmann sat between concave spherical mirrors so that the concentration of sound, their heads occupying the foci, would presumably be an equivalent for the hyperaesthesia of a *hypnotized* "percipient." Each in turn acted as agent, to see if figures could be conveyed by "involuntary whispering," and seemed to have a large degree of success. How it is possible to test whether audible whispering can be produced with closed lips and do so without the exercise of volition is something of a mystery. And how they could be certain that some factor of telepathy did not enter into their own experiments is not clear.[26] But Professor Sidgwick, who five years before Hansen and Lehmann's pamphlet had considered and discussed the possibility of "unconscious whispering,"[27] later instituted experiments of his own and concluded that something in this

---

[26] There was one experiment with drawings. One of the Danish experimenters drew a candlestick, with a lighted candle in it. The other in response drew what in the cut looks like a crooked milk-bottle with a short curved line proceeding from one end and two short curved lines proceeding from one side. The latter says he meant it for a cat, but does not know why he furnished it with only two "legs." The only use made of this drawing in the pamphlet is to compare it with a selected and very poor example from the Richet series and to assert that it is as good a reproduction. The utmost I should grant for the Richet drawing is that, regarded as one of a series containing a number of far more impressive ones, it is Suggestive, and the most I could grant for the "cat," is that it may possibly be Slightly Suggestive. But did Hansen and Lehmann think there was any resemblance between their reproduction and original? If so, how did they know that there was no thought-transference and why did they not continue to experimen[t] with drawings? Were they afraid that if they did, they might have an intractable problem on their hands? But if they thought there was no real resemblance, what possible weight had their failure against a series of experiments wherein a large percentage of the reproductions beyond question did notably resemble the originals?

[27] S. P. R. Proceedings, VI, 164–5.

direction was possible. But he, William James and others thoroughly riddled the Hansen and Lehmann dream that perhaps they had explained the published S. P. R. series of experiments for the transfer of numbers. For one thing, a part of the experiments had been with the parties in different rooms. And the notion that when the voluntarily involuntary whisper[28] of a digit was misheard, a digit whose name somewhat resembled it was most likely to be selected by the agent, was riddled too, so far as it applied to the English experiments. The Danish gentlemen had never claimed that their explanatory theory was proved, but only that it was probable. Later they quite frankly acknowledged that the Sidgwick and James "experiments and computations" had weakened even its probability.

Since their pamphlet had attracted much and widespread interest, as it deserved to do, and since if they could establish or even strengthen the probability of their theory it would mean a restoration and enhancement of their prestige, set back by the counterstrokes of Sidgwick, James, Schiller and others, it would seem that the inducement not to stop short, but to go on with the experimentation would be almost irresistible. But they either did stop there or their results were disappointing, for nothing more, so far as I can learn, was ever heard from them on this subject.

Nevertheless, the possibility, especially on the part of a hyperaesthetic percipient, of catching, to some extent, the sound of unintended whispering by the agent stationed nearby, especially where there is no guarantee that his lips are always closed, must be admitted. This possibility has impressed some investigators, and especially Herr Richard Baerwald, even beyond all logical grounds. The named writer has said *also fort mit den Nahversuchen* (so away with near-experimentation)! I certainly agree that experiments for telepathy should be made with sufficient space between agent and percipient to make the suggestion that there may have been some perception of involuntary whispering manifestly incredible and absurd. Such was Mrs. Sinclair's success under such conditions as to make it probable that if there had been many scores of experiments under the same conditions a like staggering ratio of success would have been maintained. Nevertheless, I must maintain that the involuntary whispering theory fails to touch many of the Sinclair experiments attended with one or another degree of success, considering their nature and the peculiar character of the percipient drawings.

In the first place, let me observe that where the experiments were to transfer numbers the range of choice on the part of the percipient, endeavoring to interpret any faintly heard indications by the posited involuntary whispering, was strictly limited. If the agent were to choose a figure from one to naught

---

[28] Professor Sidgwick declared that the whispering of himself and his colleagues was certainly voluntary, and that there was no success otherwise.

inclusive, the percipient's range for guessing would be but ten digits. If the agent was to choose some figure from one to ninety-nine inclusive, the range for guessing would of course be greater, yet more limited than at first appears to be the case. There would be the ten digits, eleven, twelve, thirteen, fourteen, fifteen, twenty, thirty, forty, fifty, and in addition only combinations from among the foregoing or made up of a digit with "teen" or "ty" added. But where the agent drew whatever he pleased, generally an object, his range was unlimited, and the task of the percipient interpreting any indications by involuntary whispering would be much more difficult. But still it would be theoretically possible. So we turn to the next and overwhelming point.

Whenever the agent's drawing was one which could be indicated by a name, and the percipient's result corresponded to the extent covered by the name, it is easy to apply the theory of involuntary whispering if the agent was near the percipient. Granting that this was the case (which often, as will appear later, we cannot grant, since the facts forbid it), it is easy theoretically to explain the response "Sailboat" to the drawing of a sailboat. We have only to suppose that the agent was so intently interested that, unknown to himself, he faintly whispered the name, and that the percipient, having *ex hypothesi*, abnormal alertness of hearing, caught the word, or enough of it so that she successfully guessed the whole. Still easier is it to imagine the transmission of Y in the series of January 28–29. The agent, being absorbed and desirous, simply whispered "Y, Y, Y," until the percipient got it. The reader may pick for himself other plausible instances in Mr. Sinclair's book, or even from the materials furnished in this Bulletin, such as the helmet experiment (Figs. 5, 5a). It is even conceivable that the agent's eye, flitting over the drawing of the peacock (Fig. 75) caused him to whisper "long neck" and "spots" or "eyes" (Fig. 75a), although no spots appear in this drawing and "peacock" is the word he would be expected to whisper, if any. But every increasing complexity in the agent's drawing, which finds duplication in that of the percipient, every increasing difficulty of defining the drawing by one or two words increases the difficulty of the explanation. Take the remarkable correspondence between Figures 7, 7a. The agent, it seems, would have to whisper the following, or its equivalent: "Cross" (or "radiating figure"), "eight arms" (or "many arms"), "arms not made of a single line but having breadth," "notches in the ends." That is a lot for the agent to whisper, and it appears improbable, but maybe it is "conceivable."

A much-esteemed friend writes me: "Those willing to press the unconscious whispering hypothesis to its extreme consequences need not invariably postulate the *transmission direct* of a word. They may go further. Let us suppose that in an experiment at close quarters the name thought of by the agent is 'Napoleon,' and that the percipient gets a small island and the name 'Helen.' It is theoretically conceivable that, nevertheless, the explanation is to be sought in involuntary whispering; the name 'Napoleon' was perceived in a normal way (unconsciously) and then in the percipient's subconscious *transformed* into an idea associated with Napoleon's name. I do not say this is my opinion, but what I do say is that such an hypothesis is no more absurd than other 'explanations' put forward in the sphere of psychical research. Anyhow, experiments at close quarters seem to be open to the grave objection that some competent investigators reject them altogether—whatever we may think of the grounds of such objection."

Conceivable, yes, though hardly likely. When a medium for "automatic" writing or speaking is in undoubted trance, she habitually makes direct response to any intimations from without, and it is common to make it a reproach that she makes direct and unblushing use of any information inadvertently dropped by a person present. Why the subconscious should act in so devious a fashion in another species of experimentation, why it should either from device or some mechanism now set in motion withhold the word "Napoleon" caught from the agent's involuntary whispering and set down instead words significantly associated with Napoleon, is something of a puzzle. The trance-medium's subconscious, according to the explanation theory, is always eager to shine, and takes advantage of every source of information or inference to improve its product. Yet the subconsciousness of the percipient in experiments for telepathy, having heard the word "Napoleon" involuntarily whispered, deliberately avoids achieving a full success! If done at all, I should judge this was consciously done, that the percipient consciously heard and consciously avoided the word. And this is conceivable.

But that there should be so many reproductions which strikingly resemble the originals in shape, yet which do not represent the objects which the agent drew, and have no more ideational connection with them than can be traced between a cockroach and an archangel, or between a violin and an eel, and yet that the explanation for the correspondences should lurk in the involuntary whispering of the agent, I maintain is practically inconceivable. Between Figures 25 and 25a there is an unmistakable close resemblance of shape, in each two lines forming an inverted and sprawling V, with a swirl of lines in each forming a similar shape of similar dimensions proceeding in the same direction from the apex. But the percipient wholly misinterpreted the meaning of what she was impressed to draw. What affinity is there between an active volcano and a "big black beetle with horns"? Run through all the terms you can think of which the agent could have involuntarily whispered descriptive of his drawing, if he whispered anything—"volcano," "mountain," "smoke," "angle," etc., and what could possibly have suggested the impression which the percipient received? Look at Figures 118, 118a in the same series, and ask what the agent could have whispered about his caterpillar which should suggest a shape considerably resembling that of the caterpillar but intended to represent a long narrow leaf with serrated edge. To be sure, a caterpillar sometimes walks on a leaf, as a big black beetle may perhaps light on the side of a volcano, but surely it will not be concluded that the agent would have whispered so discursive a remark. Whispering "caterpillar" would not result in "leaf," and if "legs" had been whispered, surely legs would have resulted and "many" would at least have increased their number beyond the number of points in the reproduction. View again Figures 108 and 108a in the same series with the two foregoing. If the agent whispered anything, would it not have been "hand," solely first and principally? Imagine, if you please, that he also whispered "thumb sticking up." But a negro's head is not a hand, nor what the word "hand" would suggest, nor does a thumb ever grow out of a negro's head, yet out of this negro's head rises that projection curiously like a thumb. Neither would "hand" suggest a "pig's head," yet the pig's ear resembles the thumb, and the rest of the head carries a certain amount of analogy with the hand. Again, "rabbit's head" is written, but little more than the ears are drawn, each a thumb-like projection, and as in the other attempts at reproduction and in the original, straight upward. There is no association of ideas between a hand and a pig's or rabbit's head. Look at Figure 45, representing a coiled snake, and read again the description of her impressions which the percipient wrote. Between the snake and much of that description there is an association of ideas which we can follow. The whispered word "snake" might naturally rouse a picture of the fright which the apparition of a snake inflicts upon birds and small animals. While it does not seem like either the conscious or subconscious, having heard the word "snake," which surely would have been the first and foremost one to whisper, to suppress it and make a clear success a debatable one, we admit that this is "conceivable." But what about the "saucer of milk"? The agent may theoretically be supposed to whisper "snake," "coiled," "tail," "head," but hardly "saucer." I may here be reminded that some snakes drink milk, whether from a saucer or any other receptacle. But in Mrs. Sinclair's imagery it is a kitten that is associated with the milk—a much more common combination. Leaving this case, which is conceivably conceivable as the result of involuntary whispering plus a strange effort to spoil a success in hand, let us turn to the series of February 15th. Most of its members are to the point, but we will mention only a few. What association of ideas is there between a spigot and a dog's leg (Figs. 96, 96a)? The name "Napoleon" might indeed cause one to think of an island named St. Helena, or another one named Elba, or a woman named Josephine. But why on earth should the whispered word "spigot" cause one to think of a dog's leg and "front foot"? The association of ideas is not there, but the curiously resembling particulars of shape are there. Whatever the agent may be supposed to whisper in connection with the drawing shown in Figure 98, surely "box" would be a part of it. And as surely, if the three marks of the box were mentioned in the whispering they would have been called "crosses," and not "stars" or "sparks" as in the reproduction. And "crosses" do not naturally suggest either stars or sparks. Figures 94 and 94a unquestionably have resemblances in general shape, in the two pedals which are transformed into feet, in vertical lines within the periphery. But why should the word "harp" bring a woman's skirt and feet peeping beneath it? Perhaps we shall be told it is because a woman plays on a harp. A *woman* does, yes, but not half a woman, and that half standing so that her skirt takes the form of a harp. If conceivable that "Napoleon" should rouse a vision of an island and induce the drawing of an island, would the island take the shape of half of Napoleon's body? The mind, conscious or subconscious, does not act in that fashion. Again, the percipient's drawing which was the sequel to the agent's balloon (Figs. 95, 95a) is not by itself recognizable as a balloon, and was not recognized by the percipient as a balloon, for she wrote, as we inadvertently neglected earlier to state, "Shines in sunlight, must be metal, a scythe hanging among vines or strings." The involuntarily whispered word "balloon" would hardly, by any association of ideas, have led to such a reaction; nor would the agent have whispered "half a balloon" or "scythe." But we can understand how the agent's eye may have dwelt upon one side or half of the balloon and how his attention may have wandered to the cords, with corresponding telepathic results. See Figures 92, 92a. Here the analogies of form, although imperfect, are nevertheless unmistakable, but what association of ideas could have led from the involuntarily whispered word "chain" or "links," to "eggs" and "smoke," or to "curls of something coming out of the end of an egg"? At a later date the agent drew a mule's head and neck, with breaststrap crossing the lower part of his neck, forming a strip curving very slightly up from the horizontal. The percipient's drawing is of the head and part of the neck of a cow, turned in the same direction. The long ears of the mule have become the horns of the cow, and matching the breast-strap of the mule there appears a narrow horizontally extended parallelogram in front of the cow's neck and extremity of its muzzle, which last the percipient seemingly tries to explain by the script "Cow's head in 'stock.'" But if the agent involuntarily whispered "mule," it would hardly suggest a cow, if he whispered "long ears," it should not have resulted in long horns, if "breast-strap" or "strap" or "harness," this would hardly bring as its reaction the narrow parallelogram, which, whatever it is, is manifestly no part of a harness. The resemblances in shape are distinct and unmistakable, but they are incomprehensible as the result of overheard whispering. Or look again at Figures 78, 78a. The percipient, especially in the first of her two drawings, very nearly reproduces the original, but the barb of the fish-hook has become a tiny flower with a curving stem. The resemblance in shape is exceedingly impressive, but what words could have been whispered about a fish-hook which by association of ideas led to the flower?

So we might go on citing examples in the same category, which the doctrine of transformation by association of ideas of words whispered and heard utterly fails to explain. But the reader may find them for himself, either in this Bulletin or from the wider range of illustrations in *Mental Radio*.*

Concluding Observations

We have remarked that if there was involuntary whispering, it could easily explain the percipient response "Sailboat," and that by no circumambulatory process but by direct reaction, since the original drawing was a sailboat and "sailboat" would be the most natural if not inevitable word for an agent, intent on the experiment, and anxious for its success, to whisper involuntarily. The same may be said of the goat (Fig. 138), the chair (Figs. 16, 16a), the fork (Figs. 1, 1a), the star (Figs. 2, 2a)—except the extraordinary correspondence of odd shape, and the man's face (Fig. 20). But the star and man's face results were obtained when the agent was thirty feet away in another room with closed door between, while the agent looked at it but probably did not whisper so as not to attract his own attention but to be audible through walls for thirty feet. The chair and the fork were reproduced when the agent was some thirty miles away. The sailboat and goat were made in the latter period when the percipient was left alone with the drawings, and involuntary whispering is not a possible explanation. Part of the other examples given are from the period when Mr. Sinclair sat in the same room and watched the percipient's work, and partly from the later unguarded period.

So, in order to explain the results of the experiments as a whole they have to be divided into three categories, and a different theory applied to each.

I. Experiments in which the agent was near the percipient. Theory: Involuntary Whispering. Insuperable difficulty in applying the theory: Many of the percipient drawings are shaped significantly like the originals in whole or in parts, yet do not represent the same objects as do the originals, or objects which whispered words relevant to the original objects would suggest, directly or by association of ideas.

II. Experiments of the later stage when the percipient was left alone unwatched with the original drawings in her possession. Theory: Conscious or unconscious inspection of the original drawings. Difficulty which the theory faces: The results did not improve or undergo alterations due to a new cause during the unguarded period.

III. Experiments when agent and percipient were either thirty feet apart in different rooms, with a closed door between, under which circumstances it is incredible that involuntary whispering could have been heard, or thirty miles apart, in which case it is unquestionably impossible that involuntary whispering could have carried. Theory: Chance coincidence. This is the only theory left

---

* Neither M. C. S. or I ever made the faintest trace of a sound during an experiment. That was the law. And I never knew which drawing she was holding. I had just one order: to watch steadily, and be able to say that she never "peeked." I did this, and I say it, on my honor. This is an honest book.—Upton Sinclair.

for such experiments, unless conspiracy is charged, and that at different times would have to include not only Mr. and Mrs. Sinclair, but Mr. Irwin, Mrs. Irwin, the Sinclairs' secretary and Professor McDougall. Refutation of the theory: The experiments in this class were of such number and had such success both in number and quality as to challenge the production of any such success by guessing though hundreds of series each of an equal number of experiments should be gone through with.

It is credible that the large percentage of Successes and Partial Successes in the first fourteen experiments and twenty-four among the latest ones should have been obtained by one method, that (aside from these) during the earlier months another and quite different method should have been employed, and that (still aside from these) later a third and quite different method should have been resorted to, and yet the whole mass of results be homogeneous? It would certainly be expected that the inauguration of any new method would in some way be reflected in the nature of the results. But the lot produced with intervening distances too great to admit of the involuntary whispering theory melts imperceptibly into the lot produced with the agent and percipient together so that the involuntary whispering process is conceivable, and this in turn melts imperceptibly into the lot where all precautions are discarded, and this again into long-distance experiments and out, without it being possible to detect any changes in the character of the results at the points of junction. Throughout there is homogeneity, some successes being correct literally, some incompletely and partially, some results only suggestive and some entire failures. Throughout we find some corresponding in both shape and meaning, some in idea but not shape, and some in shape only and misinterpreted by the percipient; in fact, all the peculiarities of Mrs. Sinclair's work are to be found in about equal proportions in all stages. There is perceptible a gradual [though] irregular tendency to decline in the ratio of success achieved, but in such a manner that the decline cannot be chronologically connected with any of the changes of method.

The "peeking" theory cannot be applied to the experiments of Class I. The "involuntary whispering" theory cannot be applied to the experiments of Class II. Neither the "peeking" nor the "involuntary whispering" theory can be applied to experiments of Class III.

Only the theory of chance coincidence can be applied as a single explanation of the experiments of all three classes. Let this be done and there is simply massed a greater amount of material for the demolition of the chance coincidence theory by anyone who will undertake a large series of precisely parallel experiments in Guessing.

For myself, I am willing to say, perhaps for the fourth time, that I am willing to rest the whole case on those experiments to which no one, presumably, will have the hardihood to apply either the theory of "involuntary whispering" or that of "peeking," that is to say, those experiments in which agent and percipient were either in separate rooms or many miles apart.

AN INTERPRETATION OF MRS. SINCLAIR'S DIRECTIONS

Mrs. Sinclair, on pages 104-114 of *Mental Radio* outlines on the basis of her own experience the method which she thinks best calculated to develop an ability to attain at will a mental state which will enable some of her readers to receive and record telepathic impressions to an evidential degree. I propose, at the same time recommending that prospective experimenters shall obtain the book and read the full directions, to attempt a condensation of them. To some extent I shall interpret them; that is, state them in other terms, which it is hoped will not be the less lucid. As a matter of psychological fact, you cannot "make your mind a blank," though you can more or less acquire the art of doing at will what you sometimes involuntarily do—you can practice narrowing the field of consciousness, so that instead of being aware of many things external and of various bodily sensations, your attention is fixed almost exclusively for a time on one mental object. Some persons at times become so absorbed in a train of thought that with eyes open and with conversation around them they are hardly conscious of anything seen or heard. But it is best to assist the attainment of such a state as Mrs. Sinclair does, by closing the eyes, and it is best that silence should prevail. When one remembers how in revery he has become oblivious to all around him, or how when witnessing an entrancing passage in a play everything in the theatre except the actors and their immediate environment has faded out of consciousness, he will have no difficulty in understanding what Mrs. Sinclair really means by saying that "it is possible to be unconscious and conscious at the same time," although taken literally that is not a correct statement.

But, according to her, in order to be in the state best fitted for telepathic reception, it is not enough to narrow the field of consciousness until, approximately, only one train of thought on a mentally conceived subject occupies it. There must be cultivated also, in as high a degree as possible, an ability to shut out memories and imaginations, and to wait for and to receive impressions, particularly those of mental imagery, which seem to come of themselves, and to expend the mental energy upon watching, selecting from and determining these.

We are told that it is important to relax—"to 'let go' of every tense muscle, every tense spot, in the body," and that auto-suggestion, mentally telling oneself to relax, will help. Along with this there should be a letting-go, or progressive quietening, of consciousness.

She wisely says that if in spite of you the selected mentally-visualized rose or violet rouses memories by suggesting a lost sweetheart, a vanished happy garden, or what not, you should substitute thinking of another flower which has no personal connotations for you. It must be some "peace-inspiring object," even a spoon might suggest medicine. The reader will understand that we are now discussing the means for cultivating ability to fall at will into the state for telepathic reception; we are not talking about experiments with that end in view.

After considerable practice of this kind one will tend to fall asleep. It seems that it is right to nearly come to that point, but one must stop a little this side of the sleeping stage.

When one feels that some success has attended the practice described above, he may proceed to actual experiments. The amateur experimenter is advised at first to experiment in the dark, or at least in a dimly-lit room, as light stimulates the eyes.

She goes on to say what means that you should induce mental relaxation and passivity, narrow the field of consciousness. But at this point I must depart from Mrs. Sinclair's precepts and recommend her own best practice. Her very first seven formal experiments were with her brother-in-law making his drawings some thirty miles away. The results were so remarkable that they deserve to arrest the attention of every psychologist. The next seven experiments were made with agent and percipient in different rooms, shut off from each other by solid walls; and their results also were very impressive. Therefore I see no reason why amateurs experimenting according to the light that they get from Mrs. Sinclair should not make their very first attempts in another room from the agent. Let the latter do as we find in the book was done; make his drawing, call out "All right" when he is done, and gaze steadfastly at the drawing until the percipient has made hers and signalized the fact by calling out "All right," then proceed to make another and repeat the process. At least part of the time, let there be another person with the agent keeping watch upon his lips and throat muscles, lest the desperate theory should be advanced that at the distance of, say, thirty feet and through solid walls "involuntary whispering" on the part of the agent reached the ears of the percipient.

But how shall the percipient further conduct herself (we are here supposing the percipient is a woman) as to the means of getting telepathic impressions? Adapting the directions given in the book, we should say that, lying on the couch with eyes closed, and having sunk into that state of mental abstraction which she is supposed now to be capable of attaining, she is to order her subconscious mind, very calmly but positively, to bring the agent's drawing to her mind.

And now we quote literally from the book, even to the expressions about making the mind a blank. Although not technically correct, it may be that to many not versed in psychology the expressions will be actually the best to suggest to them what they are to do.

Mrs. Sinclair warns that "the details of this technique are not to be taken as trifles," and that to develop and make it serviceable "takes time, and patience, and training in the art of concentration." There are special difficulties, at least in her case. In undertaking a new experiment what she last saw before closing her eyes again, particularly the electric light bulb which she lighted in order to make her drawing or drawings, appeared in her mind, and also the memory of the last picture. "It often takes quite a while to banish these memory ghosts. And sometimes it is a mistake to banish them," a fact which we have noted several times in the account of her work. Another difficulty is to restrain one's tendency when a part or what may be a part of the original appears, to guess what the rest may be, and to keep the imagination bridled.

It is quite probable—and this Mrs. Sinclair recognizes—that the procedure, now fairly clearly outlined, may not in all its details be suited to all minds capable of telepathic reception. Mr. Rawson, as we shall see in Part II, when successful, was nearly always so almost instantly. On the other hand, the percipients in the Schmoll and Mabire series were often as long as fifteen minutes making their choice. But it would be wise to begin along the lines of the instructions, and make modifications of method, if any, in the light of what personal experience suggests.

It is hoped that there will be readers of this Bulletin disposed to school themselves and to experiment in conformity with the above instructions, patiently and persistently, and that, successful or not, they will make careful records and report to the Research Officer.

APPENDIX I

WHY ARE WE LIKE THIS?

(Parts of a Hitherto Unpublished Manuscript by Mrs. Sinclair)
There comes a time in the life of each of us when we begin to wonder what it is all about—this life. I mean, to want, with all one's bewildered and troubled heart, to *know*. What is life, what is the purpose of it, above all, what is the reason for the preponderance of the pain of it? This brief earthly existence, with its series of cares and sorrows and bafflements—what is the purpose of it? It seemed so full of purpose in our youth—full, rather of purposes, for youth has no one purpose. Youth's purpose is to fulfill what seems to be the little purposes of each day, such as evading unpleasant things and pursuing the pleasant ones. But as we pass on through the days of our youth, toward early middle-age, we realize that these eagerly, zestfully pursued purposes of youth were thwarted, one by one. If achieved, they brought some penalty, or disappointment.

Three years ago, being ill and not happy,[1] I reached the crisis of questioning. I wanted to know how to get well, and I wanted to know why I wanted to get well. And so, I began to ask, where is the path toward knowledge? In which little store-house will I find a clue to the answer? I went to see the medical men who have access to one little store-house. I went to the psychological healers who have access to another little store-house. And I went to the only religious group in the world today which seemed to have any real, or living religion.[2] From all three of these sources, one clue, one hint, stood out as a real clue. From the mass of purported knowledge it appeared to me to be the most significant. It seemed to be the thing which produced results in all these three domains, though the priests and priest-esses of but one of them seemed aware of the great significance of this hint.

It had to do with man's mind, to begin with, but it seemed to lead into the very heart of all the universe—into our "material bodies," as well as into our mental hopes and longings and joys and despairs. So I set to work to experiment first with telepathy and clairvoyance. If clairvoyance is real, I said, then we may have access to all knowledge. We may really be fountains, or outlets of one vast mind. To have access to all *knowledge*.

If telepathy is real, I said, then my mind is not my own. I'm just a radio receiving set, which picks up the thoughts of all the other creatures of this universe. I and the universe of men are *one*. I had long known, of course, that my body was not my own—that it picked up sun-rays, and cold-waves, and sound-vibrations, which shook the atoms of my being into new forms; that I picked up iron and sulphur, and phosphorus, and vitamins, and what not, when I ate the plants and animals of my universe; in short, that I had to pick up the constituents of a new body in the form of "fresh air" and "water" and "food" every day of my life in order to maintain the hold I had on the thing I called my body. But somehow, in the vague way in which we think of the mind, I had felt that mine was entirely my own. Surely it was not dependent on, nor at the mercy of, outside forces—except in the one horrible, inexorable way of its dependence on my own body. It was free, of course, to accept ideas from other minds, if it wished; but it did not have to, unless it wanted to. So I had believed. Now, with my new clue, I began to wonder if all my life I had not been in error in my thinking, if I had not got the scheme of things turned upside down. Had I been looking at an image in a mirror, a reversal of the truth? Was my body dependent on my mind when I had thought my mind was dependent on my body? Was it sick when my mind was, and did it die when my mind died—of discouragement? And was my mind my own, or did it receive and accept thoughts constantly from all the other creatures of the universe without my being able to prevent it, without my even knowing it?

---

[1] She was undergoing the menopause; hence the special depression. It is important that every such fact should be stated. It might even be that the condition heightened the telepathic faculty.

[2] Of course Mrs. Sinclair is solely responsible for this as every other of her expressed opinions.

What is myself, anyway—body or mind, or both, or one and the same thing, or—what? I must find out! Is my mind a hodge-podge of its own thoughts and the silent, ever-changing thoughts of all other creatures, just as my body is a hodge-podge of the elements of the plants and animals and light-rays it is fed on and made of?

Here were a lot of questions which had become terribly important, and I couldn't answer them, I couldn't really answer any of them. But I had a clue— a new clue which might lead—anywhere—to heaven or to hell.

Some of the best scientific minds of the world have experimented with telepathy and believe that it is a proven fact. I have read much of this evidence, and I have watched a "medium" demonstrate telepathy. But perhaps he was deceiving himself—perhaps he used some trick without realizing it, such as listening to the breathing of the sender of the thoughts he received. I do not see how this could be, but it is possible, so I am told by experienced investigators of psychic phenomena. However, there is this mass of evidence, in books, written by men of the highest scientific training who have made experiments in telepathy and who are convinced that it is a fact.

But despite all this evidence, I seem to be uncertain. And this is too serious a matter to leave to uncertainty. So I set to work to make my own experiments. I have experimented already with a "medium," but I have been warned about the mediumistic temperament. These psychically sensitive persons are, thanks to the very quality of mind which causes them to be sensitive, overly prone to unconscious thinking which is supposed to take a form of conscious instability. So I must find a hard-boiled materialistic-thinking person to experiment with—one who is prone to object thinking, who can maintain a wide-awake consciousness with which to watch his own thoughts to prevent any self-deception, while I, by a trustworthy mechanical device, *i.e.,* a writing pad and pencil, protect my mind from deceiving itself. I find such a hard-boiled object mind in the person of my brother-in-law, who is a most capable, practical businessman, and whose philosophy of life does not include any "mysticism," or unconscious knowledge. Being ill, however, and with no better way to pass the time, he consents to act as sender of telepathic messages to me. He is domiciled thirty miles away from me, and so we cannot look over each other's shoulders at drawings, nor listen to each other's breathing.

We proceed as follows: Each day at one o'clock, an hour which suits the convenience of both of us, he sits at a table in his home and makes a drawing of some simple object, such as a table-fork, or an ink-bottle, a duck, or a basket of fruit.[3] Then he gazes steadily at his drawing while he concentrates his mind

---

[3] This was written when it was expected that the experiments with the brother-in-law would continue some time. The general character of the objects is stated. In fact neither duck nor basket of fruit figured. The experiments with "Bob" soon ceased, not only because they involved a strain upon him in his then condition of health but because Mrs. Sinclair suspected that she was telepathically having her own feelings of depression increased by his.

intently on "visualizing" the object before him. In other words, he does not let his mind wander one instant from the picture of the fork, or the ink-bottle, or whatever he has drawn. He may gaze at the original object instead of at his drawing, but he must not think of anything else but how it looks. The purpose of the drawing is for proof to me that this was actually what he thought of at the appointed hour. If his mind wanders off to thoughts of something else, which he has no drawing of, I may get these wandering thoughts. Then he will forget these wandering, unrecorded thoughts, and I will have nothing to prove that he ever thought them.

When he has finished the fifteen minutes of steady concentration on one object, he dates his drawing and puts it away, until the time when we are to meet and compare our records. At my end of the "wireless," I have done a different mental stunt. I have reclined on a couch, with body completely relaxed and my mind in a dreamy, almost unconscious state, alternating with a state of gazing, with closed eyes, into gray space, looking on this gray background for whatever picture, or thought-form may appear there. When a form appears, I record it at once. I reach for my pad and pencil and write down what I have seen, and then I make a drawing of it, and then I relax again and look dreamily into space again to see if another vision will appear, or if this same one will return to assure me that it is the right one. At the end of fifteen minutes, the period of time we arbitrarily agreed upon for each day's experiment, I date my drawing and file it until the day comes to compare notes with my brother-in-law.

Each day thereafter, for several days, my brother-in-law goes through this same performance, varying it only by his choice of a different object to draw and concentrate upon each time. Every three or four days we meet and compare notes.

One day, while I lay passively waiting for a "vision," a chair of a certain design floated before my mind. It was so vivid that I felt absolutely certain that this was the object my brother-in-law, thirty miles away, was visualizing for me. Other objects on other occasions had been vivid, but this one was not merely vivid; in some mysterious way, it carried absolute conviction with it. I knew positively that my mind was not deceiving me. I was so sure that this chair had come "on the air" from my brother-in-law's mind to mine, that I jumped up and went to the telephone and rang him up. His wife was in the room with him and my husband was in the room with me, and we called on them as witnesses—for we had set out on the experiment determined that there was to be no deception, of each other, nor of ourselves. I wanted the truth about this matter—I was at life's crisis, at the place where my whole soul cried out, "What is the meaning of it all, anyway?" And my brother-in-law knew my mood, and a painful, lingering illness was rapidly bringing him to share it. My vision of the chair, and my drawing of it, were entirely correct. This was our first thrilling success. Others followed it, and in the meantime, my husband and I had made together some similar experiments, with success. Before the summer was over, four persons—my husband, my brother-in-law, his wife, and I—had become convinced of the reality of telepathy. Then, having read a book by an English physicist *(An Experiment With Time,* by J. W. Dunne), I began keeping records of my dreams according to Mr.Dunne's method, in order to see if, as he thought, they would render evidence of foreknowledge of future events. Clairvoyance is the usual term for this form of psychic phenomena, but Mr. Dunne, being a physicist, is averse to mixing it with psychic things to the extent of using the regular language, so he calls it "an experiment with time" and writes a book about it in the language of physics. Not being a physicist, I'm quite willing to stick to the well-known word, clairvoyance, even at the risk of repelling those ignorant persons who think that all psychic phenomena is trickery. There are hordes of charlatans who call themselves mediums, just as there are hordes of physicians who are charlatans, and of Christians who are cheats, and of bankers who are dishonest. So, having read Mr. Dunne's useful book, I set out to record my dreams and to watch for their "coming true." Some of them did. Some which could not be accounted for by coincidence. Some others came true which were clearly due to telepathy between my husband's mind and my own. I dreamed that I was doing things which it turned out he was actually doing, at a distance from me, and at the time at which I was having the dream. Also, during these months, I made some experiments on a young hypnotist I knew. I had no intention of letting him hypnotize me, but I asked him to try to. I knew he would never consent to the telepathy experiment if he suspected it; he would not want me reading his secret thoughts. But he had played some tricks on me, so I felt justified. And so, when he concentrated on the task of putting me into a hypnotic sleep, I concentrated on "seeing" his thoughts. Again and again I succeeded in this experiment. I discovered his sorrows, his sins, his hopes, his daily adventures. And I recorded them and faced him with them and became his "Mother Confessor,"—and most generously rewarded his unintentional confidence. I am sure he will agree that I made a full return to him for the knowledge he inadvertently enabled me to obtain—the knowledge of the interaction of minds.

APPENDIX II

Classified complete list of drawings made by Mr. Upton Sinclair in his experiments with Mrs. Sinclair, plus those by his secretary, mostly diagrams, and the seven by her brother-in-law, from July 8, 1928, to March 16, 1929, inclusive, being the period covered by his book.

DIAGRAMS, ETC.

Asterisks—five, Circles—five small, Circles—ten small, Circles—six concentric, Circles—three interlinking, Circle and Center, etc., Crescent—approximate, Cross—pattée, Cross—swastika, Cross—swastika, Cross—eight arms, notched at ends, Diamond, Heart, Hexagon, Horn-shaped figure, Oblong—vertical, Oval—over larger oval and touching it, Spiral, Spiral, Squares—four concentric, Star—odd-shaped, Star—six-pointed, Triangles—three concentric, Wheel—figure like rimless.

LETTERS OF ALPHABET

(Script) B, E, M, Y. (Print) KKK, M.C.S., M.C.S., T, UPTON, W—lying on its side?

FIGURES, ETC.

2, 5, 13, 6, $

HUMAN BEINGS

Boy—with hoop, Eye—dropping tears, Face—grinning, Face—grinning, Face—hairy, Face—man's, bearded, Face—round, with round ears, Foot—with roller skate, Girl, Hand—with pointing finger, "Happy Hooligan," Head—of boy, wearing hat, Head—of girl, wearing hat, Head—of man, bald, profile, Head—profile, Head and Bust—of woman, bundle on head, Leg and Foot—in buckled shoe, Leg and Foot—with roller skate, Legs—two, one of wood, Man—line and circle, Man—profile, waiter, Man—walking, Man and Woman, Mandarin, Men—line and circle, Skull and Crossbones, Woman—nude.

MAMMALS

Bat, Bat—with wings spread, Cow—head, Cow—head, tongue protruding, Cow—homed, Cow—rear half, Cow—rear half, Deer—running, front part, Dog—and man's foot, Elephant, Fox—running, Goat (probably), Horse—head,

Animal—running after string, Monkey—hanging from bough, Rat, Reindeer, Walrus, Whale—spouting, Wolf—head.

BIRDS

Bird—baby, Bird—head, Chicken—coming from shell, Chicken—cooked, on plate, Duck—with feet, Eagle, Heron, Nest—with eggs, Parrot—head, Peacock, Rooster.

INSECTS, FISHES, ETC.

Butterfly, Caterpillar, Crab, Fish, Inch-worm—curved, Insect—eight-legged, Lobster, Shell—sea, Snake, Snake, Spider, Turtle.

VEGETATION

Acorn, Apple, Bean—lima (?), Cactus—branch, Carnation, Cat-tail, Cat-tail, Celery, Clover—three-leaf (?), Clover—three-leaf (?), Daisy, Flower, Flower—on stalk, Flower—with narrow leaves, Leaf, Leaf—poplar (?), Melon—on inclined plane, Plant—potted, Roses—pink, with green leaves, Tree—branch, Tree—odd, Tree—palm, Tree—bare, with pointed limbs.

HOUSEHOLD

Ash-can—with bail, Bed, Bottle, Bottle—milk, Bottle—square, lower half shaded, Broom, Broom, Bureau and mirror, Campstool, Candelabrum, Chair, Chair, Chair—easy, Cup—with handle, Desk—four-legged, Dish—with rising steam, Door-knob, Electric Light Bulb—*(object itself)*, Electric Light Bulb, Fork—table, Fork—three-pronged, long handle, Glass—drinking, Key, Key, Lamp—burning, Lamp—burning, Picture—black frame, Spigot, Table, Table with curved legs, Telephone, Telephone, Vase—ovoid, Wallhook.

PERSONAL

Bag, Bag—round, with protruding top, Belt-buckle, Book—black, Bottle—pen and ink, Box—rounded, with cover up, Cane, Cane, Cap, Cigarette—smoking, Clock—alarm, Eye-glasses, Eye-glasses, Fan—partly spread, Fan—spread, Hat, Hat, Hat—with feather, Necktie, Pin—diamond, Pipe—smoking, Pipe—smoking, Ring—with stone, Scissors, Shoe, Soap—cake, Suit—man's, with knee breeches, Tooth-brush, Tooth-brush, Watch, Watch, Watch, Watch—face.

WAR, HUNTING, ETC.

Arrow, Bow and Arrow, Cannon, Cannon—muzzle, Daggers—with hilts, crossed, Epaulet, Fish-hook, Fish-hook, Fish-hook, Helmet, Trench-mortar—pointing up.

RECREATION

Balloon, Cart—child's, Dumb-bell, Dumb-bell, Football, Hammock—slung from post, Indian Club, Skyrocket, Sled, Tennis Racket, Tennis Racket, Tennis Racket.

TRANSPORTATION

Automobile, Elevated Railroad, Railroad Engine, Sailboat, Sailboat, Sailboat—side view, Sled—drawn by dogs, Steamboat—on water.

OBJECTS RELATED TO SOUND

Bell, Bell, Bell—lines radiating from tongue, Harp, Horn—straight, Mandolin, Musical Staff, Notes—musical, Tuba—brass, Violin.

BUILDINGS, ETC.

Column, Derrick—oil, Derrick—oil, Door—with grating, Frieze Design, Gable end—with tall chimney, House—with many dots for windows, House—with smoking chimney, House—with smoking chimney, Obelisk, Pillar, etc., Pillars—row, etc., Windmill.

MISCELLANEOUS

Ax and written word "Ax," Box—open, Box—with three crosses, Butterfly net, Flag, Flag—Japanese, fringed, on staff, Fleur-de-lis, Gate, Gibbet and Noose, Globe—world, Hearts—two, pierced by arrow, Hill—with birds above, Hill—with sun above, Hoe, Hook—in hasp, Hose—end, with water, Hourglass—with running sand, Hydrant, Ladder, Machine—scraper (?), Mail Bag, Money—five-cent piece, Mortuary monument (?), Police Billy, Rake—head, Rule, Screw, Shovel, Sun, Telegraph Wires and Pole, Trowel, Volcano, Wheel.

EPILOGUE

SUCH WAS THE END of Dr. Prince's study; as careful and precise a piece of scientific investigation as I have ever come upon. She did not fail to appreciate it, and to thank him. He died a couple of years later.

Craig survived him by a quarter of a century; but she did no more experimenting. She had satisfied herself, her husband, and such authorities as Dr. Prince, Prof. McDougall, and Albert Einstein, and that was enough. Her mind went on to speculate as to the meaning of such phenomena; to psychology, philosophy, and religion. What was the source of the powers she possessed and had demonstrated? What was the meaning of the mystery called life? Where did it come from, and what became of it when it left us, or appeared to? She filled a large bookcase with works on these subjects, studied them far into the night, and discussed them with a husband who would have preferred to wait and see.

At the age of seventy she had her first heart attack, and from that time on was never free of pain. For eight years I had her sole care, because that was the way she wished it. Her death took many weeks, and to go into details would serve no good purpose. I mention only one very curious circumstance: During her last year she had three dreadful falls on a hard plastone floor, and I had taken these to be fainting spells. A few days after her death I received a letter from a stranger in the Middle West, telling me that he had just had a seance with Arthur Ford and had a communication from Mary Craig Sinclair, asking him to inform me that her supposed fainting spells had been light strokes. I called the doctor who with two other doctors had performed an autopsy; I did not mention the letter, but asked him the results, and he told me that the brain lesions showed she had had three light strokes.

I tell this incident for what it may be worth. I myself have no convictions that would cause me to prejudge it, to say nothing of inventing it.

INDEX

Page numbers ending in *n* refer to footnotes on that page

S

Savage, Minot J., 1
self-deception, 108
Semmelweiss, Ignaz Philipp, 135*n*
Sinclair, Mary Craig. *See* Craig
Sinclair, Upton
        bio, 137
        'healing' with Craig, 13
sleep, auto-hypnotic, 106
Society for Psychical Research, *x*
Sterling, George, 12-13
subconscious mind, 110, 111-112
'superstition,' 1

T

telekinesis experience, 15
telepathy
        See also ESP
        basis of, 119-121
        causing of, 115
        danger of, 103
        distance of effect, 3
        essence of, 3
        evidence for, 1
        how to do it, 105-114, 191-193
        issues in study of, 139*n*-140*n*
        meaning of, 119, 194
        observations of, 16
        questions surrounding, 3, 194-195
        Richet's thought on, 101
Telepathy and Clairvoyance, 121
tension, 105
thought-rays, 120
Tischner, Rudolph, 121

W

Walter, Bruno, 130
whispering, 183-189

Hampton Roads Publishing Company

. . . for the evolving human spirit

Hampton Roads Publishing Company
publishes books on a variety of subjects including
metaphysics, health, complementary medicine,
visionary fiction, and other related topics.

For a copy of our latest catalog,
call toll-free, 800-766-8009,
or send your name and address to:

Hampton Roads Publishing Company, Inc.
1125 Stoney Ridge Road
Charlottesville, VA 22902
e-mail: hrpc@hrpub.com
www.hrpub.com